The I

The Debt Doctor

A guide to getting – and staying – out of debt

Robert Leach FCCA ACA

CANTERBURY
PRESS
Norwich

First published in 2007 by the Canterbury Press Norwich
(a publishing imprint of Hymns Ancient & Modern Limited,
a registered charity)

13–17 Long Lane, London ᴇᴄɪᴀ 9ᴘɴ

The diagram on page 127 is © the Money Advice Trust
and is used with permission.

www.scm-canterburypress.co.uk

British Library Cataloguing in Publication data

A catalogue record for this book is available
from the British Library

ISBN 978–1–85311–769–5

Typeset by Regent Typesetting, London
Printed and bound in Great Britain by
William Clowes Ltd, Beccles, Suffolk

Contents

Introduction

One in five British households now has a debt problem. This problem is not confined to any particular social classes. Accountants, doctors, ministers, financial advisers and celebrities have debt problems. Probably people you know have serious debt problems but are unwilling to admit it.

Households that appear to be comfortable may have serious debt problems. People with large houses, smart clothes and impressive cars can have debt problems.

On 29 June 2004, the Bank of England announced that consumer debt was £1 trillion. That is £1 followed by 12 zeros. This figure has continued to increase by more than 10% a year. The biggest single cause is over-spending. On average, we each spend £105 for every £100 we earn.

In itself, debt is not necessarily a problem or an evil. Borrowing money to buy property or start a business is quite responsible provided the loan is readily repayable. Debt becomes a problem when repayment is not readily possible. This often arises from ineffective budgeting or irresponsible spending. Such indebtedness is like an illness, which is why this book is called *The Debt Doctor*.

Chapter 1 introduces the subject of debt and a guide to determining how serious is the problem.

The financial advice starts with Chapter 2 on budgeting and Chapter 3 on economizing. Even people with no debt problems may find advice helpful. Chapter 4 deals with maximizing income, and Chapter 5 explains social security entitlement. These should help a debtor, though debt recovery is more about reducing expenditure.

The 'main course' comprises chapters 6–8, which deal with types of debt, serious debt and how to clear debt.

Chapter 9 explains many basic legal principles behind debt, many of which are not properly appreciated. Chapters 10 and 11 deal with debt at different stages of life, and the particular problems of business debt.

Chapter 12 deals with insolvency, the ultimate method of debt recovery. The last two chapters give warnings about scams and advice on staying out of debt.

In 1992, I faced a debt problem from a failed business venture. The methods in this book allowed me to recover. They have also been used to help others with problems.

This book is written from a specifically Christian perspective that believes in the dignity and worth of every individual, yet recognizes that simply spending more and more does not bring happiness and fulfilment. However, the book is not a theological text, but a practical hands-on guide, and it certainly doesn't set out to preach at anyone. It is unlikely that any guidance here will contradict the received wisdom of secular debt agencies.

I am grateful to Credit Action and its director Chris Tapp for help on practical advice and for reviewing the manuscript. I also thank many other bodies for their help in answering specific questions.

Debt is a serious problem. This book aims to provide serious help.

Robert Leach
Epsom
April 2007

I

Debt – the diagnosis and first aid

Introduction

Debt can be a problem even to the most careful handler of money. It is an area where many people are reluctant to admit any problems even to those closest to them or to those best able to help. There is often a tendency to maintain a facade that all is well when it is not.

As with all problems, debt gets worse when left. The first step to resolving any problem is to **acknowledge** that it exists. This can be surprisingly difficult. The sooner a recovery plan is started, the sooner the problem is solved, and the sooner the pain ends.

The good news is that no debt problem is incapable of resolution. The bad news is that the most painful stages are the first ones:

- acknowledging that there is a problem
- quantifying the problem by adding up all current debts
- preparing a budget for future income and spending.

Once those early stages have been overcome, a debtor can even be pleasantly surprised at how easy and painless it can be to recover. However, resolution requires full co-operation in a proper procedure.

Often the hardest task faced by a debt doctor is to get the debtor started on the process of recovery. Sometimes, even these first hard steps have another step to take first. That is preventing the debtor from doing anything without thinking it through. Despite what the television advertisements say, rolling up your debts into one loan is not the best option. Moving to a smaller house is rarely a wise move. And no-one gets out of debt by living on economy baked beans and not switching on the lights at night. A debtor may be at a very low ebb, possibly even contemplating suicide. A debt doctor must be aware of these problems and be prepared to help. Appendix 3 gives general comments on counselling skills.

Cause and effect

Financial problems do not happen in isolation. There is usually a non-financial cause, and there are always non-financial consequences.

There are always causes and **effects**. Sometimes the effects can be the causes of further problems. Worrying about debt can make a person withdrawn and moody, which leads to problems in relationships, and can lead to marriage breakdown and problems at work. This in turn can lead to defeatism, making the person even less willing to face up to the debt problems.

If the cause is not addressed, any debt counselling is treating the symptoms and not the disease. If the effects are not fully treated, all the symptoms have not been treated. A person may recover from debt in financial terms but still face the wreckage of a broken marriage, alienated family and friends, loss of self-worth and more.

Debt arises in the context of illness, stress, divorce, business failure or other problems. It is usually good practice to separate the financial aspects from the non-financial.

The **cause** of debt can include such factors as drug or alcohol dependency, gambling, compulsive spending, failing to run a business properly, spoiling children or just being silly with money. Any change of circumstance, such as divorce or job loss, can be a primary cause of debt. In all debt counselling, the root cause of the financial problem must be identified and addressed.

First aid is concerned with stopping a problem getting worse, such as stopping any bleeding. Similarly debt counselling must start with stopping the situation getting worse before we can start making it better. For a parent simply to bail out a debtor may treat the symptoms but it does not cure the disease.

Identifying the problem is the first step to solving it. Gambling and drinking do not automatically lead to debt problems as millions of our fellow citizens routinely gamble and drink with no problem. The real issue is when the gambling or drinking or something else is being done to excess. For example, the book *Gambling – A Family Affair* by Angela Willans (SPCK) identifies four reasons why people gamble:

- hope of winning money (usually a huge amount)
- a social life
- to relieve boredom
- the 'buzz' of the risk.

Dealing with gambling requires identifying which of these reasons apply to the gambler and confronting them. For problems such as gambling, alcohol and drugs, there are specialist groups such as

Gamblers Anonymous and Alcoholics Anonymous which provide the necessary help.

Not all debt arises from irresponsibility. Debt can arise from a big customer going bust owing a large sum to a small business. Someone may be the victim of fraud or theft. A person may suffer from unexpected illness or injury, or from an uninsured risk.

The Debt Doctor's Advice

Whatever the problem is, it must be identified and it must be treated.

Sometimes a debtor may blame the underlying problems on others: parents for an unhappy childhood, other businesses for unfair business practices, or a family member for being irresponsible with money. Sometimes the debtor may be right.

However, what matters in debt counselling is not in apportioning **blame**, but getting the debtor to accept that his debt is *his* problem and *he* must solve it, whoever is to blame. In the final analysis every one of us is answerable for our own conduct and what we make of what life presents us. A person *may* have had an unhappy childhood, been the victim of unfairly denied opportunity or been the victim of a fraud. However, passing the blame does not help to solve the problem. A person must take charge of their own life and accept responsibility.

Just as debt frequently has non-financial causes, it will certainly have non-financial effects. Most debt recovery plans involve significant changes in lifestyles which can affect a person's esteem and friendships. There will often be strain within families and relationships.

Arguments about how to deal with a debt problem are best solved by following the advice of a debt counsellor rather than letting one partner unthinkingly rush into an impulsive or dramatic solution. Further advice is given on page 6.

Acknowledging the problem

The first step to solving any problem is to admit that the problem exists. If someone denies that they have a problem, commonly known as **denial**, there is little that can be done until the issue of denial has been cracked.

Those close to the debtor may discern or even have hard evidence of a debt problem, but be unable to shift the debtor's obstinate denial.

It can also become obvious to those close to a person that something is seriously wrong, even if the nature of the problem is not instantly discernible. A person can seem distracted, behave out of character, not respond positively when you would expect them to, or always seem to be 'busy doing nothing'.

There is no painless solution to such a problem. The worst option is simply to bail the person out, such as by paying their bills or confirming their view that there is not a problem. While such an approach may be well-intentioned, it is the wrong approach and will only make matters worse. You never help a debtor by pretending that there is no problem.

If a person has cancer, you do not help them by covering this up and saying they do not need treatment. You must do all you can to force the person to accept medical treatment. Anything else is a waste of time and, worse, will allow the situation to deteriorate. The principle is exactly the same for financial illness.

The only help is to force the debtor to confront the problem. A wife trying to get her husband to face the issues is in a desperate situation, as the husband can react abusively or even violently. It can poison the family relationship, involving children in matters to which they should not be exposed. The husband may retaliate by pointing out all the wife's failures. Another common situation is a wife running up debts and hiding them from her husband. Other relatives may become involved by taking sides (which is always the wrong course of action).

If other family members have funds or are able to borrow money, their refusal to provide financial help can be seen as showing a lack of love or support. There is always the difficult situation where a relative *is* prepared to bail out the debtor, such as when the debtor's father gives his son money and thus helps the son avoid confronting the issue.

This is an area where those close to the debtor must:

- make a particular effort to show love and support in a way consistent with dealing with debt
- avoid the temptation to take soft options which avoid the problem
- ignore all forms of retaliation, however hurtful
- never let up on the need to confront the debt problem.

This is not easy. In many situations this will be a 'make or break' time. A couple which survives this will have a much stronger relationship afterwards.

Acknowledging the problem is stage one of the debt recovery process. Until this has been accomplished, there is no stage two.

Seriousness of problem

For convenience, we classify debt problems into two broad types:

- standard debt problem
- serious debt problem.

This book attempts to assist debtors with both types of problem. It also contains general advice which should assist people with no debt problems at all.

A person has a standard debt problem if they:

- have had a cheque dishonoured in the last year
- have been refused cash from a dispenser in the last year because of insufficient funds
- have four or more hire purchase or similar consumer credit agreements
- carry forward balances from one month to the next on any credit card
- spend 25% or more income on consumer credit (excluding mortgage)
- spend 50% or more income on consumer credit *and* mortgage
- use more than five credit cards on a regular basis
- have problems paying utility bills, such as telephone, gas, electricity and water
- must borrow money for normal household expenditure.

A person has a serious debt problem if they:

- have had three or more cheques dishonoured in the last year
- carry forward balances from one month to the next on more than one credit card
- have problems paying the minimum amount on a credit card
- routinely spend more than their income
- do not know how much debt they have
- do not open bills and related letters.

A standard debt problem can usually be addressed simply by economizing and budgeting. For a serious debt problem, the debtor must seek help, and will need to follow more extensive procedures explained in Chapter 8. It is no use a debtor saying that he can cope when he is already not doing so.

About 41% of the population have a standard debt problem, and 10% have a serious debt problem, affecting about one in five households.

The government itself is no better, and sets a poor example of not living within its means. The national debt is more than £8,000 for every person in the UK. Your taxes pay the interest on that huge debt.

What *not* to do

Having got to the position where the debtor accepts the problem, stage two is to stop the debtor doing anything unwise.

If a debtor has been forced to accept the seriousness of his situation, it is easy for him to indulge in some dramatic gesture or rush into a scheme without proper consideration. Acknowledging that you have a serious problem (be it debt, illness, addiction, relationship breakdown or anything else) is very demoralizing and debilitating. It is at such a time of weakness that irresponsible actions can happen.

Examples of irresponsible behaviour are:

- not opening mail – 'it's always bad news'
- refusing to work – 'what's the point?'
- selling items without considering whether this is appropriate or whether a better price may be obtained – 'I'm desperate for cash'
- paying some bills without considering other bills
- refusing to spend money on essentials such as food – 'you know we can't afford it'
- allowing utilities to be disconnected
- making over assets to someone else
- refusing to do anything about the debt – 'let them do their worst'
- irresponsible spending – 'I might as well as enjoy myself while I can'
- rushing into debt consolidation or bankruptcy – 'problem solved'.

All such irresponsible behaviour must be resisted. This may be difficult, particularly for those close to the debtor who may still be recovering from the pain of getting the debtor to face up to the reality.

Dramatic gestures are always wrong. It may make the person feel better for three seconds, but it creates an additional problem at a difficult time. No-one should live their life as a **soap opera**. In soap operas, dramatic gestures such as walking out of the room and hanging up on the telephone are a necessary part of the drama. Picking needless quarrels with friends and family comprises much of the plot, and refusing to resolve quarrels allows this plot to extend over several episodes. No sensible person ever behaves like a character in *Neighbours*. There is a risk that television entertainment can provide role models.

The issues raised by the debtor all have answers, if the debtor is committed to overcoming the problem and going on to lead a financially responsible life. Here are some possible answers:

1 Why should I open my post? It's only bad news
Any debt recovery must start from a position of quantifying the position. You must know how much is owed, what interest may be accruing, and what steps the creditor is considering.

2 What is the point in working? Anything I get will go to someone else
Any debt recovery plan depends on the creditors seeing that the debtor is being responsible in clearing old debts and living within means for the future. No creditor will tolerate a situation where the debtor simply refuses to do what he can to help.

3 I'm selling it because I'm desperate for cash
Self-martyrdom plays no part in debt recovery. Selling the family television is unlikely to make any significant contribution to clearing debts. A glance at eBay or in classified advertisements shows that a second-hand television may sell for as little as £40, which will make no impression on a debt of £100,000. But selling the television will have a massive negative impact on your family life. Denied televiewing, children will find other things to do which may create far more serious problems.

4 You know we can't afford it
Refusal to spend money on essentials, such as heating, utilities and food, is another form of self-martyrdom likely to create more problems than it solves. Even bankruptcy recognizes that people must spend to live. Economizing is an essential ingredient in any debt recovery programme – to a point. Many supposed economies are fool's economies which can end up costing more.

5 Let them do their worst
The problem with this attitude is that 'they' *will* do their worst, and this is worse than what they will do if you co-operate. Goods may be seized which could be saved, a person may be bankrupted when a plan could have been prepared, legal restrictions may be imposed which could have been avoided. Acknowledging the problem is an essential step in addressing the problem; non-co-operation has no part to play.

6 I might as well as enjoy myself while I can
This is another form of denial and non-co-operation. It is likely to lead to a greater reluctance by creditors to agree to any sensible financial recovery, and could therefore considerably delay the day when the debtor can enjoy himself again with a clear conscience.

7 Problem solved
A debtor must be told not to rush into a scheme advertised on television, such as 'roll up all your debts into one single repayable loan'. It seems too easy and simple to be true – because it isn't.
    The dangers of simply rolling up a loan like this are:

- the debtor replaces unsecured debts with a secured debt, increasing the chances of losing his home
- the debtor loses any opportunity to negotiate the debts
- the debt increases, as the company usually charges the equivalent of one month's debt repayment for its costs, and may charge fees on top
- the debt takes longer to repay, and ends up costing more.

As part of a debt recovery plan, it may be sensible to consider debt consolidation, but that is a matter to consider at a much later stage, not now. If rolling up a debt does prove to be a sensible option, there is no need to use a company advertised on television; you simply take out a personal loan and pay off all your other creditors.

In general, you should avoid all financial products advertised on television or with glitzy advertisements in magazines. Such products tend to be laden with charges to pay for the advertising when there are less expensive products available. A financial product advertised on television is not always bad – it just probably is.

Attitude to money

Avoiding debt, recovering from debt and staying out of debt is made much easier by a healthy attitude to money.

An often misquoted Bible saying is that money is the root of all evil. The Bible does not teach this; the actual quote is 'the *love* of money is the root of all evil' (1 Timothy 6.10). Money itself is neither good nor bad; it is simply an asset that can be used for good or evil.

Money should always be seen as a means to an end, and not as an end in itself.

One of the biggest practical problems with debt recovery is that debtors do not see borrowed money as 'real money'. A credit card facility of £5,000 is treated as a windfall of £5,000 to be spent. If the balance on the credit card statement shows £3,000 owing, this can be seen as £2,000 worth of facility 'wasted'.

This is entirely the wrong attitude. A credit card should only be used as a convenient method of paying for goods *where the whole balance is cleared each month*, reducing the balance owed to nil. In many cases, a debt recovery plan may involve cutting up and cancelling all credit cards, and reverting to using actual cash – pieces of paper and metal with a picture of the Queen on. An objection is that this imposes a security risk as cash can easily be lost or stolen. While true, the real risk it represents is usually much less than the risk of getting carried away with a credit card. Also credit cards can themselves be stolen and fraudulently used for much greater sums.

Outline of debt recovery plan

1 Quantify, list and categorize all debts.
2 Identify income and expenditure for current lifestyle.
3 From income and expenditure statement, work out how to economize.
4 Consider possible sources of additional funding.
5 Establish how much income can be spared to repay debtors.
6 Prepare a financial plan to repay creditors.
7 Negotiate terms with creditors.

2

Budgeting

Introduction

Preparing a budget involves two steps:

- recording income and expenditure
- controlling them.

These steps are accounting and budgeting. The accounting is known as **personal accounting**. It is a useful discipline for all individuals, even those who do not have a debt problem.

Income is the money coming in from all sources. For most people, it simply comprises their pay. There may be some other amounts such as child benefit, interest or dividends on savings, and perhaps earnings from a second job or from renting a room. In every case you record the amount you actually receive, after any tax or other deductions.

Expenditure is where the money goes. Expenditure is really just another word for spending.

Accounting

The first step is simply basic **accounting**. You record all the money you receive and all your spending. This means that every last penny must be recorded. There must be no category of 'spending money'. This must be analysed into fares, entertainment, food and suchlike.

The simplest way to do this is to buy a notebook and record all the money coming in on the left-hand page, and all your spending on the right-hand page. There will usually be many more items on the right-hand page. That is normal.

If you are computer literate, a program such as *Microsoft Money* is an effective way of keeping records, but you must be disciplined into keeping it up to date. The purpose is defeated if you find you cannot remember what you spent money on two weeks ago.

At the end of each month, you analyse income and expenditure. In practice, there will usually be little to analyse under income. It is the expenditure side where the real work is done.

Categories

A common mistake in setting up a personal accounting system is to make it too complicated.

All you need is to identify about 15 or so categories of expenditure and put all your expenditure into those categories. Many items can be lumped together. For example, electricity, gas, water, TV licence and telephone can all be included as 'utilities'. You could include council tax with utilities. Petrol, MOT tests, breakdown cover, repairs, servicing, road tax, motor insurance and car accessories can all be included as 'car expenses'.

A typical list might include:

- mortgage (or rent)
- utilities
- council tax
- car expenses
- insurance
- fares to work
- entertainment
- food and other household spending
- gifts and presents
- clothes and personal items
- children's expenses
- interest paid, bank charges and other financial charges
- holidays
- charitable donations
- sundry.

Ready-made forms are available from Credit Action (see Appendix 2) free of charge.

Where you are not sure how to classify an item, remember that it is the *purpose* of the spending that matters, not its nature. Accounts are always prepared for a purpose, to paint a picture of what we are doing with our money. We need to know how much we are spending in entertaining ourselves, how much we spend on our children – that sort of thing. We do not need to know how much we spend on vegetables, on fruit and on meat. We do not need to know how much we spend at the convenience store. So motor insurance is classified as a car expense, and not under 'insurance', which is limited to house and contents insurance, life insurance and perhaps some other items.

Similarly it is usual not to have a single category for travel, but to split it between travelling to work, holidays, and travelling in the course of entertainment.

Food, newspapers and household items such as light bulbs, matches, nails, bin bags and cooking foil can be a single item.

The final item in any list of expense categories is always **sundry** for those things which do not fit into any other category. This category should be used as little as possible.

In some cases, there may be additional categories which are appropriate for you, particularly if the amounts are significant. A self-employed person may wish to split all spending between business and personal use (and will need the former anyway for tax purposes). If someone has an expensive hobby, that could be a separate heading.

All spending must be included whether paid by cheque, standing order, direct debit, cash or credit card. The spending must be recorded *when incurred*.

If you use credit cards, you should include the whole cost of whatever you buy on the card when you buy it, even if you do not pay the whole balance when you receive the credit card statement. Thereafter you should include any interest or late payment charges under 'interest paid etc'.

If you have savings or pay into a pension fund, that should be a separate category of expenditure. An exception is where the pension contribution is deducted from your pay.

Always make sure that you check the bank statement *before* completing your monthly analysis. You must ensure that all standing orders, direct debits and bank charges are included. This process also checks that no cheques have bounced, and that neither you nor the bank has made any mistakes.

If using a computer system or a more sophisticated accounting system, you will keep a separate account for each bank account and credit card, and one for cash. The statements can then be **reconciled** to your records. Note that it is your record which is the 'correct' account, so always reconcile the bank statement to your records, not the other way round. On-line banking makes this process even simpler. However, this is only needed for operating a computer-based accounting system or where you have a particular need for a proper accounting system. For most personal systems a notebook simply listing items is quite sufficient. A notebook is preferable to pieces of paper as it is less easily lost and the pages cannot get out of order.

Always start each month on a new page, even if there is only one item on the last page. Always head each page with something like 'Expenditure: February 2007' so you know what the page is recording. Write neatly.

How you do the analysis is a matter of choice. The simplest method is to list all spending as incurred. Provided you keep each month separate, it does not matter that the days do not always run consecutively. You then go through the list taking one category at a time, adding up the items on a calculator and recording the total for each category on a separate page. Make sure that the totals are themselves totalled and checked against the total of all items of spending, to ensure that no item has been missed. Record the totals in the notebook, not on a separate piece of paper. Always write neatly; there must never be any doubt as to what you have written.

A more sophisticated but still simple system is to use a **cash analysis** book, available for a few pounds from most stationers. The difference is that different columns are used for different categories of spending. This is known as the **columnar system** of record keeping.

You will not usually have enough columns for every category of spending, so it is normal to allocate a column for those items where you have the *greatest number* of items (not the greatest value). The final column, which is usually wider, records all items in categories which do not have their own column. Once you have decided which categories to allocate to which column, keep to that for the whole notebook. Do not change from one month to the next, as it will lead to mistakes.

If more than one page is needed for a month (as will almost always be the case), all pages except the last for each month have each column totalled and marked **c/fwd**. This stands for 'carried forward'. These figures are then the first items in each column on the second and every subsequent page for that month. The 'details' are **b/fwd**, which stands for 'brought forward'.

A page from a cash analysis notebook may look like Figure 1.

Figure 1. Page from a cash analysis notebook.

Expenditure: February 2007

Date	How paid	Details	Car	Household	Entert.	Children	Other
2.2.07	Cheque	Gas bill					Utility 147-29
3.2.07	Cheque	Road tax	175 —				
3.2.07	Cash	Milk bill		21-06			
5.2.07	Cash	Cinema			27-00		
5.2.07	Cash	Popcorn			3-20		
5.2.07	Cash	Taxi home			11-00		
6.2.07	Cash	Bar of chocolate			1-20		
6.2.07	Cash	Fares to work					Travel 6-30
7.2.07	Card	Petrol	51-19				
7.2.07	Cash	Pocket money				4-00	
8.2.07	D/D	Phone bill					Utility 47-16
		c/fwd	226-19	21-06	42-40	4-00	200-75

Note that we record the date, details and how the bill was paid. D/D means direct debit and would be taken from the bank statement. You may prefer to write the six-digit cheque number rather than 'cheque' in the 'how paid' column. You may want to write the name of the credit card used, rather than 'card'. That is fine.

It is also possible to have another column headed **Amount** which lists the total spending for each item separately from the columns which analyse that spending. In the example above, this column would total £494.40, which is how much has been spent on those days. The five columns on the right then analyse that total spending. The advantages of having an Amount column are that you have a running total of all spending on each page, and having to check that the totals for each column add up to this Amount total provides an additional check against mistakes.

Even from such a simple and short example, a picture is emerging of spending. We can see that the night at the cinema cost £41.20 if we include the popcorn and taxi home. All this is needed for when we prepare a budget, and if we decide to economize.

Each month you find the total for each category of spending. At the end of the year you add up the total of each monthly category and find out how much you spent in each category for the whole year.

The **year** may be any period of 12 months, but it is usually sensible to keep to the calendar year. It also provides something useful to do in the cold days of early January. But you can make up accounts for any 12-month period, such as from 1 April to 31 March, if you wish. A 12-month period which spans two calendar years is described in the form '2007/08'.

Before leaving the subject of accounting, it is important to clear up confusion over the words **debit** and **credit**. In normal speech, we talk of a credit meaning money going *into* our bank account, as in 'my account has been credited with £100 I paid in'. In bookkeeping terms, the words have the exact opposite meaning. A bookkeeper will record a payment of £100 into your account as a *debit*. Money going out of your account is a *credit*. This arises because bank statements are produced from the bank's perspective, not yours.

In terms of a bank account, debit means 'in' and credit means 'out'. If you go on to study double-entry bookkeeping, you will find that debit and credit mean much more, but that need not concern an individual who simply wants to keep control of spending.

Budgeting

Accounting involves receiving and spending money which is then recorded. Budgeting does this the other way round; you prepare the budget *before* you receive and spend the money.

A budget is a plan of how much you expect to earn and spend in a defined period, usually one year. The spending is per category, with one exception.

In strict accounting terms, a **budget** is an order. In a business, a sales budget is how much business the sales department is required to find. The premises budget is how much the premises manager may spend. In contrast, a **forecast** is simply what the accountant *expects* to happen. However, the word budget is often used to mean a forecast even in the business context.

The two main types of budget are the **fixed budget** and the **zero-based budget**. The fixed budget simply adjusts the spending of the previous year to reflect factors known about the next year. For example, you may increase figures to allow for inflation. If you know that your income will go down, you reduce the figure for income. A zero-based budget starts from scratch where every item of spending is zero unless you can justify it. In practice, the two methods are much closer than they may seem and tend to produce similar results.

There is also a **flexible budget** which relates expenditure to income, so the more income is generated, the more expenditure is permitted. This is appropriate only for commercial activities where there is a clear nexus between income and expenditure. For example, if income is derived from selling a product, you obviously need more expenditure to buy more products to sell more. Using a flexible budget without such a clear nexus is a false justification to fritter away money, and defeats the object of debt management.

You must budget for all items whenever payable. In 2007, a car probably costs at least £700 a year to maintain. A monthly budget should include £60 for car maintenance.

In most years there are **one-off expenses**. These are items which are unique to that year, such as buying a new household item or a new car, or settling a legal bill or paying for a training course or exam. Where these items have been incurred in one year, they should not be reflected in the budget for next year. Instead you add a new expense category called **contingency**. This may be as much as 10% of all your spending. Contingency simply means items not thought of at the time. They are next year's one-off expenses. Without this category, you will almost certainly not live within your budget. Contingencies are included in the government's accounts and in company budgets and building contracts. It is how accountants plan for the unplanned.

A budget must be realistic. If you decide that your figure for entertainment will be half what it was in the previous year, you must know how you will meet that budget.

> ## The Debt Doctor's Advice
>
> Never put a figure in a budget unless you know how you will meet it.

The objective of budgeting was most eloquently expressed by Mr Micawber in Charles Dickens' novel *David Copperfield*:

> Annual income twenty pounds, annual expenditure nineteen nineteen six, result happiness. Annual income twenty pounds, annual expenditure twenty pounds ought and six, result misery.

For those not familiar with Victorian English and pre-decimal currency, he is saying that happiness comes from having expenditure sixpence less than income; misery comes from having expenditure sixpence more than income.

A budget which plans to spend more than is earned is known as a **deficit budget**. There are a few limited circumstances when a deficit budget may be appropriate, such as when starting a new business or having a gap year for training. In each case, the budget should have been planned years in advance to build up funds to cover the deficit. Normally, a budget should always plan for a **surplus** of income over expenditure.

There is an accounting concept known as the **prudence concept**. This can be summarized as 'fear the worst'. Where there is uncertainty, income should be understated and expenditure overstated. Suppose your income is likely to be in the range of £16,000 to £17,000, and your expenditure in the range of £14,000 to £15,000. Your budget shows income of £16,000 and expenditure of £15,000. This concept reflects the reality that finances have a habit of not turning out as well as planned. There is not a problem if the finances do perform better than expected.

If the first budget shows a deficit, you should look to see what can be done to address that. Chapter 3 gives advice on economizing.

Most guides on economizing look at marginal savings. Changing your electricity supplier may save you £10 a year, paying by direct debit can save you £20 a year, Nectar points from Sainsbury's can save you £15, and so on. While these are all usually worth having, they will not address the problem of a deficit budget. Small savings do add up, and also have the advantage of forcing a debtor to appreciate the value of items. Serious debt recovery is usually addressed by a lifestyle change, such as only running one car, making lunch rather than buying it, and not buying any new clothes for a year.

When you prepare your monthly accounts the next year, you should compare them with your budget to see how well you are doing. If your annual budget for entertainment is £1,800, your monthly budget is £150. After three months you should have spent no more than £450. If you have actually spent £550, you are £100 over budget and must rein in future expenditure.

In accounting terms, your **actual** is £550 against budget of £450. This is a **variance** of minus £100.

Some sense is needed in comparing budget to actual. Some expenses such as TV licence and road tax are usually paid once a year. Depending on when in the year this is paid, you could have a positive or negative variance during the year while still being on budget for the whole year. The monthly check should not automatically see every positive variance as an opportunity to spend more and every negative variance as a need to rein in spending. The question to ask is 'Am I still on target to hit my budget at the end of the year?'

Budgeting must also consider **cashflow**. This is when the money is available. It is cheaper to tax a car for 12 months than twice for six months, but the latter may be the only option if you cannot find sufficient funds when the tax is due.

Attitude to borrowing

It is quite likely that the debt doctor will hear views that all debt is immoral (possibly excluding mortgages) and borrowing money is always wrong: 'You should save up for what you want as we did in the good old days'.

Such comments are questionable both historically and logically. Historically, borrowing money for business has existed from Old Testament times. Borrowing money to buy household goods was common in the 1930s and was only halted by the war and post-war austerity. Credit was resumed from around 1954 when rationing ended and consumerism resumed.

While it is usually better financially to pay outright for possessions rather than borrow, it is difficult to see that borrowing is morally wrong. Taking out a loan to buy a car and repaying it during the life of the car simply means that you are paying for the car as you use it, in the same way that you pay for the petrol. In effect, the purchase price of the car has become a hire charge.

What is important for debt management is not the enforcement of arbitrary values based on sentiment, but for any borrowing to be responsibly managed within proper financial controls.

3

Economizing

Introduction

Economizing should be part of everybody's mindset, whatever the health of their finances. If your finances are healthy, economizing makes them more healthy. If your finances are a bit rocky, economizing can sort out the problem. If you have serious debt problems, economizing is *part* of the solution but you need to do much more.

Economizing means spending money more wisely; it does not necessarily mean spending less money nor having fewer products and services. In some cases, you can end up with more products and services.

Financial products are a particular area where significant economies can be made. These include insurance, banking, pensions, mortgages, savings and suchlike. For some reason, many people do not see these as 'products' at all and just take whatever is offered. Always think of a bank as a shop – the bank does.

A couple may spend hours deciding which fridge to buy and yet not spend even ten minutes choosing a mortgage. A fridge is a box which keeps food cool and where your choice is basically between a big one or a little one. Shopping around may save you £20. A mortgage typically costs about twice the sum borrowed, so a £250,000 mortgage costs about £500,000. Shopping around could easily save you £10,000. More information is given on page 90.

In particular, do not believe that a financial product is good just because the company's other products are good. There are many retailers selling excellent household goods at excellent prices, but also offering dreadful extended warranties or credit terms for them.

Bad buys

Some products and services are such bad buys that it is most unlikely that you should ever waste your money on them. These include:

- extended warranties
- credit card protection insurance
- dread illness insurance
- book clubs and record clubs
- National Lottery tickets
- packaged bank accounts
- telephone competitions and TV quizzes
- collectables
- savings plans
- most DVDs.

Extended warranties

Extended warranties are heavily marketed whenever you buy an electrical product and extend the period for which you are entitled to free repair or replacement.

Whenever new consumer goods are sold by a trader, there is a legal requirement that they must be 'of satisfactory quality' under Sale of Goods Act 1979 s14(2). If the goods are faulty, from 31 March 2003 you are entitled to repair or replacement within 'a reasonable time' under *Sale and Supply of Goods to Consumers Regulations SI 2002/3045*. Under an EC directive effective from 1 January 2002, it is assumed that any failure in the first six months is down to faulty goods unless the supplier can demonstrate otherwise, such as by misuse. For the next 18 months, up to two years after the purchase, you can still claim but you must prove that the fault existed at the time of supply.

These provisions you have under the law. Note that they do not apply when you buy second-hand goods, nor if you buy from a non-trader, such as from a person selling goods by a classified ad or on eBay. You still have some protection, but not as much.

Most reputable suppliers offer their own guarantee which may only be *additional* to what the law imposes. For example, many suppliers of electrical goods guarantee their products for 12 months. The extended warranty extends that, typically to three, four or five years for an additional fee.

In practice, electrical goods tend not to break down these days. If they do break down within the extended period *and* you can find your receipts *and* you can take it to the supplier who is still in business, they will repair it for you, which can take two months. It is usually cheaper simply to throw the product away and buy another one, either second-hand or new.

The worst extended warranty offer the author has seen was for a radio sold by Comet in February 2006. The radio cost £18.99, which seems a good price for what looks like a good product. The extended warranty was another £34.99. You could save yourself £16 simply by buying a second radio as a spare!

Credit card protection insurance

Credit card companies offer 'protection against illness and unemployment' for 'only 75p per £100'. You may even be offered this as a 'special offer' for a 'privileged customer'. This is not a special offer for a privileged customer, it is a rip-off available to anyone daft enough to fall for it.

These schemes are deceptive in the extreme. The 75p is *per month*, so you are paying £3 a year to insure £100 against an eventuality that will probably not happen. If you do claim, perhaps on becoming unemployed, it does not wipe out the balance, but reduces it a little until you start work again. If you do not work again, you could still find that half the balance remains payable. Further explanation is given on page 257.

If you do want to insure your ability to pay your debts if unemployed or ill, obtain income protection insurance. Typically it will give you better cover for about one fifth of the amount.

Dread illness insurance

Dread illness insurance was invented by insurance companies around 1990 to find something else to sell us. At the time there were scare stories about everyone dying from AIDS on top of normal fears about cancer. This insurance sought to exploit that fear.

The policy pays out a sum if you contract HIV (AIDS), cancer or any of a defined list of illnesses. Much criticism of these policies arises when a policy holder contracts a serious condition not on the list and finds the insurance company will not pay. About one fifth of all claims are rejected for this reason.

However, the real issue is why insure at all? Insurance is intended to protect a person against a loss they cannot otherwise bear. For many of these illnesses, there is no loss at all. Thousands of people are HIV-positive or have cancer and lead perfectly normal lives with no loss of income. Doubtless these people enjoy having some extra cash from their policy, but this is not compensating them for a loss and is not insurance.

More significantly, far larger numbers become disabled through accidents, and from strokes and arthritis. A vast number of illnesses are caused by stress. These more likely eventualities are not covered by a policy. Illness rarely kills in the first half of life. Up to the age of 40 you are more likely to be murdered than die of a dread illness. By far the commonest cause of death for those under 40 is a road accident followed by other types of accident. None of these are covered by dread illness.

As with the previous item, you are better advised to take out an income protection policy which covers you regardless of what you may contract.

Book clubs and record clubs

Book clubs and record clubs are honest organizations and do not involve any deception. Their terms are spelled out quite clearly. You know what you are getting. There are some magazines which come with a CD every month. These usually represent excellent value for money.

Book clubs and record clubs are not *always* a bad buy. They usually are because most people simply collect what is supplied and never read or listen to what is provided. However, they tend to concentrate on the initial offer to get you 'hooked'. Typically you can buy £40 worth of books or records for £2, or something like that. You simply sign up and undertake to buy one book or CD every month or so for a minimum period, though some now allow you to cancel at any time. The club guarantees that the books or CDs offered will be less than their full retail price, and that you will have a choice. All this is true. These clubs rely on customers' inertia. If you do not choose a book or CD one month, you receive the editor's choice.

It may seem unfair to describe these clubs as a bad buy when they provide what they offer and almost without exception provide goods at a good price. But look again at what people buy. A book on English trees or a CD of opera themes may indeed be sold at a good price, but do you really want it? Most of such books and records simply sit on a shelf, probably unheard or unread despite your best intentions. In most cases you would never buy the CD or book in the first place.

If you do decide that you want to build up a collection of classical CDs or romantic novels, there is plenty of choice at charity shops or on the Internet at much less cost.

Collectables

Anything which is described as a collectable almost certainly is not. Few tangible items can be justified as an investment.

There is no market for current commemorative stamps or special £5 coins, nor for 'limited edition' collections of china plates depicting flowers. If you really do want such items, then budget for them as expenditure.

Most of the items which gain any significant collectable value are those which were *not* considered collectable when acquired. Even those items which do have a collectable value represent a loss in value in real terms. A nineteenth-century farm implement may have cost several weeks' wages when bought, yet be sold for the equivalent of a few hours' wages more than a century later.

Similarly, consider carefully **magazines** that build up into a set. Typically the first edition is heavily promoted with a generous gift. By the time you have bought all the editions and the binders, you have probably paid hundreds of pounds to acquire the equivalent of a book which could be bought for £20.

Even **jewellery** is not an investment. For all but the most expensive jewellery, the value of the item is half the price. So a ring which costs £200 is worth £100. Jewellery tends not to hold its value against inflation, so even this £100 will slowly lose value.

Sometimes people believe that gold is a good investment. Historically this is not so, as gold tends to do well only when other investments are doing badly. Over long periods of time, gold loses value, as do most metals and gems. If you want jewellery for its beauty and pleasure, buy it as part of your budgeted expenditure, but do not believe there is any investment value.

National Lottery tickets

'It could be you', but it never is. All forms of gambling are bad buys. Further comment is given on page 40.

Packaged bank accounts

Banks now have a love of offering bank accounts which carry a monthly charge but offer all sorts of goodies. Typically they include travel insurance, low-commission foreign currency, discount rates on various items and similar.

Such accounts are often billed as 'Gold' or 'Privilege', implying that you are given exclusive treatment, you are important and a member of this in-crowd. This is all a nonsense playing on your vanity.

All packaged accounts represent bad value for money. Discounts on car hire and suchlike are easily obtained. Travel insurance is cheap if taken out for a year at a time. Foreign currency can be converted free at the Post Office. A bank account should be a piggy bank where you pay money in and take it out, and nothing else.

Telephone competitions and TV quizzes

Telephone competitions are another rip-off designed simply to accumulate money from callers.

Never dial a number starting 09. That is a premium rate number which can cost £1.50 a minute. When you get through, you may find that you are kept waiting before speaking to a very friendly person who just needs to take down some details, and is only too delighted to help you in any way possible. When you are paying £90 an hour, they can afford to be. A simple call to answer a question seen on television can easily take six minutes. You have spent £9 to enter a competition where you have a 1 in 100,000 chance to win something worth perhaps £100.

Competitions are also sometimes used as scams, as explained on page 42.

Savings plans

Savings plans are often bad buys as they can be stuffed full of charges and offer a very poor rate of return.

People in financial difficulties can be very reluctant to give up a savings plan as it represents some hope for them of cash for the future.

You should never invest in anything you do not understand, and should always read the small print. The author has seen supposedly wonderful savings schemes which offer:

- 10% over six years, not 10% a year, which would be excellent (and was what the person thought he had bought) but 10% after six years, a pathetic return of 1.6% a year;
- a 'guaranteed' rate of 6% a year, except that there is a clause which states that they may reduce this rate if interest rates or share prices fall. In other words, there is no guarantee at all.

These 'investments' were respectively held by a professor and a company director, showing that even intelligent people can be tricked by slick marketing.

By far the best long-term investment is shares. Despite their much-publicized fall during the years 2000 to 2003, over a 20-year period shares outperform any other investment, including unit trusts. This is because there is just one charge when you buy them and no more while you leave the certificate in your files and bank the dividend cheques.

In 2007, Lloyds TSB sells various savings accounts offering around 4%. This means that either your capital grows at 4% a year or you can take 4% a year as income and leave the capital alone where it will slowly reduce in value through inflation. Yet you could get a Lloyds TSB product which gives you 7% income a year *and* sees the capital grow by at least 5% a year. You do not buy from the bank, you buy the bank itself in the form of Lloyds TSB shares.

If you are not convinced, there are plenty of straightforward and safe investments from National Savings available at any Post Office.

As a general rule, a savings plan is likely to be a bad bargain if:

- sold by a bank
- advertised
- (worst of all) if offered by a phone call.

DVDs *and videos*

DVDs and videos are honestly sold. The question a purchaser should ask is how many times will the DVD or video be watched? If the honest answer is dozens of times, then the DVD or video is not a bad buy. Very young children will watch the same DVD or video dozens of times, just as they will repeatedly listen to the same bedtime story.

For most of us, a DVD or video of a film or television programmes will be watched once. Then perhaps once more in a few years' time and then never again. Ask yourself how many times have you ever watched one film. In most cases, a person is better off subscribing to Sky television or renting DVDs from Blockbusters.

Spending less

On average, a household has no control of 57% of its expenditure. This 57% covers the mortgage, council tax, house insurance, loan repayments and most utilities. This figure is usually much higher for those starting out in independent adult life, and is much less for the retired or those approaching retirement.

Economizing usually involves saving as much as possible from the other 43%. This is sometimes called **free money** or **disposable income** because it is the money where we have freedom over how it is spent. The rest is sometimes called **committed money**.

The distinction is not always clear cut, as road tax could be saved by not having a car, and mortgage payments could be reduced by living in a smaller home. However, the distinction is useful in planning economies.

Shop around

Before any significant expenditure, ask yourself:

- do I really need it? If, in truth, the expenditure is for a status symbol, or to satisfy a want rather than a need, save your money.
- where is the cheapest source? Look at different sources, check prices on the Internet, read the *Which?* report.
- wait for sales. If necessary ask your loved ones if they will accept a Christmas present in January or Valentine flowers at the end of February.

Remember to shop around for financial products and not only tangible products. Look for the best deals on loans, insurance, pensions, bank charges and suchlike. You do not have to accept whatever poor terms you are offered.

Suppose you visit a new supermarket and are greeted by someone aged 22 in a sharp suit and reeking of cheap after-shave. They welcome you to the store and ask you how many oranges you intend to buy each month. They then ask you to fill in a form committing you to buy 10 oranges a month for the next 12 months with a penalty clause of £35 should you be naughty enough to buy 11 oranges one month. They explain that you have the option to renew your contract for oranges after 12 months, they offer you expensive insurance against not being able to pay for the oranges, and they charge you £100 arrangement fee for setting all this up.

You would probably never use that supermarket again because the terms are so ludicrous. Yet these are exactly the terms quoted by most banks for loans! Understand that banks sell loans in the same way that supermarkets sell oranges. A bank is not doing you any favour by providing you with a loan – it is simply trading with you.

The Debt Doctor's Advice

Remember, a bank manager is just a shopkeeper.

Sometimes people say 'My bank manager has told me to . . . ' Understand that a bank manager is not a doctor or priest, giving you proper advice in your best interests. A bank manager is just a shopkeeper whose sole purpose in life is to sell his wares and make big profits for his employer (and possibly commission for himself). A bank manager can never *tell* a person what to do. A bank manager may advise a person. In the author's experience this will usually be bad advice.

Someone may receive conflicting advice and not know who to believe. The first test is to ask if the adviser has a vested interest. Anyone trying to sell you something is likely to offer poorer advice than someone with no interest. Second, look at the adviser's experience. The lady in the cake shop may be right in her advice, but she won't have the knowledge and experience of an accountant. And you can always check the advice with what this book says.

Consider second-hand

Ask yourself if you really need a new product. For some items, such as low-cost items and electronic goods, this is probably not an option. For other items, including clothes, it is.

Immediately you use a new product, it becomes a second-hand product. So what disadvantage is there in starting with a second-hand product?

Regular expenditure

Any item of regular expenditure should be reviewed. Suppose you have a special coffee or two pints of beer every day at work as your little indulgence.

There are about 240 working days in a year (48 weeks of 5 days). The £4 you pay for a coffee and a cake each day is £1,000 a year. The £5 for two pints of beer is £1,250 a year. This does not make it wrong, but it does mean that you should consider whether this expenditure is really necessary. Would you rather make your own coffee and have that £1,000 for something else?

Even fares to work may be avoidable if the journey could be made by walking or cycling. Alternatively there may be scope for sharing cars with a colleague.

Particular items of spending

Food

Considerable savings can be made by preparing your own food rather than by eating out or buying prepared food.

At 2006 prices, a mug of coffee typically costs £2 in a coffee shop or about 4p to make at home.

A pub lunch for perhaps £6 is good value compared with restaurants. However, a varied and balanced nutritious two-course adequate lunch at home can be provided from ingredients costing 60p or less per meal. In April 2005, one London school was providing dinners for just 37p a pupil.

At 2007 prices, £30 to £40 per person per week is more than enough to buy the ingredients for normal home cooking. This allows for the occasional steak and smoked salmon. It allows for some prepared foods, such as frozen vegetables. It allows for crisps, sweets, nice desserts and soft drinks.

Supermarkets are always offering promotions which can make huge savings. Details of supermarket promotions are given on the website www.fixtureferrets.co.uk.

Cars

Define what you want from a vehicle, and look for that. Here is an example from the author's experience:

Example: replacement car

In 2005, a man needing a new car found an old Mercedes which exactly matched his needs: large, comfortable, reliable, powerful, capable of carrying his family of five, a boot big enough to carry his equipment, fairly economical for his limited mileage, and it looked good. It cost just £2,600.

The salesman tried to sell him a newer Mercedes for £30,000, concentrating on what a bargain price this was and how much the car normally cost.

When asked what he would get for an extra £27,000, the salesman paused and said that it was newer and a more modern shape. After another pause, he added, 'but it's probably not so well built'. The £2,600 car was bought and proved ideal.

The AA calculates that an average car used for 10,000 miles a year costs £5,639 a year to run, the equivalent of 56.4p a mile. (An average car is one which cost between £13,000 and £20,000 when new.)

But of this figure, £2,343 is depreciation – the cost of the car itself. This is more than 41% of the whole cost of motoring.

For any car there are two sets of costs: standing charges and running costs. The **standing charges** are the cost of *ownership* – those costs you pay anyway even if you do not use the car. They comprise depreciation, road tax, insurance, cost of capital (interest on the bank loan), and breakdown cover. The **running costs** are the cost of *usage* – those costs which relate to using the car. They comprise petrol, tyres, repairs, servicing, tolls and parking.

A summary of AA figures for 2006 is given in Figure 2.

Figure 2: Cost of running a car (provided by the AA).

	Cost of car				
	up to £10,000	£10,000 to £13,000	£13,000 to £20,000	£20,000 to £30,000	over £30,000
Depreciation	£1,161	£1,611	£2,343	£3,266	£5,178
Total standing charges	£1,933	£2,608	£3,541	£4,979	£7,471
Petrol per mile	9.5p	10.9p	12.1p	16.0p	18.7p
Total running costs	16.0p	18.3p	21.0p	26.1p	30.4p
All costs per mile:					
5,000 miles	54.2p	69.8p	90.9p	£1.24	£1.78
10,000 miles	35.4p	44.3p	56.4p	75.9p	£1.06
15,000 miles	29.2p	36.1p	45.2p	60.2p	81.5p
20,000 miles	26.3p	32.1p	39.9p	52.7p	70.3p
30,000 miles	23.0p	27.7p	33.8p	44.1p	57.5p

A full analysis and latest figures can be obtained from the AA website www.theaa.com.

Even for the smallest car, the annual depreciation cost of £1,611 is more than enough to buy a comfortable, roadworthy and reliable second-hand car. Just look at *Autotrader*, *Loot* or any local newspaper. Let us assume that this car cost £1,400 and lasts eight years (the average). Its depreciation figure is just £175 a year.

So the cost of motoring for someone who drives 10,000 miles a year is:

- £1,775 in a reliable small second-hand car
- £3,540 in a new small car
- £5,640 in a new medium-sized car
- £10,600 in a Chelsea tractor.

It should also be noted that petrol consumption is significantly affected by how you drive. The most obvious scope for economy is that driving at 50 mph can use 25% less petrol per mile than driving at 70 mph.

Of other factors, a gentle acceleration can use 30% less petrol than fierce acceleration, and removing unnecessary weight can lead to a 5% fuel efficiency.

Cosmetics

Cosmetics can cost a fortune, often for very little effect.

On this subject, I can do no better than quote wise words from Anita Roddick, founder of The Body Shop, a leading bodycare and shampoo company:

> There is no cream in the world that will restore youth to a 50-year-old woman. But for some reason, we let the beauty industry sell us that hope.
>
> No matter what chemical formula is on the label, no cream will make your breasts bigger or your thighs thinner. No shampoo will get rid of split ends, no matter what the manufacturers claim. If you want to get rid of split ends, cut your hair. All a shampoo will do is clean your hair. That's it.
>
> Most of what we think of as ageing is actually exposure to sunlight, so the most effective anti-ageing product is a sun hat.
>
> *Business as Unusual* by Anita Roddick (Thorsons)

Roddick further explains that the only skincare products that do anything are soap and moisturizer, and any will do.

Even in healthcare products, there are many cheaper alternatives.

Warm salty water is effective as oral antiseptic, for example, and costs almost nothing.

Clothes

Economizing does not mean that a debtor must dress unfashionably or wear rags. It does mean that a different choice of supplier may be appropriate and that a different approach is needed.

Using 2007 prices, a man's suit can cost £400 from a tailor, £150 from a high street retailer or £20 from a charity shop. A woman's dress can cost £300 from a designer store, £60 from a high street chain or £10 from a charity shop. The cheapest goods may be as good as the most expensive.

Perhaps a more fundamental approach is to look at your wardrobe. It probably contains many garments worn just once or twice, perhaps bought on a whim.

A more effective approach is the **capsule wardrobe**. For most people there are some colour combinations which particularly suit their complexion, perhaps green and brown. Clothes are bought in those colours with several accessories. Thus a large number of combinations can be created from few garments. The concept was invented by Susie Faux in the 1970s.

For a woman, the wardrobe need only comprise:

- two pairs of trousers
- a dress or skirt
- well-fitting jacket
- coat
- knitted jacket or smart cardigan
- one pair of flat-heel shoes and one pair with higher heels
- a small formal bag, and a larger bag.

The advice is that the garments should be well made and fit perfectly. The list is completed with accessories and underclothes.

Fuel costs

Heating the home is a major expense. Following soaring fuel prices in 2005 and 2006, it can now easily cost £1,000 a year to heat a home. For many homes, savings in hundreds of pounds can easily be made.

Simple economies can reduce that bill significantly. A heating bill can be cut by:

- 35% by fitting cavity wall insulation
- 32% by replacing a boiler more than 15 years old with a new and much more efficient one
- 30% by turning the thermostat down by 1 degree C
- 25% by insulating the loft
- 20% by fitting draughtproofing
- 17% by careful timing of when the heating is on
- 5% by fitting double glazing or secondary glazing
- 1% by having fitted carpets over floorboards.

Insulating a hot water tank saves 75% of the heat used. The capital cost of lagging hot water pipes and tanks is usually recovered in a few months.

There may be grants available for insulation. The local authority should be able to advise. Retired people may receive an allowance for winter fuel.

Switching off lights can save a small sum. Suppose electricity is sold to you at 12p a unit, equivalent to 1000 watts for one hour. Leaving a 60-watt light bulb switched on for eight hours while you sleep uses 0.48 units, costing 5.75p a day. For 365 days, this is £21 a year.

A more effective cost saving is to use low-energy **light bulbs**. This can save £78 in electricity costs for the lifetime of the bulb.

Leaving televisions, videos and computers on **standby** uses between 10% and 60% of the energy when the appliance is on. This is saved by switching them off completely.

Another common saving is to boil only the amount of water needed for hot beverages. In an unscientific experiment in the author's kitchen using a common 2.2 kilowatt **electric kettle**, it took 82 seconds to boil one mug of water, and 128 seconds to boil two mugs. At 12p a unit, this costs 0.27p for one mug and 0.43p for two mugs. If you drink five mugs of tea or coffee a day, you will save £232 a year by only boiling the water you need.

Other energy-saving tips are:

- use lids on saucepans
- do not leave fridge and freezer doors open
- don't set the hot water above 60C (140F)
- fix leaking hot taps (a dripping tap can fill a bath in a week).

The author's young daughter wishes me to add that, in addition to saving you money, you should do all these things to protect the environment and save penguins.

At present, microgeneration is not a cost-effective option. **Micro-generation** is when a home generates some of its own electricity. A solar panel can save 75% of the fuel bill in summer and 25% in winter.

A typical fitting cost in 2007 is £12,000, so it will take about 24 years to recoup the cost. However, this period could reduce sharply as costs reduce and energy prices rise. A wind turbine cannot yet be built big enough to provide enough electricity to justify its expense. However, all this is likely to change. Modern wind turbines are already eight times more efficient than those first installed.

Family

One hopes that the decision to marry or have children is not based on financial criteria. However, they both have financial implications, particularly children.

Marriage imposes less of a financial strain, as two people can live together for about 1½ times the cost of a single person. If both parties own property, there can be a significant saving in selling them and buying one bigger property.

Children are much more of an expense. Prospective parents should look at the price of children's shoes. Actual parents quickly find that free education is very expensive.

A survey for the Liverpool Victoria Society in November 2005 found that bringing up a child can cost as much as £176,449 to the end of their university education. This is the equivalent of £22 a day. The two biggest items are:

- £46,000 childcare while the mother works
- £25,572 for university.

The cost is £50,000 for the first five years of a child's life.

A survey by the bank Egg found that parents spend £715 a year on toys. By the age of 16, a child has owned more than £11,000 worth of toys.

Holidays

There are always bargains for holidays. Try one of these websites:

www.ebookers.co.uk
www.expedia.co.uk
www.travelocity.co.uk

Other money-saving tips

- Borrow books from the library rather than buy them.
- Buy magazines on subscription, for a significant saving.
- Read most newspapers free on their website.
- Review all life insurance policies, mortgages and bank accounts every three years. There are often new cheaper products to which you can switch.
- Use direct debit to pay bills, which could save £169 a year according to BACS.
- Use term life insurance rather than whole life insurance. (Term life insurance pays if you die within a specified period; whole life insurance pays whenever you die.) Term life insurance is much cheaper and probably more exactly matches your needs.
- Ask for pay rises and be prepared to haggle with your boss.

Mindset budgeting

There are at least two areas where a person needs to make a mindset decision. These relate to indulgences and voluntary giving.

An **indulgence** may be defined as any spending which is primarily designed to give pleasure rather than meet any human need. It includes holidays, meals out, entertainment, hobbies and much else.

Help is sometimes available. For example, help with holidays may be obtained from the Family Holiday Association, 16 Mortimer Street, London W1T 3JL. Telephone 020 7436 3304, website: http://www.fhaonline.org.uk.

The Church has had an ambivalent attitude on such matters, mainly because its moral teaching tends to follow society's values rather than lead them. There is a concept of **holy poverty** which requires its adherents to lead a non-material monastic life. For most people, the obviously correct course is not to feel guilty about the occasional indulgence, but to keep it within reasonable bounds between extravagance and austerity.

There is little in the Bible to support extreme **austerity**. Jesus' first miracle was to produce over 200 gallons of wine for a wedding feast in Cana. A loving parent does not just meet his child's needs; the loving parent also provides some indulgence for the child, sweets and parties for example. The occasional indulgence can be beneficial. Here is an example from the author's experience:

An occasional indulgence

A married couple worked full-time in a successful Christian charity they founded. Both they and the charity were always just adequately funded which they took to be a sign of God's providence. Despite all this, they started to get a bit scratchy with each other and did not enjoy their work as they once did. They believed something was missing.

One day they received a cheque for £1,000 for their charitable work. With it was another cheque for £150 payable to them and subject to the condition that they were to spend it on personal luxury.

The wife bought a handbag she had admired, and they both went out and enjoyed a good meal together, the first they'd had since their wedding. This opportunity for a guilt-free indulgence together changed their attitude to their work and to each other. They described it as 'a great blessing'.

For serious debt, the usual problem is too much extravagance and self-indulgence. But in preparing a budget, extreme austerity is not to be recommended. A budgeted indulgence can provide motivation which can easily cost-justify itself.

The other mindset decision relates to **charitable giving**. It may seem odd to suggest that someone with serious financial problems should give away money unnecessarily, but that is exactly what the author does suggest. Research has shown that those who include charitable giving as part of their normal finances have a much better record of managing their finances and staying out of debt.

Several of the world's major religions teach **tithing**, giving away one tenth of one's income. Passages such as Leviticus 27.30–32 give the Old Testament law that one tenth of the harvest and every tenth animal belongs to God. In Matthew 23.23 Jesus commends tithing in a passing reference on another matter. Some take this to mean that giving away one tenth is still obligatory on Christians. Perhaps a better understanding comes from 2 Corinthians 9.7: 'each person should give as he has decided for himself; there should be no reluctance, no sense of compulsion; God loves a cheerful giver'.

The author suggests that the best policy is not to take a legalistic view but to decide how much seems appropriate in your circumstances. It seems perfectly reasonable to be more generous in those times when one enjoys prosperity. If you find you really cannot make a 5% or 10% contribution, make a nominal gift rather than no gift at all. However poor a debtor may become, there are always millions much poorer.

Sometimes Christians have 'given God his 10%' and regard the other 90% as theirs to fritter away as they like. Christian teaching is that all

100% belongs to God. We are just stewards who should spend what we have been given wisely.

Some Christians have gone as far as to promote the doctrine of the **prosperity gospel**, that God financially rewards donors, so giving £100 means that £500 will be given back which would not otherwise happen. To the author, this seems more like the love of money than the love of mankind. A better explanation is that those who practise charity demonstrate good judgment and compassion, both of which are essential qualities in proper financial management.

4

Maximizing income

Introduction

Debt recovery is primarily about bringing spending into line with income rather than bringing income into line with spending.

Nevertheless seeking ways to maximize income should still be part of the debt recovery plan. Even if such measures generate little additional income, the fact that you have looked at this matter demonstrates to the creditors how seriously the debtor is considering his position.

A debtor should seek to maximize his or her income. However, this is only likely to help ease the situation. Resolving the fundamental problem almost always involves reducing expenditure.

> ### The Debt Doctor's Advice
> Debt recovery is mainly about reducing expenditure.

The main methods of income maximization are:

- borrowing (strictly not income maximization at all, but it can help)
- selling items, or even selling the home
- additional work
- renting a room or garage
- equity release.

These are looked at below. It may also be possible to claim social security as explained in the next two chapters.

First, it is necessary to issue some cautionary warnings on what *not* to do.

What not to do

1 Immediately consolidate your debt

Do not be beguiled by television advertisements saying that all a person's debt problems can be solved just by making one free telephone call to the advertiser. The attractive female presenter and the testimonies of people whose monthly payments have halved are telling the truth, but not the whole truth.

This process is known as **debt consolidation**. It *may* be a useful step in getting out of trouble, but it is always a *later* step only to be considered once the debtor has identified all debts, and produced an assets statement and an income and expenditure account, and these have been properly considered by an accountant or debt counsellor. Even if it does prove to be advisable, there are better ways of doing this than listening to Carol Vorderman.

The usual consequences of debt consolidation are:

- an additional fee may be incurred, making the debt greater
- the debts are 'secured', which means that the debtor risks losing his home if still unable to pay the debt
- there is no scope to negotiate individual debts.

Although the rate offered in debt consolidation will usually be less than that charged by credit cards and store cards, it is still likely to be higher than other sources of finance such as extending the person's mortgage. In 2006, a typical rate for debt consolidation was 12.8%, whereas almost every mortgage then offered had a rate below 6%.

Someone paying 28% interest on £20,000 worth of debt will benefit from paying 12% interest on £21,000 debt. What may be overlooked is that the debtor will benefit far more if able to pay 6% interest on £15,000 debt.

2 Fall for get-rich-quick schemes

Serious debt problems can tempt a debtor to fall for a scam, as outlined in Chapter 13. Beware of any **get-rich-quick** scheme. The Office of Fair Trading routinely gives the sound advice that if something seems too good to be true it almost certainly is too good to be true. And if someone really did find a simple way to make money easily, they would not share it with you.

Investments that promise huge returns are usually just gambling. They will always be hedged with conditions that excuse the provider when the huge return fails to materialize. One such guaranteed scheme required people to pay £50 to find out how it worked. Those foolish enough to pay found it consisted of finding other mugs to pay £50 – there was no scheme at all.

Many schemes offer wonderful riches with testimonies of those who have made vast fortunes from little or no effort. Sometimes the literature can have page after page of such testimony and hype without saying what is involved. While writing this book, the author was contacted by such a company wanting their literature written. It took some effort to get the barely literate director to explain to his would-be copywriter that this wonderful mega-percent growth plan to untold riches was guidance on how to trade on eBay. There is nothing wrong in selling guidance – after all, that is what this book is doing. The difference is that the company was trying to sell what might justify a £15 book for a much larger figure by pretending it is something else. The work was declined.

There are also **debt vultures** who prey on individuals with debt problems, particularly where the debt arises in the course of business. Typically they are 'smooth' operators, immaculately dressed and driving an expensive car. Their typical approach is that the business looks sound, they know investors who may be able to help, and for a fee they can probably fix it up. The fee is always payable in advance and no guarantee of success is ever offered. Predictably no deal is ever arranged and the fee is lost, making the debt worse.

It is possible to obtain finance for a business in difficulties. This is known as **distress financing** and is explained on page 211. There is no need to use any intermediary for this. Distress finance may be obtained in exactly the same way and from the same sources as any other form of business finance.

3 Break the law

Desperate people do desperate things. For example, a business person in difficulty may be tempted to:

- evade tax
- pay staff less than the national minimum wage
- compromise on health and safety
- short-change customers in quality or quantity of goods.

All of these activities are illegal and carry heavy penalties. The penalties will increase the debt and the criminal record will make debt recovery more difficult.

Under English company law, there are also offences of fraudulent trading and wrongful trading. **Fraudulent trading** arises where a business is set up for the purpose of fraud.

Of more relevance is the offence of **wrongful trading** where a business is allowed to continue even though it should be obvious that the business cannot continue and innocent parties are likely to lose money. The law is contained in the Insolvency Act 1986 s214. The consequences of wrongful trading are:

- the directors become liable to contribute to the loss of the company, so the protection of limited liability is lost
- managers and others in sufficiently senior positions can also be made personally liable for the company's debts
- the person may be disqualified from being a director of *any* company for up to 15 years
- the person may be prosecuted for breach of duty or for offences under company law or insolvency law.

While the temptation and opportunity to break the law may be greatest for business debtors, non-business debtors may be similarly tempted to commit offences such as tax evasion and shoplifting. A desperate person may seek to justify such action on the basis of 'I need the money more than they do'. That may be so, but it does not justify theft. If the moral and legal arguments do not persuade a debtor (assuming that you are even aware of such matters), stress the consequences of being caught.

4 Gamble

It is not possible to **gamble** out of debt. All forms of gambling are designed to make a profit for the bookmaker. Only a portion of the bets are returned as winnings. As a rough guide, typical portions are:

- Internet gambling: 98%
- roulette: 97%
- horse-racing: 90%
- football betting: 86%
- football pools: 50%
- national lottery: 45%
- television quizzes: 20%

It is unlikely that anyone would ever enter a sweepstake on the basis that the boss kept half of all the money and shared out the other half. Yet that is exactly how football pools and the national lottery work.

The **National Lottery** was launched in November 1994 with the slogan 'it could be you', which is true. Punters soon found that while it could be you, in practice it never was (see Figure 3).

Figure 3: The chances of winning a prize in the National Lottery.

Prize	Average win	Odds to 1	Average return on £1
Jackpot (6 numbers)	£2 million	13,983,816	14.3p
5 numbers + bonus	£100,000	2,330,636	4.3p
5 numbers	£1,500	55,491	2.7p
4 numbers	£62	1,032	5.8p
3 numbers	£10	56.7	17.6p
any prize		54	44.7p

What this means is that if you bought enough tickets for long enough, you could expect to get back about half of the money you spent. However, to buy 14 million lottery tickets would require you to spend £1,000 every week for 269 years. The odds of winning the jackpot are the same as a middle-aged healthy man dropping dead in the next 40 minutes.

Joining a syndicate does not increase your winnings at all. If you are one of ten members of a syndicate, your chances of winning are ten times greater, but your prize will only be one tenth, so you will still see only 45% or so of your stake.

Do not be beguiled by gamblers telling you of their winnings. Usually they conceal from you (and sometimes from themselves) their losings. There will always be some winners in gambling; that is an essential part of keeping gamblers interested. In the long term, the gambler loses.

Casinos use all sorts of tricks to keep you losing money. All natural light is excluded, there are no clocks anywhere, and services operate continuously all day and night so that gamblers lose all sense of time. Free food and other facilities are provided so that the gambler does not need to leave the premises. Some even offer free sleeping accommodation. Fruit machines are programmed to keep coming up with near-wins to make the punter believe that the jackpot is about to be won. Tape recordings of jackpot wins are played in the fruit machine area to make punters believe that jackpots are being won. The surroundings are lavish and the staff dress and act to make you feel important. The air is fragranced and temperature-controlled to give you the feel-good factor. And where do you think the money comes from to pay for all this?

If you really must nurture the faint hope of winning a million pounds, buy premium bonds. At least you are only gambling with the interest you would otherwise earn.

Television quizzes, also known as **participation quizzes,** started in 2004. They are a new and iniquitous form of gambling, mainly because people do not even realize they are gambling. ITV currently promotes a late night quiz called ITV Mint which is reported as making £100,000 profit *per night*. There are also some dedicated game channels on satellite television. They are all presented by personable individuals who keep the encouraging patter going. This is supported by flashing graphics. The programmes are designed to be compulsive viewing, and are targeted for those likely still to be watching television after midnight.

Typically a simple question is asked, such as think of a word which follows 'water' (such as fall, butt, lily etc.). If your answer is one of six they have preselected, you can win £1,000 or whatever. You simply dial a number beginning with 09. If you have a big TV screen and good eyesight you may see that calls cost 75p each. What you are not told is that as few as one caller in 100 is selected to have a go. They simply lose their 75p. Because this is charged to the telephone bill, gamblers do not realize how much they are spending. Indeed most of them probably do not realize they are gambling at all.

Under pressure from regulators, the television companies limit the number of calls they will accept from one number in one day. ITV's limit is 150 and Channel 4's is 140. This means that you can lose £112.50 a day on ITV and £105 on Channel 4. ITV says that quiz participants spend an average of £6 a week. To its credit, Sky Television made a policy decision not to run such shows.

It should also be appreciated that many financial investments have more of the nature of gambling than investment. Depending on the circumstances, this can include **options** and **futures** and similar financial instruments. The use of such instruments is perfectly legitimate for purposes such as hedging other investments, when the instruments assume the nature of insurance. Otherwise a debtor should stay away from such financial instruments and probably from all forms of investment. If you do not understand this paragraph, don't worry – you probably don't need to.

Dealing with gambling is a separate problem from debt advice. Agencies such as GamCare can help.

5 Leave bills unopened .

Always open all mail, however tedious it may be to read yet another statement or final demand. Not opening mail is a classic symptom of someone with a serious debt problem.

6 Ignore summonses

Never ignore a summons to attend court. However bad the situation is, it will be far worse if you treat the court with contempt. If you really cannot attend when requested, at least write to the court to tell them why.

Courts are sympathetic to those who are trying to sort themselves out of a mess. Courts are unsympathetic to those who show no responsibility to others and treat the courts and creditors with contempt.

Assistance

Look at all the organizations to which the debtor belongs. Many clubs, professional bodies, Masonic lodges and similar bodies have funds for the relief of distress. Sometimes these funds can be very large because so few claims are made.

There are often charities designed to assist in particular occupations or in particular circumstances, such as if debt has been exacerbated by a particular illness or injury.

Many areas have parochial charities. These collect up what are often small charities established before the welfare state was introduced in 1948. Often such charities have funds which are much smaller and less relevant than when created in a previous century. A parochial charity allows an application to be made to the Charity Commissioners to merge funds and relax outdated conditions. A problem is that such charities tend to be largest in areas where they are least needed.

Loans are often covered by insurance policies. See if it is possible to make a claim.

Borrowing

Borrowing money does not reduce a debt as it simply replaces one debtor with another. However, it can assist a debtor if the new rate is less than the old rate.

Borrowing by a debtor is likely to take one of two forms:

- family borrowing
- commercial borrowing.

Debt counsellors have found individuals who seek loans with the highest rate of interest, believing this must be the best deal – 'I was offered 12.9% by my bank but I then found this company which gave me 14.9%'. That is why many lenders now extol their rate as 'good' without saying why. When borrowing money, the borrower should seek the *lowest* interest rate.

Family borrowing

A family member or close friend may lend money to assist a person. Although the motive may be admirable, great care is needed for any such arrangement. Whatever the intentions may be when the loan is made, it is highly likely that a debtor will default on a family loan. This can cause further problems of broken relationships, particularly if other family members or friends then take sides.

A lender should only lend such money as he or she can afford to lose, because they probably will. It should therefore be considered a gift which is repayable at the discretion of the borrower. In practice it is often difficult to make a cash gift because of the debtor's pride. In such cases, it may be better to provide help indirectly such as paying a bill.

There is also the more fundamental issue that the lender is more likely to be treating the symptoms than curing the disease. Indeed, providing a soft loan can be counter-productive in stopping the debtor facing up to the fundamental problems.

The first responsibility of those who love the debtor is to force him or her to face up to the problems. This is much easier to say than do, particularly if the potential borrower can easily afford to help. Many parents have paid off the debt of an adult son or daughter from the finest of motives, only to find that 12 months later their child is back in debt. It is difficult and painful not to offer the help which is demanded by someone you love, and such refusal can create its own problems.

The following is a recommended code of practice for family loans to debtors:

Recommended code for family loans to debtors

1 A loan should only be made as part of a debt recovery programme. This will usually mean that the arrangement has been approved by the debt counsellor. Money should never be lent to anyone, however close, who refuses to disclose their debt problems to the lender or debt counsellor.

2 The loan must always be documented, giving the names of the borrower and lender, the amount lent, and the expected date of repayment.

3 The loan should not carry any interest or any other charge (as otherwise it starts to become a commercial loan).

4 The loan should be regarded as a gift by the lender. Therefore the lender should not lend money which he or she cannot afford to lose.

Commercial loans

A commercial loan is one where interest or another charge is made for borrowing the money. Borrowing money to pay off other loans is known as a **consolidation loan**.

A consolidation loan is advisable if:

- the rate offered is less than that currently being paid
- there is no opportunity to reduce the debt further
- the rate offered is the lowest readily available
- either the loan is unsecured, or the security is not a real problem.

For the last item, a secured loan is one where you can lose your home if you do not keep up payments. Offering this security is only appropriate if:

- the home is worth significantly more than the total borrowings secured on it
- there is no serious likelihood of not keeping up payments.

A consolidation loan should only be considered when:

- the financial statements have been prepared and sent to creditors
- all creditors have had a chance to respond
- every opportunity has been taken to reduce the amount of debt
- every opportunity has been taken to offer payment in instalments.

Banks and other finance companies operate on a system of credit scoring, explained on page 184. The higher your score, the lower the interest rate charged and the less you pay.

There is a new form of borrowing known as **ZOPA** (zone of possible agreement) formed in 2005 and supported by the people who gave you eBay and Skype. Like eBay, it is a website which matches suppliers and customers, except that the product being sold is money. The lenders pass the money to ZOPA and state the rate and terms for lending. Borrowers decide whether to accept the terms, having first been screened and credit scored. The beauty of the scheme is that the turn (difference between lending and borrowing rates) is about 1% compared with 4% or more for commercial lenders. This means that rates are comparatively good for both parties. Amounts are lent in multiples of £10, so someone lending £1,000 could be lending money to 100 different people. A borrower of £1,000 could be borrowing from 100 people.

It is also a friendly person-to-person scheme. Someone cannot become a borrower unless they have a good credit record and have been on the electoral register for six years. The website can be accessed on www.zopa.com.

There are companies which specialize in lending to people with poor credit ratings. Norton Finance offers rates from 8.9% to 19.9%, with a typical rate of 12.9%. It advertises that it will offer secured loans to those with county court judgments or who have missed repayments on existing loans. Despite this, more than nine million people are refused credit each year. About one adult in five cannot borrow money from a recognized lender. More information is given on page 48.

Where not to borrow

Places and people where it is usually advisable *not* to borrow money are:

- pawnbrokers
- cheque shops
- loan sharks.

A **pawnbroker** takes possession of goods, which are said to be 'pawned' or pledged. It is in effect a simple short-term secured loan. The goods are then redeemed for the amount of loan plus a charge. A pawnbroker usually only lends for up to half the value (often a great undervaluation) and charges interest of between 5% and 12% for a month. If goods are unredeemed after six months and the amount lent was £75, the goods belong to the pawnbroker. If the value exceeded £75, the pawnbroker may sell the goods but must return any excess proceeds to the customer, which rarely happens in practice.

Originally pawnbrokers operated in back streets with a sign of three balls outside the premises. These days they operate more openly but prefer to call themselves pledge agents or some other euphemism.

It is believed that the seventeenth-century nursery rhyme 'Pop Goes the Weasel' is a reference to pawnbroking. 'Pop' means to pawn, and 'weasel' probably means a coat, from Cockney rhyming slang 'weasel and stoat'. This is a reference to the 'Sunday best' being pawned on Monday and redeemed on Saturday, when the worker was paid, ready for wear the next Sunday. This was to buy half a pound of twopenny rice and half a pound of treacle, two cheap foodstuffs which just provided a reasonably balanced diet.

A **cheque shop** allows someone to borrow money on the strength of a cheque which the shop agrees to delay paying in, usually for a month. The typical charge is 10%, so £45 will be paid now for a £50 cheque paid a month later.

Some suppliers offer **retail credit**, also known as **buyback stores**. These offer credit in the form of regular payments. These only apply to specific goods supplied by the store. Such arrangements are similar to hire purchase. Another form is the **catalogue club** whereby a person can buy goods from a catalogue and pay in weekly instalments. This involves a form of revolving credit, as a new purchase may be made when sufficient has been paid on a previous one. Typically a catalogue club is run by a neighbour who collects from people she knows (most agents are female).

The worst option of all is the **loan shark**. Unlike the above, a loan shark is illegal. Typically a loan shark charges a massive rate of interest, perhaps many hundred percent. They secure their loans by taking possession of social security books (which is illegal) and often enforce collection by threats and violence. On 19 February 2007, consumer minister Ian McCartney MP put it more concisely in a DTI press release: 'loan sharks are scum'.

Loan sharks operate illegally, but efforts to stamp them out have proved difficult. In December 2006, the government estimated that 165,000 people were using loan sharks just in Liverpool, Sheffield and West Yorkshire.

A DTI report shows that loan sharks target two sorts of victim. About one-third are defined as **chaotic lifestyle**, often with drug or alcohol addiction, but who do occasionally work. Such people have worked their way down the **credit ladder** until only loan sharks will lend to them. The other two-thirds are **credit-excluded**, who cannot get normal credit because of their poor credit record or because home credit company agents (see below) are not prepared to collect money in their neighbourhood. The credit-excluded are often on benefits and among the most vulnerable section of society.

The government plans to extend its anti-loan shark scheme through the whole of the UK by the end of 2008. Information on loan sharks may be given to a special team on 0141 287 4900.

Home credit companies

Opinions vary within the Church about **home credit companies,** also known as home-collected debt companies or doorstep lenders. They are usually the last resort (before loan sharks) for people who do not have access to normal credit facilities. Such people typically have no bank account, and are paid weekly in cash. The home credit company provides the loan in cash and collects it weekly in cash through collectors, called agents, many of whom are former customers. The interest rates are high in absolute terms. Home credit companies, with pawnbrokers and cheque shops, are collectively known as **sub-prime lending.**

The market is dominated by four companies:

- Provident Financial
- Cattles
- London Scottish
- S & U.

The National Consumer Council believes these companies have 69% of the home credit market. The other 31% is shared by about 500 small lenders.

The most well-known company is probably Provident Financial. Their website http://www.providentpersonalcredit.com promotes loans of between £50 and £500 which can be arranged on-line. Its own example is a loan of £300 repaid at £9 a week for 55 weeks. The total repayment is £495, with an APR of 177% (and, no, we have not lost a decimal point in typesetting). A £100 loan may be repaid at £5 a week over 25 weeks, a total of £125 and APR of 152.3%. Loans are paid for periods of 23, 31 or 55 weeks starting one week after the loan.

It should be appreciated that the APR is fairly meaningless over short periods. If someone was desperate for £100 cash a week before pay day, being lent £100 on condition that £101 was paid a week later probably seems a good deal. But £1 for one week represents 52% simple interest or 68% compound interest over a year.

About 10% of households have used a sub-prime lender, and 5% have used one in the last year. About 7.8 million people are refused credit by mainstream lenders, and many more are believed to be self-excluded because they know they will be refused.

The company has often been criticized by the Church for charging such high rates to the poorest and most desperate members of society. The author does not share that view. The company is commendably honest and straightforward in its business dealings, clearly setting out its terms. There are no hidden charges or early payment penalties. Home collection is expensive, and the risk of bad debts is high. Home collection costs typically account for 15% of the amount collected, about half of which is paid to the agent. Bad debts can be as high as 20%.

Home credit customers would otherwise be at the mercy of loan sharks. Instead their customers report high satisfaction levels. It should be remembered that the best way to drive down any charge is via competition, for more banks and finance companies to find ways of meeting the needs of the less affluent sectors of society.

Organizations campaigning for reform in this area include Debt on Our Doorstep, whose website is http://www.debt-on-our-doorstep.com. A leading member is Church Action on Poverty, whose website is http://www.church-poverty.org.uk.

Selling items

Most houses contain junk – items that have not been used for a year or more. Some of these items can be sold. This does not generate a regular income, but may generate some one-off income which can be used to pay immediate debts and ease the situation.

The first consideration for the debt doctor is to see if the item may be 'sold' back to the supplier. Under the Consumer Protection (Distance Selling) Regulations SI 2000 No 2334 (as amended), anyone who buys consumer goods by mail order has seven days from receipt of the goods in which to send written notice cancelling the sale. Written notice includes fax and e-mail. The supplier must refund the whole cost of the supply less any reasonable charges for collecting the goods.

In practice the customer usually pays the postage to return the item, but a customer cannot be compelled to do so – a supplier must offer collection at a reasonable charge. The customer must have taken 'reasonable care' of the goods while in his possession. If a customer does send goods back, the responsibility for the goods then passes to the supplier. So a customer is not liable for returned goods which do not arrive or are damaged in the post.

If goods were accepted in part-exchange, those goods must be returned to the customer if possible. If not possible, the supplier must refund a sum equal to the value of the goods.

This statutory right is a legal right given in addition to rights the supplier may offer. A supplier may offer greater rights, such as return within one month on whatever terms he likes, but cannot reduce this statutory right.

If the goods have been bought by any consumer credit arrangement, such as hire purchase or credit card, the credit arrangement is automatically cancelled. Any charges for credit must be refunded.

In practice, a debt doctor will be fortunate if he finds goods that can be returned within this seven-day period. However all is not lost. A compulsive spender may have acquired all sorts of items still in good condition, possibly still in their original packaging. A debt doctor can always ask the supplier if they will agree to take it back even though the seven-day period has expired. The supplier will say no, particularly if the bill has been paid. If the bill has not been paid, the debt doctor can explain that the customer has serious debts and that there is a possibility the supplier will receive nothing at all.

In many situations, it is not possible to return unwanted items to the supplier. In such cases, unwanted goods are commonly sold by:

- local car boot sales, advertised in local newspapers
- local auction
- magazines such as *Loot* and *Exchange and Mart*
- websites such as eBay on www.ebay.co.uk.

There is an art to selling goods by advertisement, whether by magazine or website. The main points are:

- describe the item accurately in the first few words
- give full details of the item, such as who made it, its material, its age, condition, function
- include a photograph
- be willing to answer questions or let someone inspect the item
- note any flaws or defects
- general information about the item, why it was used, how it was used, when it was used
- explain why someone may be interested in buying the item.

Remember that old documents and magazines can be sold. So don't throw out old magazines, tax discs, Green Shield stamps and driving licences.

If selling at auction or on a website, ensure that you either have a **reserve price** (the minimum price you are willing to accept), or be prepared to sell the item for a nominal sum. Ensure that the buyer pays postage or delivery on top, and ensure that this is adequate.

Selling the home

Selling the home to clear debts is an extreme measure, but one which may be necessary. If most of the debt is in the form of mortgage or other secured loans, selling the home may be better than allowing the lender to repossess the home. Typically the debtor can lose out significantly as repossessed homes sell for much less than normal (see page 112). Moving from a large home to a small one is known as **downsizing**.

The expenses of moving must always be costed. It is quite normal for a move to have more than £10,000 of 'dead costs'. This is money which you pay out for no return.

Suppose the debtor has a home worth £350,000 and debts of £150,000. The debtor concludes that he could live in a home costing £200,000 and use the other £150,000 to clear the debt.

Typically, most houses are sold at an 'offer', typically around 5% less than the asking price. So the home may only sell for £330,000. This may be partly mitigated by buying the house at an offer, though offers tend to be more common and larger on the more expensive properties. The most reliable (and free) source of finding out house prices for your area is to consult the Land Registry website at www.landregistry. gov.uk. This also gives prices for houses recently sold near you. Looking in local newspapers and estate agents' windows also gives a good idea.

These are typical charges for the move:

estate agent, perhaps 1.75% of £330,000	£5,775
stamp duty land tax: 1% of £200,000	£2,000
legal fees, say	£2,000
removal expenses, say	£3,000
Total moving expenses	£12,775

And this is before we consider such expenses as travelling to view new properties, taking time off work, buying new carpets and curtains, storing furniture, and reprinting stationery.

Estate agents' fees are always negotiable, despite what they say. It is usually advisable to choose a sole agency, which is less expensive. You may, with some persuasion, negotiate a sliding scale of 2% for more than £350,000, 1.75% for at least £330,000, and so on. A good estate agent should value your property and send a genuine buyer round at least once a week to view. If not, call the estate agent each week and ask for progress.

Stamp duty land tax is a tax on buying property. There is no tax on properties costing up to £125,000; 1% to £250,000, 3% to £500,000 and 4% above. The tax is charged on the *whole* price. So if you buy a house for £200,000, you pay 1% on the whole price; the first £125,000 is not tax-free.

There is no shortage of advice on how to make a house look attractive to quicken the sale, and possibly increase the price. In outline:

- the house should have **kerb appeal**: it should look good from the road, with a front garden able to park cars and have some greenery
- rooms should be uncluttered
- paint and surfaces should be clean
- colours should be light, and the building have a sense of space
- kitchens and bathrooms should have modern accessories if the basic fittings are old-fashioned
- each room should have an obvious *single* purpose, so remove computers from bedrooms
- generally furniture should be minimal to make the rooms look bigger and functional.

If still in doubt, a visit to any show house will indicate exactly what is required.

Returning to our example, the debtor hoped to sell the £350,000 house and buy a £200,000 one to clear a £150,000 debt. What actually happened is:

house sold for	£330,000
less expenses of sale	£12,775
net proceeds of sale	£317,225
less new house	£200,000
amount raised from move	£117,225

The debtor raised £32,775 less than he had expected. Although most of these figures and situations are variable, the above is typical.

Second job

Additional work is an obvious source of extra income. Local newspapers, newsagents' windows and the JobCentre may advertise suitable vacancies. In addition to the money gained, it is likely that extra work will also save expenditure, as the client will not be down the pub or running up an electricity bill at home.

Against this, the client must consider whether he has the energy and time to do additional work and still attend to debt problems and be able to sustain the main job. A second job would be counter-productive if the client was so tired at his main job that he was sacked.

Taking a second job can have other advantages, as this true story illustrates:

Unrealized talent

An unemployed office worker took a temporary low-paid job as a studio supervisor. He noticed that there were many odd jobs that needed to be done round the studio, and so he agreed with the owner that he could work additional hours to fix the jobs. In truth, he had no experience in handyman jobs and was just desperate for more money.

He discovered that he could do these jobs quite easily and found them enjoyable. As a result he obtained a full-time job as a handyman at a care home. There it was discovered that he had an aptitude for working with residents of the home. He was trained and qualified, leading to a job that was better paid and more satisfying than his old office job.

Sometimes a person is put off doing extra work because of all the additional income tax that seems to be payable. In fact, this is an illusion. Until someone starts earning more than about £36,000 a year, they pay income tax (from April 2008) at a maximum rate of 20%. The illusion arises because all taxpayers have a slice of income on which no tax is paid at all.

Suppose in the main job the client earns £1,200 a month. The tax-free slice is about £400, so the monthly tax bill will probably be around £176, which is less than 15%.

Suppose the client gets a second job and earns £700 a month. The tax is £140, or 20%, which looks a much bigger slice. This is simply because the tax-free slice has been given in the main job. Suppose the client got a job paying £1,900 a month. The tax would be about £330, which is exactly the same amount of tax as the two jobs.

For national insurance there is an advantage in having two jobs rather than one, as there is a limit (£97 a week for the year to 5 April 2007) on which you pay no national insurance. Unlike income tax, the national insurance limit is *per job*. Thereafter, the person usually pays national insurance at 11%. So in our example, the client pays £85.80 a month NI in the main job and £30.80 in the second. This gives a total of £116.60. If the client simply earned £1,900 in one job, he would pay £162.80 NI. By earning money in two jobs rather than one, he saves £46.20 national insurance.

The tax and national insurance systems work in a strange way. Figure 4 shows how much combined tax and national insurance a person will typically pay on various slices of income. These figures use the rates for the tax year 2008/09 and include much approximation as they are only intended to illustrate a principle.

Figure 4: Tax and national insurance.

Slice of income	Percentage taken in tax and national insurance		
	Total	Tax	NI
£0 to £5,000	0%	0%	0%
£5,000 to £34,000	31%	20%	11%
£34,000 to £36,000	21%	20%	1%
over £36,000	41%	40%	1%

It seems crazy that the rate goes down, but this is how the system works. The point to note is that, until someone starts to earn about £36,000 a year, they will never pay more than 31p out of each extra £1 earned, and so will keep at least 69p.

This situation changes dramatically if the client is receiving any means-tested social security payment. These are income support, working tax credit (WTC), housing benefit, council tax benefit, and some payments from the Social Fund. These are explained in detail on pages 62–76. The benefits have different rules, but all work on the basis of reducing benefit for every additional pound of income. The withdrawal rate is 100% of net income for income support and 70% for WTC.

This means that clients on income support have no real incentive to earn any more money. Although they will receive 69p for every extra £1 earned, that 69p will be deducted from the benefit so the person is no better off.

Even for WTC, things are not much better. A client may receive an extra 69p for every extra £1 earned, but lose 70% of that 69p in reduced benefit. This means that the client will only receive 20p out of every extra £1 after tax, national insurance and loss of benefit.

The system is that a poor person on WTC struggling to make ends meet keeps just 20p out of every £1 earned, while a millionaire keeps 59p out of every £1.

Although the government has come up with various schemes to reduce this effect, the truth is that the systems for income tax, national insurance and social security do not easily fit together. It will take a radical overhaul to address this anomaly.

Renting a room or garage

A room or the garage may be rented out. This does involve a loss of privacy but can bring in significant sums.

One problem is that a person can acquire the right to stay permanently. This could make it difficult if you later need the space or want to sell the house. Never assume that your nice lodger will move out when you want. He could ask for money for leaving. Advice should be sought first. Some landlords only let to students for this reason.

There is a special tax relief known as rent-a-room which allows a person to receive up to £4,250 a year (£81.73 a week) without having to pay tax. In terms of what to charge, look in local newspapers and ask local estate agents.

Equity release

Equity release allows the value of the home to be turned into income without selling the home. It can be popular for 'asset rich, cash poor' individuals, such as an elderly widow or widower whose mortgage is long paid off but who is struggling on a small pension.

All schemes allow the person to continue living in their home for the rest of their lives. For a couple, the scheme will allow the survivor to continue living in the home when their partner has died. It should be appreciated that the ages of the people are the main factor in determining how much money can be released. The younger a person is, or their partner is, the less money is released.

Before taking the big step of equity release, the borrower should consider all other alternatives. If the funds are needed to improve the property, it may be possible instead to obtain a house renovation grant from the local council.

Anyone receiving means-tested benefits, such as income support or pension credit or council tax benefit, is unlikely to benefit from an equity release scheme. The income generated will largely be deducted from the benefits, so the person will simply lose part of their home for no overall benefit.

The person who takes out an equity release plan is still responsible for all repairs and maintenance on the property, and for paying council tax and all other bills, and for keeping the property fully insured.

It should be appreciated that all equity release schemes impose restrictions on the borrower which need to be carefully considered before signing anything. It is essential to obtain independent professional advice before making any equity release arrangement.

Factors to consider before taking out any equity release scheme include:

- there is less to leave to children and other beneficiaries in your will
- there are additional factors should you wish to move house or move into a care home, sheltered accommodation or with children
- there can be a hefty charge for paying off a scheme early, particularly in the early years – this can make it difficult to move into a care home or to move into a granny flat with children
- there are fees for arranging an equity release scheme – these typically include solicitor's fees, surveyor's fees and a charge by the lender
- the plan may impose stricter conditions regarding maintaining and insuring the property, which could impose additional costs
- there can be restrictions on allowing someone else to move into the property (see below)
- there will be restrictions on obtaining further funds from the property
- an equity release scheme will almost certainly reduce or end any means-tested benefits.

It may be advisable for an elderly home-owner to discuss the matter with potential beneficiaries. Children may be willing to provide the income themselves rather than lose their inheritance. Such an arrangement must be clearly documented and understood by all parties involved, particularly if the lender is to be given a greater inheritance as a result.

An equity release plan can impose restrictions on allowing someone else to **move in** to your home. This could restrict the borrower's freedom such as on remarriage, taking in a lodger, or letting a child come back home. Such a person usually has no right to remain in the property after the borrower's death. It may also affect the financial terms of the equity release.

As for **moving home**, this depends on the terms of the scheme. Points to watch are:

- whether the scheme allows the terms to be transferred automatically to a new property, or if moving home automatically ends the plan or requires further approval
- if the borrower moves to a cheaper home, whether any part of the proceeds must be used to pay off part of the mortgage
- if the interest rate remains the same for a scheme transferred to a new property.

An equity release scheme is not usually approved quickly. It can take two or three months to gain approval, and approval cannot usually be assumed. It is a slower process than obtaining a normal mortgage.

A borrower may change their mind during this time. Once the equity release scheme has been agreed, it is not usually possible to change your mind. If there is a realistic possibility that a scheme may need to be ended before death (such as if a windfall is expected, perhaps from an inheritance or sale of business or sale of another property), any equity release scheme should be a mortgage-based one, as a reversion cannot be cancelled.

Taking out an equity release scheme restricts the borrower's ability to realize future funds in any way. Some schemes do not allow any further equity release. If you sell 40% of your home, you may not be able to sell a further 20% later. The scheme details should make clear whether such further release is permitted. Also, if you have sold 40% of your home in a reversion scheme, you will only have up to 60% of the home's value to purchase a new home.

Most schemes have a lower age limit. This can be as low as 55, but is usually nearer 65 or 70.

Schemes usually require the mortgage to be paid off or at least to be just a small amount (which is immediately paid off under the equity release scheme). Most schemes only include freehold properties, or leaseholds with at least 75 years still to run. Some schemes are not available for flats or maisonettes. There is usually a minimum value, though this is typically around £50,000 and so is unlikely to exclude many properties.

All mortgage-based equity release schemes are regulated by the Financial Services Authority (FSA) to whom any complaints may be addressed. Reversion schemes are not regulated though the government has said that they will be. The better companies offering equity release schemes conform to the **SHIP Code of Practice**. SHIP stands for 'safe home income plans'. Details are available from PO Box 516, Preston Central, Preston PR2 2XQ, telephone 0870 2416060, or from their website www.ship-ltd.org.

Different types of equity release scheme

The different types of scheme may be summarized as:

- mortgage schemes
- reversion schemes.

In an equity release mortgage scheme you raise a loan secured on your home, in a way similar to an ordinary mortgage to buy a home.

In a reversion scheme you sell some or all of the interest in the home, while keeping the right to remain in your home.

There are two types of equity release mortgage schemes:

- lifetime mortgages
- rolled-up interest plans.

Equity release mortgage schemes

A **lifetime mortgage** allows you to borrow a sum from a bank or other lender, repayable over your lifetime. Typically these are **interest-only plans** in which the borrower pays interest on a mortgage but repays no capital. The advantage is that the loan is fixed at the sum originally borrowed, so the borrower continues to enjoy the growing value of the house.

A **rolled-up interest plan**, also known as a roll-up loan, allows the borrower not to repay any capital or interest on the mortgage. The interest is added to the sum borrowed and is deducted from the sale proceeds of the house when the borrower dies. Such a plan is very risky as the interest can build up very quickly, particularly if the plan runs for a long time. It is easily possible for the sum owed to exceed the value of the home. This situation is known as **negative equity**. Some roll-up loans offer a 'no negative equity' provision whereby the loan can never exceed the value of the home.

The **home income plan** is when you use a mortgage to buy an annuity. An annuity is an arrangement whereby a lump sum is converted to regular income. Exactly the same arrangement is used when a pension starts to be paid. The amount of income depends on your age and interest rates. The amount which may be borrowed is usually limited to a maximum 75% of the value of the home. Interest is charged on the mortgage. This is deducted at source from the payments of income.

Home income plans were popular before 1999 when the returns were higher and there were income tax advantages for mortgages. Such plans have become much less popular since 1999. A home income plan is unlikely to be cost-effective for anyone under 80 as it is only at such an age that the sums realized make a plan comparable to other forms of equity release.

As with all forms of mortgage, the borrower has a choice between fixed and variable interest rates. Variable rates tend to be more generous but obviously are more risky, which tends to defeat the purpose of having the plan. It is usually advisable to seek a plan offering a fixed-rate mortgage.

Equity release reversion schemes

Under a reversion scheme, the home-owner sells all or part of his/her home to a lender.

The individual no longer owns all his home, and so is a tenant for that part of the home which he no longer owns. The rent is usually a nominal figure, perhaps £1 a month. The real benefit to the lender is the capital value of the property.

Under a reversion scheme, the individual can receive a lump sum or an annuity. An annuity simply turns a lump sum into an annual income for the rest of the person's life.

A reversion scheme has the advantage that there are no repayments (other than nominal rent). The sum owed is linked to the value of the property.

Suppose someone lives in a home worth £250,000 and sells 60% of it. This will release either a lump sum of £150,000 or an annuity based on that sum. (An annuity based on £150,000 for a man aged 65 would provide an income of about £1,000 a month for the rest of the man's life.)

The person now owns only £100,000 worth of house. When the person dies, the home is worth £500,000. In other words, its value has doubled. The lender is entitled to 60% of the proceeds as he owns 60% of the house. The lender receives £300,000 and there is just £200,000 left in the estate.

5

Social security

First ensure that the debtor receives all the social security benefits to which he is entitled. Claiming social security should never be seen as a form of begging. Citizenship is like a contract between the individual and the state whereby the individual must pay tax on earnings but is entitled to certain benefits in return.

The old age pension and child benefit are both social security benefits which are claimed by almost everyone who is eligible regardless of their need. In contrast, many means-tested benefits, intended to help the poorest members of society, have a take-up rate of less than 80%. This means that at least one eligible person in five is not receiving the help to which they are legally entitled.

It should be appreciated that social security regulations are constantly being changed. This chapter was written in 2007 on the law as it then stood. Also, the government sometimes tries out new ideas in pilot schemes limited to particular parts of the country before deciding whether to apply the scheme generally.

General guidance can be found on the website www.entitledto.co.uk or by calling the Benefit Enquiry Line on 0800 88 22 00.

Types of social security

Social security benefits fall into five broad categories:

- statutory payments
- contributory benefits
- non-contributory benefits
- tax credits
- means-tested benefits.

Some contributory and non-contributory benefits are also defined as **earnings-replacement benefits**. These are asterisked in the lists below. Generally, a claimant is only entitled to one earnings-replacement benefit at a time. Also, earnings-replacement benefits are subject to income tax if sufficiently large.

The lists below are of benefits which may be claimed from 2006. Some benefits which are no longer available to new claimants may still be paid to existing claimants. For example, severe disablement allowance may still be paid to those who first claimed before 6 April 2001.

Statutory payments are made by an employer to an employee. There are four statutory payments:

- statutory sick pay*
- statutory maternity pay*
- statutory paternity pay*
- statutory adoption pay*.

These must be paid by the employer by law. In addition the contract of employment may give the employee an additional right to **contractual pay**, which is always *in addition to* statutory pay. For example, statutory maternity pay is generally paid for six months. A contract of employment may give you the right to be paid for 12 months.

Contributory benefits are only payable to claimants who have sufficient national insurance record. The conditions vary from benefit to benefit.

The following are contributory benefits:

- bereavement allowance
- bereavement payment
- incapacity benefit*
- jobseeker's allowance*
- state retirement pension (category A and B)*
- widowed parent's allowance.

Non-contributory benefits depend on the personal circumstances of the claimant but not on the claimant's national insurance record. The benefit may be claimable by someone who has paid no national insurance at all.

The following are non-contributory benefits:

- attendance allowance
- carer's allowance*
- child benefit
- disability living allowance
- guardian's allowance
- industrial injuries benefit
- maternity allowance*
- Category D retirement pension*.

Tax credits are neither tax-based nor credits. This misnomer is used to conceal what are really means-tested social security payments. There are two tax credits:

- child tax credit
- working tax credit.

A particular problem with tax credits is that they are assessed according to circumstances at the start of the year. If these change, a person could be asked to give money back! Tax credits have also been plagued by computer problems and long delays.

Means-tested benefits do not depend on contributions. Like tax credits, they are payable to those whose income is particularly low. These are the means-tested benefits:

- income support
- income-based jobseeker's allowance
- council tax benefit
- housing benefit
- pension credit
- Social Fund payments.

Claiming a means-tested benefit can entitle the claimant to other help such as free school meals, legal aid and reduced fees for various services.

Social security benefits summarized

The following brief notes provide guidance on entitlement to social security benefits. The special provisions of the Social Fund are given separately because of their particular relevance to those in serious financial difficulties.

In addition to the specific conditions given below, there are many general conditions for claiming benefit. Most benefits may only be claimed by someone resident in the UK and may be restricted for certain types of accommodation, such as homes, hospital or prison.

Rates of benefits and entitlement thresholds are reviewed each year roughly in line with the tax year (which runs from 6 April to 5 April). If someone cannot claim in one tax year they may be able to claim in a future year, particularly if their income has not increased significantly.

The notes below outline the main elements of the benefits. They do not provide exhaustive explanations of entitlement, which would need a much larger volume. The best available such book is the *Welfare Benefits and Tax Credits Handbook* published by Child Poverty Action Group and updated annually.

Attendance allowance is payable to someone who is at least 65 and needs attendance or supervision with regard to personal care. The tests for this are the same as for disability living allowance. There are a higher and a lower rate.

Bereavement allowance is payable for 52 weeks to a widow or widower who was between 45 and state retirement age when their spouse died.

Bereavement payment is a single lump-sum payment to a widow or widower who was either under pension age when their spouse died, or whose spouse was not entitled to any state retirement pension.

Carer's allowance is payable to someone who provides 35 hours or more care to someone entitled to attendance allowance or disability living allowance at the middle or higher rates. Claiming carer's allowance automatically entitles you to the carer's premium if you are also claiming income support.

Child benefit is a weekly sum paid (usually) to the mother looking after a child who is under 16, or who is 16 or 17 and in full-time education. The benefit is paid at a higher rate for the oldest eligible child. The premium for lone parents was abolished in 1998.

Child tax credit is for a household containing a child and where the net household income is sufficiently low, though incomes up to £50,000 a year can still qualify. The credit has up to four elements depending on the circumstances of the household:

- child element
- disability element
- severe disability element
- family element.

There is an 'income threshold figure' set for each tax year. If the net household income is below this figure, the relevant amounts for each element are paid in full. If the income exceeds the figure, the child tax credit is reduced by 37% of the excess.

Council tax benefit is a payment towards council tax for people with sufficiently low incomes and with savings of less than £16,000. Entitlement is based on either main council tax benefit or second adult benefit. Second adult benefit is payable if there is another adult resident with you but not paying you rent. Someone claiming income support, income-based jobseeker's allowance or the guarantee credit of the pension credit is automatically entitled to council tax benefit.

The benefit is calculated by comparing net income against an applicable amount. If net income is below this figure, the maximum council tax benefit is payable. If net income exceeds this figure, the maximum benefit is reduced by 20% of the excess. Deductions may be made in respect of income of other household members.

Disability living allowance is not means-tested. It is paid to anyone under 65 who needs help with mobility or personal care. It has two components:

- mobility component
- care component.

The mobility component is paid at a higher rate for those who cannot walk, and at a lower rate for those who can walk with great difficulty.

The care component is paid at a higher, medium or lower rate. The higher rate is paid for those who need care day and night. The medium rate is paid for those who need care during the day. The lower rate is paid for those who need some attention during the day or who cannot cook themselves a meal.

Guardian's allowance is payable as an addition to child benefit when the child is an orphan.

Housing benefit is a means-tested benefit for people on low incomes who live in rented accommodation. The benefit can be the entire rent, though this is subject to many exceptions, restrictions and special provisions.

Incapacity benefit is payable to people unable to work because of illness or injury. It is a contributory benefit, like jobseeker's allowance (with an exception for young claimants), but is paid at a higher rate and for longer. The government has announced plans to tighten up conditions for claiming. It is payable after any period of statutory sick pay (SSP). Benefit may only be paid after 196 days (28 weeks) of incapacity, regardless of whether any SSP or other benefit has been paid in that period.

Incapacity benefit is payable at three rates for these periods of incapacity:

Rate	Period
lower short-term	first 28 weeks
higher short-term	29–52 weeks
long-term	after 52 weeks

There are additions for an adult dependant or dependent children.

An age-related addition is payable to a claimant under 45 at the start of the claim period, with a higher age-related addition for a claimant under 35.

There is no upper age limit for benefit, but if the claimant receives certain types of pension, that may reduce the amount of incapacity benefit payable.

Income-based jobseeker's allowance is means-tested and non-contributory. It is payable indefinitely while the relevant conditions remain satisfied. The rate is the same as for contributions-based jobseeker's allowance, but is not time-limited nor dependant on having paid sufficient national insurance. It is payable to claimants whose income and savings are sufficiently low.

Income support is payable to claimants aged between 16 and 60 who are neither in full-time work nor full-time education, who are in one of a defined list of eligible categories, and whose income is sufficiently low. Claimants over 60 may claim pension credit instead.

Income support may be paid in addition to other benefits. Further details are given later in this chapter.

Industrial injuries benefit is payable to someone who suffers from either:

- a personal injury from an industrial accident; or
- a prescribed industrial disease.

Jobseeker's allowance, commonly known as 'the dole', is paid for up to 26 weeks to someone out of work who is actively seeking work. The claimant must have been an employee paying national insurance for the two previous tax years. The allowance is reduced for claimants under 25 or who have £8,000 or more in savings or who have a high income from other sources. The allowance may not be paid in some circumstances, such as if the claimant was sacked for misconduct from the last job. Such restriction may apply just for a period or may make the claimant completely ineligible.

This allowance is sometimes called 'contributions-based jobseeker's allowance' to distinguish it from income-based jobseeker's allowance, which is an entirely separate benefit (see above).

Maternity allowance is payable to a woman in connection with childbirth and who is not entitled to statutory maternity pay, such as when her earnings are too low or when she is self-employed. She must earn at least £30 a week. The benefit is payable for 26 weeks starting up to 11 weeks before the expected birth. The amount payable is the lower of:

- 90% of weekly earnings; and
- a fixed weekly sum revised each year (£108.85 in 2006/07).

Pension credit is a means-tested benefit payable to older claimants. It has two elements:

- guarantee credit
- savings credit.

The *guarantee credit* is payable to a claimant of 60 or over to ensure that the person receives at least a 'minimum guarantee'. There are additions for married couples, disability, housing costs and care needs.

The **savings credit** is payable to a claimant of 65 or over. This is a curious benefit, the opposite to normal means-tested benefits in that the more income you have, the *more* benefit you receive – to a limit. The maximum savings credit is 60% of the amount by which your income exceeds the savings credit threshold, subject to a maximum figure. This figure is then reduced by 40% of the amount by which your income exceeds the appropriate minimum guarantee.

Someone entitled to pension credit may also be eligible to have their mortgage paid.

The object of the pension credit is to ensure that a retired person or couple has a minimum income from all sources. For 2006/07, that minimum is £114.05 a week for a single person, and £174.05 for a married couple or civil partnership.

State retirement pension is a contributory benefit payable to those who have reached the state retirement age. The pension is not means-tested. It is not necessary for the claimant to have retired; the pension may be paid in addition to earnings.

Retirement age is 65 for men. The age is 60 for women born before 6 April 1950, 65 for women born after 6 April 1955, and an age between 60 and 65 for women born between 6 April 1950 and 5 April 1955. In other words, the state retirement age for men and women is progressively equalized between 2010 and 2020.

The main contribution requirement is that the person has paid class 1, class 2 or class 3 national insurance for at least nine years out of every ten of working life. Class 1 is paid by employees, and class 2 by the self-employed. Class 3 is voluntary and may be paid by anyone who otherwise has insufficient contributions. The Department of Work and Pensions (DWP) should advise of any incomplete years, though it is easily possible to find out by completing a form. For missing years the contributor may be able to pay class 3 national insurance to complete the record. It is almost always advisable to do so.

Category A pension is the commonest. It is payable to individuals on the basis of their own contributions. For a widow, widower or divorcee, a category A pension may be paid on the basis of their former spouse's contributions.

A **category B pension** is paid to the husband or wife of a person who has reached state retirement age but who does not qualify for a category A pension in his or her own right. It can also be paid to a widow whose husband dies of an industrial injury or illness. A category B pension may be paid to a widower in more restricted circumstances. Those restrictions are abolished from 6 April 2010.

A **category D pension** is a non-contributory pension payable to those 80 or over.

(In case you wondered, a category C pension was payable to those who were over retirement age in 1948. The last one was believed to be paid in 1995.)

At the age of 80, all pensioners receive an additional 25p a week (unchanged from 1970). In addition there are various other benefits such as heating allowance, free bus pass, free television licence, married couple's allowance for income tax and no further liability to pay national insurance.

The state may also pay out *additional pension* in the form of graduated pension, SERPS or state second pension (S2P).

Graduated pension accrued on earnings between 1961 and 1975. Graduated contributions were an addition to national insurance which bought units, each of which buys a small amount of additional pension on retirement.

State Earnings Related Pension Scheme or *SERPS* is an additional pension which may accrue by paying additional national insurance on earnings between April 1978 and April 2002. A person could contract out by having an appropriate occupational pension or (from 1 July 1988) a private pension. SERPS provides an additional pension calculated as a percentage of 'average earnings' (which has more than one definition).

State second pension (or S2P) is an additional pension which accrues on earnings from 6 April 2002 under rules similar to that for SERPS though more generous for those with low incomes. The government has announced its intention to move to 'second stage S2P' around 2007 or 2008, though details have yet to be announced.

The Department of Work and Pensions provides a service whereby a person may complete form BR 19 available from any social security office. This provides details of a person's pension entitlement from the state under all these schemes.

Note that occupational pensions or private pensions are in addition to any state pension. Such pensions are paid under the rules of the scheme or policy, usually offering the scheme member or policy holder considerable choice.

Special *war pensions* are paid to those killed or injured on military service, or to their dependants.

Statutory adoption pay (SAP) is paid by an employer to an employee (male or female) on adopting a child. It is paid for 26 weeks. It is paid at the same rate as statutory maternity pay. If a couple adopts, the partner not claiming SAP may claim statutory paternity pay.

Statutory maternity pay (SMP) is paid by an employer to a female employee in connection with childbirth. The woman must have sufficient qualifying service, which usually means that she must have become pregnant *after* starting work with that employer. SMP is paid for up to 39 weeks starting up to 11 weeks before the expected birth with effect from 1 April 2007 (for 26 weeks previously). For the first six weeks it is paid at 90% of average earnings. For the rest, it is paid at a fixed weekly rate.

Statutory paternity pay (SPP) is paid to the father of a naturally born child, or to the partner (male or female) of whoever claims statutory adoption pay. It is paid for two weeks at a set rate.

Statutory sick pay (SSP) is paid to an employee who is off work sick with sufficient earnings, regardless of their age. Before 1 October 2006, it was only paid to an employee aged between 16 and 65. SSP is paid from the fourth day of absence for up to 28 weeks. It is paid at a set rate each week.

Widowed parent's allowance is a weekly benefit paid to widows or widowers with children.

Working tax credit (WTC) is a means-tested benefit paid to a person who is in work (or whose partner is in work) and whose income is sufficiently low. It is calculated by comparing the claimant's net income with an 'income threshold figure' based on the claimant's circumstances. If the income is below this threshold figure, the maximum WTC is payable. If the income is above the figure, WTC is reduced by 37% of the excess.

Checking entitlement

Checking entitlement to social security is a specialist area. As a rough guide the following lists the benefits to which a person *may* be eligible, provided the relevant conditions are met.

Personal circumstances	*Social security benefits*
Bereavement	Bereavement allowance
	Bereavement payment
	Social Fund funeral expenses
	Widowed parent's allowance
Caring for someone	Carer's allowance
Child responsibility	Child benefit
	Child tax credit
	Cold weather payment
	Guardian's allowance
	Health benefits (such as free milk)
	Social Fund maternity grant
	Statutory adoption pay
	Statutory maternity pay
	Statutory paternity pay
	Working tax credit

Disability/incapacity	Attendance allowance
	Social Fund cold weather payment
	Disability living allowance
	Incapacity benefit
	Industrial injuries benefit
	Statutory sick pay
	War disablement pension
Low income	Council tax benefit
	Housing benefit
	Income support
	Social Fund payments
	Working tax credit
	Retired Pension credit
	State retirement pension
	Social Fund winter fuel payment
Unemployed	Jobseeker's allowance

Social Fund

The Social Fund is the sweeping-up provision of the social security system. Because of its possible importance in serious financial difficulty, more detail is given to this than to other social security benefits.

There are two types of payment from the Social Fund:

* regulated
* discretionary.

There are four types of **regulated payment** from the Social Fund:

* cold weather payments
* funeral expenses payment
* Sure Start maternity grant
* winter fuel payments.

Cold weather payment is a fixed weekly sum paid for weeks of cold weather. It is automatically paid to those receiving income support, pension credit, or income-based jobseeker's allowance. It is also paid to those claiming contribution-based jobseeker's allowance if the household includes a child under five, disabled child or pensioner. A week of cold weather is where the temperature for your area is or is expected to have a daily average temperature of 0°C or less on seven consecutive days.

Funeral expenses may be paid from the Social Fund to someone who is responsible for arranging a funeral and who is receiving income support, income-based jobseeker's allowance, housing benefit, council tax benefit, working tax credit or pension credit. For these purposes, someone is responsible for a funeral of a

- partner, such as husband or wife
- child, depending on circumstances of other parent or guardian
- parent, and it is reasonable to assume responsibility
- other relation, and it is reasonable to assume responsibility and there is no other relation to assume responsibility.

The payment covers the whole cost of burial plot, cremation fees, documentation, certain travel expenses of the body and bearers, other fees up to £700. The payment is restricted by any amount the claimant inherits from the deceased, or which is covered by insurance or by a funeral plan.

Sure Start maternity grants are awarded to a woman who gives birth and is claiming income support, income-based jobseeker's allowance, pension credit, or other tax credits in certain circumstances. The grant is £500 per child.

Winter fuel payment is a single lump-sum paid each autumn to someone who is aged 60 or over on the third Monday in September. It is paid at higher rates at age 70 and 80.

Social Fund discretionary payments

Social Fund discretionary payments are the long stop of the social security system. Sadly, this arrangement still fails to meet all needs.

Discretionary payments are significantly different from other social security payments because they are

- budget-limited
- usually given as loans which must be repaid
- not subject to appeal.

The discretionary budget is set annually by the government for each Social Fund district. This is controlled by an area decision-maker, usually the district office manager. There is no monthly limit on expenditure, so it is possible for an area to run out of funds. Claims early in the tax year (from April) can be more successful than claims later in the year. There is provision for additional funds to be allocated to a district, but this is not automatic. The existence of a budget can mean that a claim may be refused because there is no fund left rather than the claim lacking merit. The law requires priority to be given to particular types of claim.

Most payments from the Social Fund are given in the forms of a loan which must be repaid. In deciding whether to make a loan, consideration must be given as to how realistic it is for the claimant to repay the loan.

It may seem to defeat the whole purpose of a long-stop welfare provision for it to be budget-limited and largely restricted to loans. These provisions have been widely criticized but they have survived a change of government, and there seems to be no impetus to change this arrangement.

There are three types of discretionary payment:

- community care grants
- budgeting loans
- crisis loans.

A **community care grant** (CCG) is the only form of Social Fund discretionary payment which is not repayable. To claim this grant, a claimant must meet all these conditions:

- the claimant must be receiving income support, income-based job-seeker's allowance or pension credit (or is about to leave residential care)
- the claimant must not have more than £500 capital (£1,000 if 60 or over)
- the claimant or partner must not be involved in a trade dispute
- the grant must not be for an 'excluded item'
- the grant must be for at least £30, unless it is for daily living expenses or travel expenses
- the grant must be for a permitted purpose.

The permitted purposes for a CCG are:

- to help the claimant, or a person for whom the claimant has a responsibility, to be re-established in the community after a stay in institutional or residential accommodation
- to prevent a person from going into institutional or residential accommodation
- to help the claimant set up home as part of a planned resettlement programme after a period without a settled way of life
- to ease exceptional pressures on the claimant or family
- to help with travel expenses within the UK in exceptional circumstances.

In terms of deciding priority for CCG, the law requires the case officer to consider:

- the nature, extent and urgency of the need
- the existence of resources which could meet the need (except that capital below the limit is not considered)
- whether any other person could meet the need
- the district budget
- Social Fund directions, and national and local guidance.

The priority of the application must be assessed before budgetary matters are considered. Each case must be considered individually, and discretion must be exercised flexibly and sensitively.

In practice, priority is set as high, medium or low. This is determined according to whether a CCG will have an effect in the immediately foreseeable future in resolving or improving the circumstances for which the grant may be made, and whether that effect is:

Priority	Effect
high	substantial
medium	noticeable
low	minor

Factors which affect priority include:

- mental or physical disability, illness and frailty
- physical or social abuse, or neglect
- a long period of sleeping rough
- unstable family circumstances
- behavioural problems, such as drug or drink abuse.

In practice, districts are usually only able to meet high priority claims.

There is no maximum amount for a CCG. Guidance states that it must be sufficient to buy an item of serviceable quality from a reputable dealer.

Someone claiming from the discretionary Social Fund should usually start by claiming a CCG before considering a loan. Details on the claim form should be made as specific as possible, and within the scope of the grant as explained above. Efforts should be made to establish that the claim is a high priority. Supporting evidence may be included, such as that from a doctor or social worker. If not satisfied with the outcome, there is no formal appeal procedure, but the claimant can ask for a review.

A **budgeting loan** is an interest-free loan to meet occasional expenses for which it is difficult to budget.

The claimant must have been receiving income support, income-based jobseeker's allowance or pension credit for at least 26 weeks before the application is considered. A loan is not granted to someone with capital of £500 (£1,000 if 60 or over).

Unlike community care grants, entitlement to a budgeting loan is made on the basis of precise legal criteria. However, by far the commonest reason for refusing a loan is that the person is unable to repay the loan.

The loan must be made for one of the following:

- furniture or other household appliances
- clothing and footwear
- rent payable in advance
- removal expenses
- improvement, maintenance or security of the home
- travelling expenses
- expenses with seeking work
- hire purchase or other debt for any of these purposes.

The loan must be for an amount between £30 and £1,000. The claimant must demonstrate an ability to repay the loan within a maximum of 104 weeks (two years).

In practice, a decision on whether to grant a budgeting loan is based on two factors:

- the weighting of the application
- the district budget.

The **weighting** is a figure calculated according to initial criteria, and possibly wider criteria. The higher this figure, the greater are the chances of the loan being granted.

There are two **initial criteria**:

- how long income support (or equivalent) has been paid
- the number of people for whom the claimant is responsible.

For the first criterion, the minimum period of 26 weeks has a weight of 1; the maximum period of three years has a weighting of 1½.

For the second criterion, a single person has a weighting of 1.0. One child is given a weighting of $2/3$. A partner and each subsequent child is given a weighting of $1/3$.

The weightings from each criterion are multiplied. So the minimum weighting is 1 (calculated as 1 × 1) for a single person who has received benefit for 26 weeks.

Someone with a wife and four children who has received benefit for three years would have a weighting of 4½ (calculated as 1½ × 3). The figure of 3 comes from:

1 for the claimant; plus
2/3 for the first child; plus
3 × 1/3 for each of the next three children; plus
1/3 for the partner (wife).

Local guidance will specify the maximum amount of loan payable for a weighting of 1. If this figure is, say, £200, the single person who has had benefit for 26 weeks is only entitled to a maximum of £200. The person with a wife and four children is entitled to a maximum of £900 (calculated as £200 × 4½).

If the initial criteria do not result in a figure of at least £50, wider criteria may be considered.

A budgeting loan is not granted for more than the amount requested but may be granted for less. If the claimant already has a budgeting loan outstanding, a subsequent loan is reduced by double the amount outstanding.

In practice, the real crunch is the ability to repay the loan. Repayments are set at 5%, 10% or 15% of the amount of income support (or equivalent benefit) received. The percentage depends on the claimant's 'continuing commitments' thus:

Percentage to be repaid	Continuing commitments
15%	none
10%	up to a set amount
5%	above the set amount.

The term **continuing commitments** is not defined other than excluding housing costs. Continuing commitments are assumed to include food, fuel and repayments of loans and hire purchase. The claimant can agree to repayments up to 25% higher than that calculated by the above method. There is now an absolute limit of £1,500 for loans. This means that if the maximum repayment is £10 a week, a budgeting loan can only be made for up to £780.

Budgeting loans are usually recovered by a deduction from benefits, so there is no possibility of a claimant defaulting or skipping some repayments. A claimant may repay a budgeting loan at any time.

For community care grants and budgeting loans, there is a list of **excluded items** for which a grant or loan will not be made. These excluded items are:

- any need which occurs outside the UK
- any educational or training need
- school uniform or sports equipment (grant only)
- travel expenses to and from school (grant only)
- expenses in connection with court proceedings

- removal expenses following a compulsory purchase order or similar (though the local authority may be able to help)
- domestic assistance or respite care
- repairs to public sector housing
- medical, surgical, dental and similar supplies
- work-related expenses such as fares to interviews and clothes (though a budgeting loan may be available)
- tax of any kind, national insurance and other statutory charges
- investments
- certain housing expenses.

Crisis loans are the third type of Social Fund discretionary payment. These are means-tested interest-free loans to meet an immediate short-term need. Unlike budgeting loans, the claimant does not have to be in receipt of any other benefit.

The claimant must be at least 16 years old and without sufficient resources to meet immediate short-term needs of the claimant or family. A claim can be refused if it appears that the claimant may be able to raise the funds from friends or relatives.

The loan cannot exceed £1,000 but there is no minimum. The loan must not exceed the reasonable purchase of a serviceable item, or the reasonable cost of repair if that is less. There are statutory limits on the maximum amount of living expenses.

The claimant must be able to repay the loan on the same basis as a budgeting loan.

A crisis loan cannot be made if the claimant has other resources, though many assets are excluded. Residents of hospitals, care homes, prisoners and most students are not able to claim.

A crisis loan cannot be made for any item excluded from community care grants or budgeting loans. In addition a crisis loan cannot be made for:

- telephone costs
- mobility needs
- holidays
- television equipment
- motoring costs.

In practice, a crisis loan may only be given for 'an unforeseen circumstance of pressing need, either of which requires immediate remedy or action' following 'an event that causes great distress or destruction', according to the Social Fund Commissioner. Self-inflicted crises are not excluded, so a claimant should seek review if a claim appears to have been prejudiced by perception of the claimant's conduct.

A crisis loan must be the only means of preventing damage or serious risk, so if there is a non-financial alternative, that can prevent a loan being made. A sudden lack of cooking, heating or sleeping facilities are examples that could justify a crisis loan.

According to the *Social Fund Guide* a crisis loan may be made for general living expenses for a short period when the claimant:

- is waiting for first payment of wages
- is suffering hardship because the employer has imposed a compulsory unpaid holiday
- has lost money or a giro
- is denied income support or income-based jobseeker's allowance because of capital owned but that capital cannot be realized quickly enough
- is homeless or sleeping rough
- has just been discharged from prison and has insufficient resources until a first benefit is paid.

The Guide also suggests that a crisis loan could be made for:

- emergency travel when stranded
- emergency fares to hospital
- fuel debts and reconnection charges
- up to four weeks' rent in advance to a private landlord
- disasters, such as fire or flood
- other urgent needs for which a budgeting loan is not available because the claimant has received relevant benefit for less than 26 weeks.

6

Types of debt

Introduction

Not all debts are equal, and not all debts should be treated the same.

Having quantified all the debts, it is necessary to distinguish between priority and non-priority debts. This is not determined by the amount or nature of the debt, but by the consequences of non-payment. If a creditor can seize your home or car, or can discontinue necessary supplies, it is clearly important to satisfy that creditor first.

A **priority** debt is one where a debtor will suffer serious consequences for non-payment or delayed payments. Priority debts include:

- fines, maintenance payments and any court orders
- mortgages (and any other secured loans)
- rent
- council tax
- gas and electricity
- hire purchase
- taxes.

Every other debt is a **non-priority debt**. These are likely to include:

- water rates
- credit card debts (including store cards)
- bank loans
- loans from friends and relations
- unpaid bills.

Being a priority debt does not always mean that it will be paid before a non-priority debt, but it does mean that it will be given consideration before a non-priority debt.

There is no reason to be in the least bit coy in admitting that a debt has been classified as non-priority. You will be dealing with professional debt collectors who understand this distinction fully. Indeed, the fact that a debtor has made this distinction as part of a debt recovery process demonstrates that the debt is being addressed properly, and is therefore likely to reassure a creditor.

First, it is necessary to understand the position of the various priority creditors. The information below indicates what to do at the start of debt problems. If action has already been started against a debtor for a priority debt, the matter is much more serious though still not insoluble, as explained in Chapter 7.

Guidance on debt collecting has been produced by the Office of Fair Trading. It may be accessed free from their website at www.oft.gov. uk or by calling 0870 6060321. It gives details on what is acceptable practice. For example, a creditor is responsible for the conduct of any debt collection agency it uses.

Types of priority debt

Fines, maintenance and court orders

Any payments ordered by a court must always be given priority.

If any payment ordered by a court remains unpaid, the court may issue a **distress warrant**. This allows bailiffs to seize goods. Although bailiffs can often be resisted (see page 101), the court has power to find that this was due to the debtor's 'wilful refusal or culpable neglect'. This can lead the court to issue a **committal warrant** which sends the debtor to prison.

If a court-ordered payment is proving impossible to pay, a letter should be sent to the court as soon as possible, even if the debt doctor has not had the opportunity yet to prepare the appropriate statements. The courts deal much more harshly with those who ignore their responsibilities than with those who are struggling to meet them.

Usually the court will be the magistrates' court. A letter should be sent asking for the payments to be reduced.

The earlier the court is contacted, the better. However, the court must always be contacted, even if recovery processes have started.

Zacchaeus 2000 Trust is a charity designed to help people taken to court for payment of small amounts of arrears or fines. It can arrange for a **McKenzie friend** to accompany a person in court. A McKenzie friend is someone who is not legally trained but who the court allows to attend to help a party to a case. The trust can be contacted on 020 8376 5455 or zacchaeus2000@blueyonder.co.uk.

Mortgage arrears

Some loans are said to be **secured**. This means that the creditor can take your property if the loan is not repaid. Any other type of loan is said to be **unsecured**. A mortgage is always a secured loan. Other types of personal loan may be secured or unsecured. The lender must tell you which type of loan you have. Only secured loans are priority loans.

Legally, any property may be used to secure a loan, such as a car or piece of machinery. For individuals, almost all such loans are secured on the home. It is usually a person's most valuable asset, it does not usually lose value and it cannot be moved.

Lenders always try to avoid evicting people from their homes. Their first concern is that their loan will be repaid. Their second concern is that the interest on the loan will be repaid. Provided these two concerns are satisfied, it is likely that the lender will agree to any reasonable scheme.

As with all priority debts, it is essential that the creditor is contacted as a matter of urgency. A lender is always likely to deal more harshly with a debtor who is in arrears and has not contacted them.

If it is not possible to make any sensible offer about payment, the debt doctor should ask for up to 28 days' breathing space in which the lender will take no action and the debt doctor will prepare an offer.

The debtor should continue to meet continuing liabilities, such as their everyday living expenses, even if not immediately able to make an offer to clear arrears.

If a debtor cannot even meet continuing liabilities, the lender may be willing to reduce the regular payment by:

- moving to an interest-only mortgage
- extending the term of the mortgage.

A lender is only likely to agree if this covers the arrears also, so such an offer should not be made until the necessary financial statements have been prepared.

Because mortgages can be difficult to understand, there are some more detailed notes on page 90. These notes explain the implications of paying interest only or of extending the mortgage term. Page 99 gives an explanation of what to do if repossession proceedings have already started.

Rent arrears

Arrears of rent may allow a landlord to evict the tenant, who becomes homeless. The process is known as **repossession**. A notice is served on the tenant requiring them to leave.

If necessary, the landlord can seize possession by force, known as **eviction**. Page 107 gives advice on what to do if eviction proceedings have started.

The landlord should be contacted immediately it is known that there is a problem paying rent or where arrears have built up. If possible, the tenant should pay the current rent and tell the landlord that the debt doctor and tenant are working on a plan to deal with the arrears. If the tenant cannot even pay the current rent, it is difficult to avoid repossession.

The landlord may be a local authority or housing association, particularly if the accommodation is **social housing**. Such a landlord will probably have a policy on repossession. Usually this allows the tenant to clear arrears at an amount which may be afforded.

If the tenant has not already made a claim for housing benefit, one should be made now (see page 64).

Council tax

Council tax is a priority because non-payment can quickly lead to prison.

As with all priority debts, the council should be contacted immediately. If possible, the debtor should concentrate on paying the current liability first and deal with any arrears later. If it is believed that a council is acting improperly or is being unnecessarily heavy-handed, it is effective to contact the local councillor. The council should also advise what complaints procedures may be followed.

There are many exemptions and discounts available for council tax. The debtor's circumstances should be checked to see if any are applicable.

Council tax is generally not payable for a home:

- which is unfurnished and requires structural alteration or repair
- which was the residence of a person now in prison
- which was the residence of a person now in hospital or nursing home
- of someone who has died
- of a student resident elsewhere or who will become a student within six weeks of leaving
- in the possession of a mortgage lender
- held by trustees in bankruptcy
- which is an annex and cannot be let separately
- student accommodation at university.

If a building is **substantially unfurnished**, the council may agree to a lower rate for up to six months. One short period of occupation of up to six weeks may be included in this period. The words 'substantially unfurnished' simply means that it lacks sufficient furnishings for someone to live there. So a home is not liable for council tax just because it contains some furnishings and furniture.

If a house is occupied by just one person, a discount of 25% is given on the council tax. If no-one is occupying furnished accommodation, a discount of 50% may be given, though councils now have a discretion to give a lesser discount down to 10%.

In other words, the full council tax generally requires two adults over 18 to be living there. For these purposes, the following people are not regarded as resident adults:

- full-time students, student nurses, apprentices and youth trainees
- hospital patients, and residents of mental nursing homes and hostels
- people with a severe mental impairment, or kept in hospital under the Mental Health Act 1983
- residents of Salvation Army hostels and similar
- monks and nuns, and service volunteers caring for a disabled resident
- those convicted or remand prisoners (other than those in prison for non-payment of council tax)
- diplomats, visiting armed forces and members of certain international organizations
- non-British spouse of a student.

Council tax is determined according to eight bands, known by the letters A to H, where A is the lowest. Each band relates to the property's value on 1 April 1991. England, Wales and Scotland have different bands. The average band is D, for properties then worth more than £68,000 but not more than £88,000.

The local authority determines the council tax each year by reference to the amount payable for a band D property. The tax for other bands is calculated as a multiple of the band D property.

The relevant council tax bands are given in Figure 5.

If the house has been adapted to cater for a disabled person, it is reduced by one band. So if a band D property has been adapted, it is taxed as a band C property.

Although only one council collects the council tax, it may collect tax on behalf of other authorities, such as police authority or a county council or parish council. The council tax bill explains how this is calculated.

Council tax is paid on a daily basis. This means that no tax is payable for exempt periods. So if a person is in hospital or prison for 63 days in the year, council tax may be not payable for 63/365 of the year.

Council tax only becomes payable when a bill for it has been issued. This must be done 'as soon as reasonably possible'. In 1999,

Figure 5: Council tax bands.

Band	Ratio	Property value threshold at 1 April 1991		
		England	Wales	Scotland
A	$2/3$	nil	nil	nil
B	$7/8$	40,000	27,000	30,000
C	$8/9$	52,000	35,100	39,000
D	1	68,000	45,900	51,000
E	$12/9$	88,000	59,400	66,000
F	$14/9$	120,000	81,000	90,000
G	$12/3$	160,000	108,000	120,000
H	2	320,000	216,000	240,000

Nottingham City Council had council tax bills for the periods 1990 to 1997 quashed by the court for 'inexcusable' delay.

Council tax is payable by one person on behalf of the household. If residents cannot or will not nominate such an individual, a bill may be issued to 'the council tax payer' and all resident adults are jointly and severally liable. That means that any one of them can be compelled to pay the whole council tax.

A local authority must allow residents to pay in ten instalments between May and February each year. Local authorities may make other arrangements, including offering a discount for a single lump-sum payment or for using direct debit. The resident must be allowed to pay in cash at the town hall, or equivalent. In practice, most local authorities allow payment by cheque, credit card, debit card or e-banking. The council tax reference number must always be quoted.

Council tenants may be allowed to pay council tax weekly with the rent.

All instalment arrangements are amended if council tax is only payable for part of a year.

If council tax is not paid when due, a **reminder** is sent. This must warn the resident that any right to pay by instalments may be lost if payment is still not received. If two reminders are issued in the financial year (May to April), the resident is liable to pay the whole council tax for the year after a third failure. This must be specifically warned on the second reminder.

If the council tax owed is a small amount, the local authority may be willing to write it off. Government guidance recommends this where someone has died early in the financial year or where the amount arose from a council error, particularly if not deducted for some years.

Otherwise, if a third failure occurs, a **final notice** is issued.

Seven days after the final notice, the local authority may seek a **liability order** from the magistrates' court. Usually a local authority will double-check to see if the resident:

- is entitled to council tax benefit
- has made a claim for benefit which is being processed
- has made an appeal.

If any of the above applies, the local authority should suspend enforcement until the matter has been resolved. It should be remembered that this is good practice rather than the law. In the case *ex parte Williamson and Young [1990]*, Bristol Magistrates' Court ordered payment even though there was a claim for benefit for community charge (which predated council tax).

A local authority has six years in which to apply for a liability order. The process is automatic with almost no discretion for the magistrates to refuse. The liability order means that a **summons** is served on the resident. This is for the year's council tax plus the court costs. A liability order may be jointly served on two or more adults, but summonses which arise from the order must be served individually.

The summons instructs the resident to attend court to explain why the council tax has not been paid. At least 14 days' notice must be given. If the person fails to attend, the normal practice is to hear the case in the person's absence. As the procedure is largely a formality, there is not much a resident could say even if he did attend. The only defences are:

- the council tax has not been demanded in accordance with regulations
- the amount has been paid
- the resident is not the person named on the summons.

If the full amount of a summons is paid, enforcement ends. Note that this must include the court costs. If the council tax is paid but the costs are not, the liability order may be pursued for the costs.

If the summons is neither paid nor successfully challenged, the local authority decides which recovery method to use. The choices are:

- attachment of earnings order, so amounts are deducted from wages or salary
- apply to Benefits Agency for deductions from income support or job-seeker's allowance
- send in the bailiffs to seize property, known as **distress**

- apply for a charging order against the property to which the council tax relates
- bankruptcy.

An authority may pursue only one method at a time, and may pursue against only one person at a time in respect of one council tax demand. The resident may be required to provide necessary personal and financial information, such as name and address of employer to allow an attachment of earnings order to be issued. A fine may be imposed for non-compliance.

If a resident continues not to pay or co-operate, the local authority may apply for a **committal warrant** in England or Wales for the resident to be sent to prison. This is a coercive act designed to enforce compliance. It does not apply in Scotland. It is used sparingly, mostly against those who deliberately refuse to pay the tax. Further committal costs are added. A committal warrant may generally only be issued by magistrates where at least two methods of enforcement have been considered, and distress (bailiffs) has been attempted.

The Debt Doctor's Advice

Note that a committal warrant may only be issued for wilful refusal or culpable neglect. It cannot be issued because a person *cannot* pay.

In Scotland, enforcement is by a **summary warrant** or **decree**. This allows the court to take similar forms of action against a resident, other than a committal warrant.

Various penalties may be imposed during the enforcement period. Appeals may be made against the tax or against a penalty, though the grounds are limited.

A council may write off unpaid council tax in individual cases. Some councils claim they do not have such authority. They do. It is given in Local Government Finance Act 1992 s13A as inserted by Local Government Act 2003 s76.

Taxes

Tax debts must be seen as a priority debt, because of the forces which can be mustered against the debtor for non-payment.

In the UK, there are two types of tax: direct and indirect. **Direct taxes** are charged on income. They include income tax, capital gains tax, inheritance tax and national insurance. **Indirect taxes** are charged on spending. They include value added tax, excise duty, customs duties, air passenger duty and insurance premium tax. Unless someone is in business, a debt doctor need not consider indirect taxes as these are simply included in the price of the goods or services bought.

Income tax is the one most likely to cause problems for a debtor. Broadly, income tax is collected in one of two ways:

- Pay As You Earn (PAYE) for employees
- self-assessment for others.

Tax is also collected at source from other types of payment such as interest on bank accounts and dividends from owning shares.

There is also a special **construction industry scheme (CIS)** for self-employed workers in the construction industry. Under CIS, an amount of tax is deducted from payments from the contractor to the subcontractor. For each tax year, the subcontractor prepares his tax return, from which the tax liability is calculated. The tax paid over by the contractor is offset against this, so that the subcontractor either has an additional sum to pay or receives a refund.

Under PAYE, almost all of the responsibility for collecting tax rests with the employer. Unlike CIS, the PAYE scheme is designed to collect the *exact amount* of tax due. This means that if someone has income from employment only, they probably need not be bothered about their tax. Every individual is entitled to a personal allowance, and possibly to other deductions from taxable income. This is reflected by the **tax code**. The taxpayer is entitled to an explanation of how their tax code has been calculated, and may question any deductions which they have not been given. If an individual has income from other sources, an employee may be asked to complete a self-assessment tax return.

Income tax is calculated in three main stages:

- adding up all sources of taxable income
- deducting the personal allowance and other eligible deductions
- multiplying the net taxable income by the various rates of tax (currently 20% and 40%) on different slices of income.

These three stages summarize a vast and complex set of rules regarding what income is taxable, what items are tax-deductible, and what rates of tax can be applied. If a person's tax affairs are complex or the tax demands seem high for the level of income, it may be advisable for a tax accountant to review them. It has been estimated that up to one in six people's tax is wrongly calculated, most commonly because the taxpayer is unaware of a tax provision in his favour.

National insurance was originally seen not as a tax at all but as a compulsory insurance premium for welfare benefits. It is now generally regarded as a tax. There are six classes of national insurance. Class 1 is paid by employees and their employers; class 2 and 4 are paid by the self-employed; and class 3 is a voluntary contribution to maintain a national insurance record to claim state retirement pension and other benefits. (The other two classes are unlikely to be relevant.) Class 1 national insurance is deducted by the employer along with PAYE, so the employee usually has no need to consider it further. National insurance rarely causes much problem for debtors.

Where tax (other than council tax) is being demanded, the debt doctor may need the advice of a tax accountant. Where a person has failed to provide details of their financial matters, the tax authority, Her Majesty's Revenue and Customs (HMRC), will assess a figure. This figure is usually on the high side, deliberately to force a person to complete the necessary forms. The good news is that when the person does complete the forms, the tax is usually reduced to the correct figure without much problem. The bad news is that the tax system now has many automatic penalties and interest charges, so there is usually a penalty for being late with a tax return.

Interest on tax cannot usually be avoided. HMRC argues that they have lost the use of your money for the period when you should have paid your tax but did not, and so the interest is compensation for lateness, and not a penalty. **Tax penalties** are intended to enforce compliance with tax laws. They are of broadly two types: automatic penalties and imposed penalties. An **automatic penalty** is produced by a computer from the data entered. Failure to submit a self-assessment tax return when required incurs an automatic penalty of £100 which is almost impossible to avoid. An **imposed penalty** is made by a tax officer on reviewing the facts.

Unlike interest charges, it may be possible to negotiate an imposed tax penalty. This process is known as **mitigation**. In some cases, it can be possible to mitigate an imposed penalty to zero. Factors which help in mitigating penalties are:

- prompt disclosure by the taxpayer
- co-operating fully with HMRC
- honest admission of errors.

Contrary to what people believe, the tax authorities do not employ an army of people secretly checking your bank statements and personal affairs. Although HMRC has formidable powers of investigation when fraud is suspected, for the vast majority of taxpayers all that HMRC knows is what they are told by the taxpayer and from a few other sources, such as an employer under the PAYE scheme. Obvious minor mistakes are corrected but otherwise usually ignored for the purposes of imposing penalties.

Debtors and debt doctors should appreciate that HMRC is simply doing its job. There is nothing to fear from honest dialogue with them.

HMRC is neither a business nor a charity and therefore does not seek to extract the maximum tax possible from taxpayers. It seeks to extract the *correct* amount of tax due under the law. HMRC is generally a helpful department which provides much general advice and can help provide specific advice to particular individuals. This service is provided willingly even if the consequence is to reduce the amount of tax available.

HMRC may write to a taxpayer or even send a notice formally enquiring into an aspect of a person's tax affairs. This is nothing to fear, and it does not mean that a prosecution will follow. If asked a question, answer it as best you can. If asked to produce a document, produce it.

If you believe that a tax assessment is excessive, a **tax appeal** may be made. In the first instance this is made to the tax office which issued the assessment. The appeal should be made in writing, to the office within 30 days. In practice, late appeals are often accepted, particularly if there was a good reason for the delay. Most appeals are settled with the tax office. If an appeal remains unresolved, it can be referred to the **Appeal Commissioners** for resolution. This arrangement was being revised as this book went to press. The hearing is less formal than a court case, and costs are rarely awarded against either side. A further appeal on a point of law (but not a point of fact) may be made to the courts.

If HMRC has a more serious concern about someone's tax affairs, there are two procedures it may use: civil and criminal. The civil procedure is known as **civil investigation of fraud** (**CIF**) and was introduced in September 2005. A taxpayer is allowed one opportunity to 'come clean' about their tax affairs on the basis that they will not face a criminal prosecution and get a criminal record. A single figure is agreed in respect of the tax owed, interest and any penalties.

The **criminal procedure** is usually reserved for the more serious tax cases. Since April 2005, tax prosecutions are brought by the Revenue and Customs Prosecution Office (RCPO), which is independent of HMRC. They follow police procedures in that a person must be formally cautioned and interviews must be recorded.

If either CIF or a criminal procedure is invoked, it is essential that the debtor gets professional advice.

Where there is no dispute about the tax owed, but the debtor simply cannot pay it, HMRC must be informed of this promptly, preferably with the financial statements (see page 125). Tax is generally only due on money the debtor has already received, so it is reasonable for HMRC to be firm in demanding what money is rightly theirs.

Against this, HMRC is realistic, particularly where it is obvious a person cannot pay, is making serious efforts to recover from debt, and is being co-operative. In such cases, HMRC may agree a **Time to Pay** scheme. For an employee, arrears of tax may be collected by adjusting the tax code, which collects the arrears over the tax year. For a non-employee, a scheme may allow payments over three months. Interest will continue to be added, but no penalties are imposed for using the scheme.

For more serious cases, the position is reviewed by a specialist officer. The officer may agree a longer period. In extreme circumstances, tax may be written off, but a debt doctor should not rely on this.

Where tax is owed, a tax collector may send a notice demanding payment or may call to collect payment. In such cases, the debt doctor should contact the collector's office and ask for a short time to make a response, such as for preparing the financial statements or to make an appeal against the tax assessment. Such suspensions are usually agreed quite readily in practice, but they only provide a temporary respite.

Failing any agreement to pay tax by instalments, HMRC will consider enforcement action. This will be taken through the magistrates' court (for up to £2,000) or the county court.

For bankruptcy proceedings, the procedure is that the tax officer sends details to a colleague called an examiner who decides whether proceedings should be issued. This decision is not just based on whether bankruptcy is likely to yield more than it costs, as HMRC's policy is to commence bankruptcy proceedings in situations where it is likely to have a deterrent effect.

Gas and electricity

Gas and electricity bills are priority debts because the supplier may be able to disconnect supply.

It should be noted that this only applies to bills for the supply of gas and electricity. Disconnection cannot be threatened for non-payment of any other sum owed to them, such as for buying electrical appliances or for servicing a gas boiler. Such a debt ranks as a non-priority debt.

Also note that gas and electricity are the only utilities for which disconnection may follow non-payment. Since 1999, water cannot be disconnected under the Water Industry Act 1999.

If disconnection is threatened, the supplier should be contacted immediately.

Hire purchase and similar

Hire purchase (HP) and similar conditional sale agreements are priority debts because the goods may be seized for non-payment. Such arrangements are commonly known as 'on tick', 'on the never-never' and similar. They all commonly mean acquiring goods without paying the whole price for them, and then making regular payments for a period.

There are several different types of scheme along these lines. Although they may seem the same to the debtor, it is important to understand the exact nature of the financial arrangement as this affects the legal rights. All the rules given below apply to agreements regulated by Consumer Credit Act 1974, which applies to agreements for up to £25,000 (or £15,000 if started before 1 May 1998). This Act has been amended by a 2006 Act as explained on page 173.

Under a **hire purchase** agreement, a person hires goods for a fixed period. The hirer is usually a finance company rather than the garage or shop who supplied the goods. This means that the HP contract is between the person and the hirer, rather than between the person and the garage or shop. Any claim for misrepresentation or faulty goods is therefore made to the hirer.

At the end of this period, the person may acquire the goods, usually for a nominal sum like £1. The goods are first hired and later purchased, hence the name.

Until the agreement has ended, *the goods belong to the hirer*. The person may not sell the goods until the final purchase has been agreed. The person may end the HP agreement at any time by giving written notice to the hirer who then repossesses (takes back) the goods. The amount owed by the person depends on how much has been paid.

If the person has paid less than half of the purchase price, the person must pay:

- half the purchase price
- LESS the instalments already paid
- PLUS any instalments overdue.

If the person has paid at least half the purchase price, the person owes nothing other than any arrears of instalments.

If the person has not taken reasonable care of the goods, the person may be liable to compensate the hirer.

This means that HP goods may simply be given up on payment of half the purchase price. As many cars, motorcycles, computers, clothes, furniture, jewellery and other consumer goods have a second-hand value below half price, the debt doctor is in a good position to negotiate a hard bargain with the hirer.

A similar looking arrangement is a **lease**. Under this, the person never acquires any rights to the goods. They always belong to the person known as the **lessor**, which is usually a finance company. The person with the goods is called the **lessee**. A lease typically has a **primary**

lease period with payments of a similar amount to those under an HP agreement. This is followed by a **secondary lease period** where much smaller payments are made.

Basically, the person pays for the goods during the primary lease period. After that, the secondary lease simply allows the arrangement to continue. In practice, the lessor will often agree to sell the goods to the lessee for a nominal sum once the secondary lease period has started. Leased goods may be returned to the lessor at any time unless the lease says otherwise. Any arrears of payment must be paid, but otherwise no payment is due. It does not matter whether half the price has been paid.

Mortgages

A mortgage is a particular form of secured loan where the security is land.

Strictly, a mortgage is not granted on buildings. In English law, 'land' includes everything on it, under it and over it (with some exceptions for things like aeroplanes and underground trains). So trees, fences, walls, minerals, soil and patios are included. Buildings are included because they are attached to the land. This can matter because if a mortgage is repossessed, **fixtures** attached to the land may be repossessed but furniture and other items are not. In the case *Berkley v Poulett [1976]*, the Court of Appeal ruled that there are two tests:

- to what degree an item is attached to the land
- why it was attached.

That case established that fixtures did not include pictures screwed to a panelled wall nor a marble statute of a Greek god. They were not essential to the room or garden.

Land also includes rights over land, such as easements and rights of way.

There are different ways of owning land. At its simplest, **freehold** means owning the buildings and land they stand on. **Leasehold** means having the right to occupy land for a finite payment (which may extend to 99 years or more). **Commonhold** is a leasehold where the leaseholders collectively own the common parts, such as halls and stairs.

When coming to **land law**, there are many ancient provisions. First is the legal definition of land as 'comprehendeth any ground, soile, or earth whatsoever. It legally includeth also all castles, houses, and other buildings; also water', according to Sir Edward Coke (1552–1634). Originally all land was vested in the Crown, under a declaration of William the Conqueror in 1066. Other common law grew from this declaration. From 1 January 1926, most land law is governed by Law of Property Act 1925 and other Acts passed in the same year, as subsequently amended. One of the provisions is that a mortgage lasts for up to 3,000 years, except for a second mortgage which lasts for 3,000 years and 1 day. (I am not making any of this up.)

Of more consequence than these antiquated niceties is the **legal date of redemption,** the date by which the mortgage must be repaid. This is when the lease represented by the mortgage is surrendered back to the borrower. In legal parlance this is known as the **cesser on redemption.**

It should be noted that the borrower is the **mortgagor,** and the lender of money is the **mortgagee.** These terms are often confused. Just remember that it is the person buying the house who has mortgaged it. A mortgagor is still the legal owner, so comments that 'my home is owned by NatWest bank' are not true. The bank simply has a legal charge on your property.

The commonest type of mortgage is the **repayment mortgage.** Here a sum is paid each month for a defined period, often 25 years. Provided there is no change in interest rates or the amount borrowed, the monthly payment remains exactly the same for the whole period. The same figure is paid in the last month of the 25th year as is paid in the first month of the first year.

In 2006, a typical rate for a repayment mortgage was around 6.5%, ignoring special offers, fees and insurance. At this rate, a mortgage of £100,000 over 25 years requires a monthly repayment of £675.21. (This and subsequent figures are calculated by using a financial calculator. Some lenders have different policies on exactly how figures are calculated and how they are rounded, so they may quote figures which differ by a small amount.)

The amount you borrow is known as the **principal.** Sometimes the principal is called the capital. On top of this the lender charges you **interest.**

As you make 300 monthly repayments in 25 years, the total amount eventually paid for the mortgage is 300 × £675.21 = £202,563. This means that after 25 years, you have paid:

principal	£100,000
plus interest	£102,563
total payments	£202,563

It can be a shock to find that the interest on a mortgage exceeds the amount originally paid for the house. However, a mortgage is still usually a good investment.

Each payment of £675.21 pays off a bit of the principal. The rest of the payment is interest. The principal reduces slowly at the start of a mortgage but more quickly at the end. A monthly payment of

£675.21 equals £8,103 a year. In the first year of a 25-year mortgage only £1,651 of the principal has been reduced, so you still owe £98,349 of the mortgage. In the last year, £7,822 of principal is repaid.

Using our example, this is how much principal is still owed at the end of each of the 25 years of the mortgage (Figure 6). This can help the debt doctor calculate how much mortgage may need to be repaid.

Figure 6: Principal owed at end of each year of a 25-year, £100,000 repayment mortgage.

1	98,349	6	88,279	11	74,354	16	55,098	21	28,470
2	96,547	7	85,843	12	70,985	17	50,439	22	22,029
3	94,707	8	83,243	13	67,391	18	45,469	23	15,156
4	92,702	9	80,470	14	63,556	19	40,166	24	7,822
5	90,562	10	77,511	15	59,463	20	34,508	25	0

These figures can be multiplied up to whatever the actual amount of mortgage is. So if £300,000 has been borrowed on a mortgage, the monthly repayment is 3 times £675.21, which is £2,025.63. After 5 years, the amount of principal owed is 3 times £90,562, which is £271,686.

Again, it can be a shock to find that over 90% of the principal is still owed after five years – one fifth of the way through the mortgage. Even after 17 years, more than half the principal is still owed. This is just the way mortgages work.

The example assumes a 25-year mortgage with an interest rate of 6.5%. It is possible to take out mortgages for shorter periods, and sometimes longer periods. It is also possible for interest rates to change.

Figure 7 indicates what the monthly repayment will be for different interest rates and different periods.

As with previous figures, the actual rate quoted by a mortgage company may differ by a few pounds. Monthly repayments for other amounts may be calculated by simple multiplication. So for a mortgage of £265,000, the relevant figure above may be multiplied by 2.65.

From this table, it can be seen that extending the period of the loan does not reduce the payment by as much as may be thought. A 30-year loan has a monthly repayment of 91.5% of a 25-year loan, even though the repayment period is 20% longer.

Mortgages are now beginning to be offered for long periods. Japan has offered 100-year mortgages, payable by three generations. At a rate

Figure 7: Monthly payments for a £100,000 repayment mortgage.

	15 years	20 years	25 years	30 years	35 years
4.0%	739.69	605.98	527.84	477.42	442.77
4.25%	752.28	619.23	541.74	491.94	457.89
4.5%	764.99	632.65	555.83	506.69	473.26
4.75%	777.83	646.22	570.12	521.65	488.86
5.0%	790.79	659.96	584.59	536.82	504.69
5.25%	803.88	673.84	599.25	552.20	520.74
5.5%	817.08	687.89	614.09	567.79	537.02
5.75%	830.41	702.08	629.11	583.57	553.50
6.0%	843.86	716.43	644.30	599.55	570.19
6.25%	857.42	730.93	659.67	615.72	587.08
6.5%	871.11	745.57	675.21	632.07	604.15
6.75%	884.91	760.36	690.91	648.60	621.42
7.0%	898.83	775.30	706.78	665.30	638.86
7.25%	912.86	790.38	722.81	682.18	656.47
7.5%	927.01	805.59	738.99	699.21	674.24
7.75%	941.28	820.95	755.33	716.41	692.18
8.0%	955.65	836.44	771.82	733.76	710.26
8.25%	970.14	852.07	788.45	751.27	728.49
8.5%	984.74	867.82	805.23	768.91	746.86
8.75%	999.45	883.71	822.14	786.70	765.36
9.0%	1014.27	899.73	839.20	804.62	783.99
9.25%	1029.19	915.87	856.38	822.68	802.74
9.5%	1044.22	932.13	873.70	840.85	821.61
9.75%	1059.36	948.52	891.14	859.15	840.59
10.0%	1074.61	965.02	908.70	877.57	859.67

of 6.5%, the monthly repayment for a £100,000 mortgage would still be £542.50, and you would, eventually, have paid £550,629 interest! In 2006, the first UK transgenerational mortgage was offered.

Any **additional payment** can shorten the term of the mortgage significantly. Conversely, any **shortfall** in payment can lengthen the term of the mortgage. Keeping with our example of a 25-year repayment mortgage of £100,000 at 6.5%, Figure 8 shows how long the mortgage will take to repay if the lender pays more or less than £675.21 a month.

Figure 8: Duration of repayment mortgage of £100,000 at 6.5%.			
LESS THAN £675.21		**MORE THAN £675.21**	
Monthly repayment	*Time taken to repay*	*Monthly repayment*	*Time taken to repay*
550	64y 8m	680	24y 7m
560	52y 9m	690	23y 9m
570	46y 4m	700	22y 11m
580	41y 11m	710	22y 2m
590	38y 5m	720	21y 6m
600	35y 11m	730	20y 11m
610	33y 9m	740	20y 4m
620	31y 11m	750	19y 9m
630	30y 4m	760	19y 3m
640	28y 11m	770	18y 9m
650	27y 8m	780	18y 3m
660	26y 6m	790	17y 8m
670	25y 6m	800	17y 5m

From Figure 8, it can be seen that a small variation from the standard payment figure does not change the repayment by much. Someone who could afford to pay £775.21 a month, another £100, would clear the mortgage in 18½ years, reducing the mortgage period by 6½ years.

Of more concern for debtors are the figures in the left-hand column, showing what happens if a borrower pays less than the 25-year repayment figure. A borrower paying £575.21 a month, £100 less, would have a mortgage lasting 43 years and 10 months – almost 19 years longer.

At £542 a month, it would take 114 years to clear the mortgage. Yet £542 is still more than 80% of the 25-year repayment figure of £675.21. At any figure below £541.67, you are not repaying any capital at all and the debt increases. The message is that shortfalls in mortgage payments can soon start to extend the mortgage period.

Debt recovery from a mortgage can therefore need careful planning. Suppose a debtor managed to repay their mortgage of £100,000 for 10 years with no problem, and then missed six payments. From the table on page 92, we can see that the principal has reduced to £77,511 after ten years. With no repayments for six months, another £2,712 interest is added (depending on what method is used by the lender). So the debt is now £80,223.

If the borrower is then able to resume paying £675.21 a month, the mortgage will take another 15 years 11 months to clear. The effect of missing payments for six months is to extend the life of a mortgage by 17 months.

It may be worth considering extending the life of the mortgage instead. If the debt of £80,223 is repaid over another 20 years, the repayment falls to £598.12 a month.

The general rule about mortgage arrears is that *small* shortfalls and short extensions can be worthwhile in debt recovery.

An alternative approach is an **interest-only mortgage**. For a £100,000 loan at 6.5%, this requires monthly payments of £541.67.

At the end of the 25-year period, or indeed of any period, the principal of £100,000 is still there, but no interest has been added. This is an extremely easy calculation as we simply have to calculate 6.5% of £100,000 and divide by 12.

The monthly repayments for other interest rates are given below in Figure 9.

An interest-only mortgage means that the person must be able to pay off the capital at some point in the future. A person may believe they will be a multi-millionaire at the age of 50, but the reality is usually different. It is true that inflation will have the effect of reducing the value of £100,000 in real terms. In the early years of the twenty-first century, inflation has been around 2.5%. If that rate were sustained for 25 years, £100,000 in 25 years' time would be worth £53,939 at current rates. In other words, nearly half the principal would have been eroded by inflation.

Inflation rates of 2.5% are historically low. Rates were above 10% as recently as 1990. In the 1970s, rates went above 20%, reaching a record 26.9% in 1975. If we look the other way at someone who

Figure 9: Monthly repayments for interest-only mortgages.

Interest rate	Monthly repayment	Interest rate	Monthly repayment
4.0%	333.33	7.25%	604.17
4.25%	354.17	7.5%	625.00
4.5%	375.00	7.75%	645.83
5.0%	416.67	8.0%	666.67
5.25%	437.50	8.25%	687.50
5.5%	458.33	8.5%	708.33
5.75%	479.17	8.75%	729.17
6.0%	500.00	9.0%	750.00
6.25%	520.83	9.25%	770.83
6.5%	541.67	9.5%	791.67
6.75%	562.50	9.75%	812.50
7.0%	583.33	10.0%	833.33

took out an interest-only mortgage in 1981 for repayment in 2006, £100,000 now was worth just £36,349 then. There has been 175% inflation in the 25 years between 1981 and 2006.

However, considerations of inflation can only put a perspective on interest-only mortgages. In terms of debt recovery, an interest-only mortgage is not a good idea. However, if it is necessary to buy some time, making payments at the interest-only rates will have the effect of pausing the mortgage. If interest-only rates are paid for six months and then the full repayment rate is resumed, the mortgage will simply be extended by six months.

House prices

It is worth understanding a little of the economics behind house prices. During the growth of suburbia around London in the mid-1930s, a three-bedroomed semi-detached house typically cost £875. Since then, inflation means that items cost about 37 times more in 2006 than 60 years earlier. This would put the value of such a property at about £32,000. Yet a quick glance at any local newspaper or estate agent's window shows that properties are actually selling for about ten times that figure. Someone owning such a house is seeing their wealth grow by over £80 a day.

House prices are determined by every seller looking for the one buyer who will pay the highest price. Over the last 60 years, not only has inflation has increased, but so has prosperity. Wages tend to increase by about 2% more than inflation, so someone may get a pay rise of 4% when inflation is 2.5%. This means that £100 becomes £104 which pays for goods that now cost £102.50. The extra £1.50 is prosperity; the person is £2 better off in **real terms** (after allowing for inflation). This means that people are able to afford to spend a little more each year. (This is a sweeping simplification, and there will be many individuals who do not conform to this pattern; but the principle being explained is valid over the UK population as a whole.)

Over the decades, this increase in prosperity translates into people spending less on routine necessities. Figure 10 shows how far incomes have risen faster than food prices by looking at the percentage of household income spent on food over the last half-century.

Figure 10: Percentage of household income spent on food.

1956	35.0%
1966	29.8%
1976	22.3%
1986	17.9%
1996	14.1%
2006	9.0%

Source: National Statistics

In 1956, the average family spent 35% of its income on food. By 2006, the average family spent just 9% of its income on food. A study of the weights used in calculating inflation shows that spending on necessities has steadily declined, while spending on luxuries has steadily increased.

All this means that people have more disposable income, so they can afford to spend more on mortgages. Using the example above over 60 years, we can see that inflation accounts for only 10% of the increase in house prices. The other 90% is determined by prosperity, and the laws of supply and demand.

The recession of 1991/92 was caused by a reduction in the money supply. In other words, there was simply less cash around to buy things.

A graph of the money supply shows a big dip for those years. It was not until 1995 that the money supply figures returned to the peaks of 1988 and 1989.

In the six years from 1983 to 1989, the average UK house price rose by 117% from £31,600 to £68,800. Prices fell by about 25% during the worst two years of the recession. Even by 1995, the average price was £61,500 – still 11% below the highest price.

In 2007, economic conditions are ripe for another property crash. In the six years from 1999 to 2005, the average UK house price rose 109% from £81,600 to £170,200. The money supply is also reducing. This does not mean that there *will* be a property crash in 2007, or 2008, or ever. Sometimes economic conditions can exist for five or ten years before anything happens. Sometimes, other things happen which overtake what is expected. And sometimes a sudden crash is replaced by a long fizzling out. Even if there is another crash in house prices, it will probably sort itself out within ten years. Such matters are only relevant if planning to buy, sell or move in the meantime.

The punch-line is that property prices are largely governed by prosperity and not inflation.

7

Serious debt

Introduction

Emergency action is needed when a debtor has already left it too late for normal negotiations and procedures to resolve a debt problem. This commonly arises either because the debtor is in denial (see page 3) or because he wrongly believes he can resolve the issue without help.

A debt doctor may not be asked to help until the bailiffs are at the door or the electricity has been cut off. It is not productive to tell the debtor he should have sought help earlier. Although this is correct, it does nothing to address the problem and can be counter-productive in getting the debtor's co-operation.

Emergency action usually involves little more than buying time to allow the debt doctor to put in place the procedures which should have been started much earlier. As such, emergency action is *additional* to other debt procedures, and not a substitute.

The four most serious areas requiring emergency action are:

- bailiffs seizing goods
- disconnection of utilities
- repossession of home
- harassment by creditors.

Each of these is looked at in turn.

Bailiffs

An explanation of the role of bailiffs is given on page 187.
The most effective ways of dealing with bailiffs are:

- pay the sum demanded
- negotiate an extended period
- refuse them access to the premises

- challenge the legality of their conduct
- have the warrant withdrawn.

It is not commonly known that bailiffs generally do not have the right to enter premises without permission. Many bailiffs may pretend otherwise.

If a debtor has any reason to believe that a bailiff may be about to call, other adults in the household should be instructed on what to do.

It must be stressed that preventing a bailiff seizing goods does not reduce the debt. In most cases, bailiffs make a charge. So obstructing a bailiff usually makes the debt worse.

Types of bailiff

Bailiffs can be instructed by the civil courts to enforce a judgment made against the debtor, or by magistrates' court to recover fines. The bailiff may be an employee of the court or may be a private bailiff.

Paying the sum demanded

The simplest way to stop a bailiff is to pay the sum demanded. If the whole sum cannot be paid, part payment should be offered. If necessary, the debtor should contact a friend or relative who may be willing to lend the money (see page 44).

Negotiating terms

A debtor or debt doctor should already be negotiating with creditors. If not, a visit from a bailiff may provide one final opportunity to do so. The bailiff should be told that negotiations are in hand with the creditors. This may be sufficient to persuade them to leave.

For some types of warrant, the bailiff may agree to **impound** goods rather than seize them. Impounding puts goods into the **custody of the law**. This means that the bailiffs can return to seize the goods later. For this, they may force entry into a person's home. This is only likely to be agreed if the bailiff believes that funds can be obtained soon, usually within a few days.

The most common form of impounding is a **walking possession agreement**. The bailiff agrees that the goods may stay in the possession of the debtor who may continue to use them. The debtor signs the agreement to acknowledge that the goods are in the control of the bailiff and may be seized and sold if the debt is not paid. A small fee is usually made for the agreement. The goods may be used normally, such as continuing to drive a car, but the goods must not be sold, given away or damaged. A walking possession agreement may be signed by any adult in the household, not necessarily the debtor.

Impounding can involve **immediate removal** of goods. This is not the same as seizure, as the goods are held with a view to returning them rather than selling them. This is most commonly used only for vehicles and readily saleable assets. When the debt is paid, the goods are returned.

For completeness, the other two forms of impounding are close possession and securing on the premises. **Close possession** is where a bailiff remains as a **possession man** until the debt is paid, such as where the debtor goes to a bank or cash machine or friend to borrow money. **Securing on the premises** allows the goods to stay on the premises under the control of a bailiff such as in a shed to which only the bailiff has the key, or by putting a wheel clamp on a vehicle.

It may happen that goods cannot be impounded, perhaps because the only goods worth impounding are too big to be removed. In such a case, the bailiff will issue a **notice of distress**. In law this is the same as a seizure of goods even though they have not been removed. Such a notice remains valid for a few days only. If not followed up after, say, a week, the court will probably regard it as having been abandoned.

For magistrates' court distraint, the procedure is different. There is no walking possession agreement as such. Instead, goods may be identified by a **conspicuous mark**. They may only be seized on the day of the sale.

Refusing admission

A bailiff is instructed to seize goods to the value of the debt. The bailiff may remove any goods he sees which appear to belong to the debtor. This includes a car or bicycle in the front garden, except for distress warrants for rent. More information on what can be seized is given on page 105.

The simplest way of preventing this is to refuse the bailiff admission to the premises. A bailiff can often be obstructed simply by standing in the doorway and refusing admission. If a bailiff pushes past or even touches you, that is assault and the police may be called. However, once a bailiff has gained admission to premises, he has acquired a right of admission again in respect of the same warrant. This includes the right of **forcible entry**. If necessary, the bailiff can force his way by smashing a window or breaking down a door.

While a bailiff has no right of admission, he does not need permission to enter. A bailiff may enter through an open door or window, or may seize goods which are not in the building. A car on the drive is therefore vulnerable. If the door is answered by someone other than a debtor, such as a child, a bailiff may be able to gain entry. Bailiffs have more experience of sweet-talking and bluffing their way into premises than occupants have in resisting them.

Before considering whether to obstruct a bailiff, a creditor should consider the consequences. Although obstruction of a bailiff is not in itself an offence, the consequences can still be serious for warrants issued by a magistrates' court. In particular:

- if the warrant is for a fine or tax, the next step is for the bailiff to return to court for the debtor to be committed to prison
- for other warrants from a magistrates' court, the bailiff will report back to the court who can decide whether this was due to wilful refusal or culpable neglect, and (if so decided) can imprison the debtor.

Wilful refusal and culpable neglect must be considered by the court separately. **Wilful refusal** means a deliberate decision not to pay *even though the debtor could do so*. This often happens when people refuse to pay their council tax as a protest. If a debtor *cannot* pay, there is no question of wilful refusal. In practice, the financial statements should be prepared. If necessary, a provisional and estimated statement of affairs may need to be prepared quickly, with a more detailed and accurate statement to follow, to persuade the court that a person could not pay. Even if wilful refusal is found by the court, this does not automatically mean that the person will be imprisoned.

Culpable neglect means a reckless disregarding of the court's orders. The commonest example is when a debtor spends money on non-essential items in preference to paying the debt. It is not enough for the magistrates to find that the debtor has enough money and did not pay; the magistrates must determine why it was not paid. Again, financial statements are the most effective weapon in court.

A debt doctor helping a debtor who is accused of culpable neglect should argue one of the following, namely that the debtor:

- had no money left to pay the debt after paying for essentials
- was suffering from stress at the time
- did not properly understand the need to pay and the seriousness of the action
- was wrongly advised not to pay.

Sometimes, a bailiff may say that to be refused admission is automatically wilful refusal and imprisonment will therefore happen next. There is no known instance of a court deciding that refusing admission to a bailiff is itself wilful refusal.

For a warrant issued by another court, such as by a county court for payment of goods or services, the consequences are much less serious. In practice, bailiffs are easily deterred and return the warrant to the court.

If a debtor has been notified that a bailiff is likely to call, or otherwise believes this is likely, preventive measures include:

- keeping all external doors and windows locked
- removing valuable items from outside the house, such as parking the car elsewhere
- moving valuable belongings to the back of the house or upstairs where they cannot be seen from a front window
- keeping the front door on a chain when answering it
- instructing all other occupants of the house in these matters.

If a bailiff cannot obtain access, he will look through the window to see what property you have. If he can see nothing of value, the bailiff will return the warrant to the court with a note of what he can see.

It must be appreciated that any action designed to frustrate a bailiff is only worthwhile if:

- the delay is to give time to raise funds
- it may lead to a less draconian form of enforcement.

It is not appropriate to frustrate bailiffs otherwise. Delays will usually only be for a few days and their costs are added to the debt.

Seizure of goods should always be resisted. Such goods are sold at auction, often for as little as one tenth of their value. Sums raised often do not even cover the costs of bailiffs, storage and auction. A debtor can have £500 worth of goods seized to pay a £100 debt, and end up with no goods and £150 debt. It can be better for the debtor to sell the goods himself, perhaps at a car boot sale or on eBay.

The magistrates' court may only send in the bailiffs under a distress warrant. In such a case, an application may be made to the court to give more time to pay. Magistrates vary in their policy, so it can be worthwhile a debt counsellor speaking to the magistrates' clerk to assess the local policy. There is legal doubt as to whether magistrates are entitled to refuse even to hear such an application. Sometimes the bailiffs themselves may be prepared to allow a debtor a few extra days.

Local authorities will often use private bailiffs to recover unpaid council tax. The authorities often give instructions to bailiffs restricting their right to seize goods from particular groups. The debt counsellor should find out the local policy. Even if there is no policy, a call to the local authority asking for the warrant to be withdrawn may be worthwhile.

For bailiff visits ordered by a county court, an application may be · made on form N245. For High Court orders, an application may be made to the court for a stay of execution.

An alternative to seizure is a **walking possession** whereby the debtor keeps the goods on certain conditions while arranging payment.

A bailiff does not have a general right of forcible entry to a debtor's home. A bailiff may enter without permission (see pages 100–02):

- business premises
- home premises that have been entered before for the same debt
- homes if access is possible without forcible entry, such as by an open window
- publicly accessible parts of homes, such as the front garden.

Challenging the bailiff's actions

It is an offence for a bailiff to make:

- illegal levies
- irregular levies
- excessive levies.

An **illegal levy** is where the bailiff has broken the law, such as forcing his way into a private home where he has not been before. This renders the entry illegal, the goods are returned and the bailiff is liable for substantial damages. In practice, this is usually the only bailiff offence worth pursuing.

An **irregular levy** is when an error in procedure later arises. This does not make the entry and seizure unlawful but gives the debtor a right to compensation. Many types of mistake are specifically excluded from this remedy.

An **excessive levy** is when the bailiff takes far more than is necessary to recover the debt. The debtor may sue to recover the excess property.

Obstructing a bailiff can be a criminal offence for debts relating to taxes (including council tax) and fines, for which the debtor may be committed to prison. Sometimes bailiffs threaten an unco-operative debtor with committal for 'wilful refusal or culpable neglect', though there is no known instance of a person being imprisoned in such circumstances.

What goods may be seized

The rules on what goods may be seized are complex, and vary for different types of warrant. In general, all goods may be seized unless exempt. These exemptions vary for different types of warrant.

For all types of warrant, protection is afforded to:

- household essentials
- tools of trade.

Household essentials include beds, a table and chairs, and facilities to wash and cook. The determining factor is *what is left*. The Lord Chancellor's Department has determined that a microwave oven may be seized if an ordinary cooker is left; a three-piece suite may be seized if dining chairs remain.

Tools of trade are those which are needed to allow the person to continue earning a living. A tool must be so essential that its loss would stop a person earning a living.

A car is only protected if it can be shown as a household essential (such as the only means of getting children to school) or as a tool of trade.

For **VAT distress warrants**, the list is more generous on what household items are protected. In particular, the exemptions also include curtains, cleaning materials, irons, carpets and rugs and toys.

For **rent distress warrants**, the law adds two further exemptions: items in use when the bailiffs call (such as any electrical appliance switched on), and perishable goods.

In practice, protection is also afforded to:

- fixtures and fittings which are attached to the building so that the building is damaged if removed
- goods belonging to someone else, including goods on hire purchase and the property of other members of the household
- items of such little value that their seizure would not even realize the cost of seizure and removal
- property owned or used by a child.

The exemption for **fixtures and fittings** can involve subtle distinctions. Light fittings, built-in cupboards, curtain rails and fitted carpets are probably exempt. Lamp shades, shelf units, curtains and loose carpets are probably not.

Third party goods are often a contentious area, as it is so easy to say that items belong to someone else. An inventory of such goods helps, as does a receipt showing that someone else paid for it or a hire purchase agreement. Bailiffs can be suspicious of such claims, and tend to seize goods first and argue later.

Goods of little value should not be seized, though bailiffs often still seize them.

Although **children's goods** are not exempt by law, the National Standard for Enforcement Agencies says that they should not be seized. Items which are essential for a child, such as a high chair, clothes and feeding bottle will be exempt anyway as household essentials. In practice the NSEA extends this to toys, children's books, bicycles and similar.

Gas and electricity

Gas and electricity cannot be disconnected:

- while there is a genuine dispute about the bill
- at pensioners' homes during winter
- at homes with children under 11 or with people with certain disabilities until social services have been notified and given 14 days to sort out the matter.

Many gas and electricity bills are estimated. A first step is always to read the meters and have the charges exactly quantified. A particularly high bill may indicate a fault on the meter, which should be checked. A charge is made for a meter examiner, though this is refunded if a significant fault is found.

Some debt counsellors routinely suggest disputing the bill as a means of buying time, even though there is no query on the bill. This is dishonest. If there are genuine reasons to resist disconnection, but the gas or electricity company is not being co-operative, you can contact Ofgem, which can prevent disconnection.

Liability for gas and electricity only arises from a contract between an occupier and supplier. If the occupier has properly ended that contract, no payment may be demanded from anyone for any gas or electricity still used. The companies may try to argue that someone else is a 'beneficial user' and therefore should be required to pay, but such argument has no validity in law.

The special provisions for gas and electricity only apply to the provision of power. If non-power items are outstanding, such as payments for a cooker or servicing, these must be pursued as for any other debt. A company may not disconnect power for non-payment of a non-power debt.

Where a person is having difficulties paying a bill, they should contact the power company who will try to make other arrangements. These may include fitting a coin meter. Some meters use tokens rather than coins, so it is essential to keep sufficient tokens in stock. It should also be remembered that power from a meter is usually more expensive than when provided by other means.

For coin-operated gas and electricity meters, the coin belongs to the company as soon as it enters the meter. This means that taking the coins out is theft. It also means that if the coins are stolen by a burglar, the householder is not liable. Tampering with a meter, or using false, foreign or forged coins is a criminal offence.

Gas and electricity are supplied on ethical terms by Equigas and Equipower. They can be contacted on www.ebico.co.uk or by calling 0845 4560170. They do not charge extra for installing a payment meter.

Further information about preventing power disconnection is available from the Social Action Plan of the Ofgem website at www. ofgem.gov.uk.

Eviction from home

It is not easy to evict a person from their home. Generally the law regards this as a last resort after all other options have been considered and all legal processes exhausted. However, action must be taken by a debtor no later than the first sign that the mortgage lender or landlord is seeking **possession** of the property. As with all such debt enforcement procedures, the longer the problem is left, the more difficult it becomes.

A person should never be advised to leave their home against their will until the proper court order has been obtained. Once the person has left their home, their chances of reclaiming it are effectively zero.

The procedures for arrears of rent are similar to those for arrears of mortgage. In addition, there are circumstances when council tenants may be evicted for non-financial reasons, such as anti-social behaviour. These evictions do not follow the procedure outlined below which deals solely with financial eviction.

A debt doctor must determine what is possible for the debtor. The choice is usually:

- agree a schedule to clear arrears; or
- sell the house to clear arrears.

If neither of these is possible, it is difficult to avoid the debtor becoming homeless and bankrupt.

Do not wait until the lender or landlord has started possession proceedings. Prepare a plan and seek to implement it.

A schedule to clear arrears is part of the financial statement process (see page 125).

If that is not possible, try to sell the house yourself before the lender sells it – for between 25% and 40% less (see page 112).

A person cannot be evicted from their home by a summary judgment or default judgment. This means that there must be a court hearing where the occupier may attend and put his case. The hearing is usually in the county court, though exceptional cases may be heard in the High Court.

More than a quarter of a million repossession orders were started in 2005.

Negotiate with the creditor

A debt doctor should always try to negotiate with the creditor, and not rely on the court hearing.

The reasons for trying negotiation are:

- it leaves the court case as a long stop
- anything can happen once a court case starts
- the occupier will usually have additional costs, as the occupier usually must pay the lender's or landlord's costs.

A lender or landlord may ask for a suspended possession order (see page 111).

Mortgage arrears

A lender cannot simply seize a person's home just because the mortgage or a secured loan is in arrears. If the mortgage was issued under the Consumer Credit Act 1974, a default notice must have been issued first (see page 113).

If the mortgage was taken out after 30 October 2004, it may be a **regulated mortgage**. This means that it is regulated by the Financial Services Authority (FSA). This brings it within the scope of the Mortgage Conduct of Business Rules, which require a lender to deal 'fairly' with borrowers, and to have a written policy on dealing with those in arrears.

Many lenders have their own policies. Typically many lenders do not consider repossession until the mortgage is three months in arrears, but you should not rely on this. The Council of Mortgage Lenders, to which many lenders belong, has a code which states that repossession is only considered as a last resort when attempts at alternative resolution have failed.

Possession claim form

A lender or landlord will start repossession by completing a particulars of claim form. In this, the lender or landlord gives all known relevant information about the debtor, including what is known about the debtor's circumstances.

Paragraph 11 of the form asks what remedy is being sought. The usual answer is repossession and the sum owed.

For rented property, the payments should be checked carefully to ensure that only rent is claimed. Rent does not include rates, water charges or overpayments of housing benefit. These items cannot be included in the possession claim.

Possession hearing

The hearing normally takes place in private, between four and eight weeks after the issue of the possession claim form.

At least three weeks before the hearing, the lender or landlord must serve the claim form and particulars of claim on the debtor. At least two weeks before the hearing a notice must be sent to the property addressed to 'the occupiers'. This is to notify anyone else who is resident there.

There is a defence form N11M which allows the debtor to resist the possession order. This should be submitted two weeks before the hearing, though the courts usually allow a later submission. Failure to file the form is unlikely to compromise the debtor's right to resist the order, but can lead to extra costs.

The debtor should pay particular attention to question 3 on the amount of arrears. If there is any reason to question the figure, that fact must be stated. The court cannot order possession if the arrears figure is wrong.

The final question on the form is also of particular importance as it gives the debtor his chance to tell his story. For arrears of mortgage, the last question asks:

- the circumstances in which the loan was made
- why the arrears arose
- what circumstances were beyond the borrower's control
- why it would cause particular hardship if eviction is ordered.

For arrears of rent, the last question asks:

- why the arrears arose
- what circumstances were beyond the tenant's control

- why it would cause particular hardship if eviction is ordered
- (if applicable) why an expensive property was rented.

It should never be assumed that the court knows any of these answers, nor any part of the answers. Nor should it be assumed that the answer is obvious.

In all proceedings, the debtor must make himself or herself look as responsible as possible. Debt must be seen as a consequence of unexpected events outside the debtor's control. If that is clearly not the case, the debtor must at least acknowledge any failing and demonstrate a determination to remedy the situation.

Mortgage arrears: dual interest rate

A debtor may have a further unpleasant shock in that the interest rate being applied increases significantly once possession proceedings start. This is known as a **dual interest rate scheme**. It is kicking a person when down.

A higher rate of interest may be imposed if:

- the terms of the mortgage specifically allow it; or
- the borrower was enjoying a special low rate (such as an introductory rate) which automatically ends if arrears build up.

In November 1997, the Office of Fair Trading said that such arrangements were unfair and oppressive and could not be applied unless:

- the difference between the rates is small, usually up to 2.5%; and
- the borrower can return to the lower rate once the arrears are cleared.

Court hearing

The court will usually hear a possession application quickly. It is usually advisable not to try to play for time by thinking up excuses for delay. Judges can see through such ploys, and they will reduce the chances of a settlement in the debtor's favour.

The debt doctor must be clear as to the situation for the debtor.

To avoid possession for rent arrears, it is essential to have a schedule to clear the arrears *and* pay future rent. Suppose someone is paying £500 a month rent and has £2,000 arrears. A scheme could include a scheme to repay £200 a month for 10 months *plus* the £500 rent. This means paying £700 for 10 months and then continuing at £500. It is most unlikely that any landlord will agree to a scheme which allows rent to build up further.

For a mortgage, possession can be resisted by one of the following:

- a schedule to make payments to clear the arrears; or
- a proposal to sell the home to raise funds to clear the arrears; or
- giving up the home to move to other accommodation.

Factors considered by the court include:

- how many previous warrants have been suspended
- whether previous arrangements have been made and not kept
- how well the case is presented to the court
- how long the debtor has been seeking help.

Unless the proceedings are for a mortgage regulated by the Consumer Credit Act, the court has a wide discretion in a hearing for a possession order. In general, the court may:

- adjourn the proceedings;
- suspend the possession order; or
- postpone the date for 'delivery of possession' (eviction).

If the proceedings are regulated by the Consumer Credit Act, the court should consider making a time order.

It is possible to seek an adjournment, of which there are three types:

- adjournment with liberty to restore – the amount is about to be paid in full, or the property is about to be sold, or a plan to clear the arrears has already been agreed
- adjourned for a fixed period (usually 28 days) – to allow the debtor to obtain advice or to clarify matters
- general adjournment – when a repayment plan seems to be working.

Conditions may be attached to an adjournment, such as payment of instalments (by the debtor) or no further interest being added (by the creditor).

Suspended possession orders

The court has power to suspend possession provided the arrears can be cleared within a reasonable time. The terms of such an order are usually to pay a specified amount at a specified interval to clear the arrears. For mortgage arrears, the court will start by looking at the remaining period of the mortgage. This principle was established by the Court of Appeal in the case *Cheltenham and Gloucester v Norgan* *[1996]*.

This does not prevent the court ordering a period longer than the term of the mortgage. The courts have tended to allow long repayment periods when the amount owed is less than the value of the property. The courts take the view that the lender has adequate security.

It may be that the debtor cannot clear the arrears and the option is to sell the property. The objective of the debt doctor in such circumstances is to get a suspended possession order to allow *the borrower* to make the sale. If the borrower does nothing, the lender (usually bank or building society) will take the property and sell it. Although the lender is required to get the best price, in practice such properties are sold by auction where prices are often less. Remember the lender is keener on getting his money sooner rather than getting the best price soon. The website www.propertyenquiries.com states that typical savings from buying a repossessed house are between 25% and 40%. Other websites indicate similar reductions.

Suppose someone owes £200,000 on a house which would sell for £300,000 if put with an estate agent and two or three months were allowed for the sale. If the debtor could arrange this, he could clear the mortgage and have £100,000 towards a new property. If the lender sells the property, the lender may put it in an auction with a reserve of £200,000. If it sells for that figure, the lender has got back his £200,000 promptly and the borrower gets nothing. The borrower has lost £100,000.

The situation is even worse when there is **negative equity**, as giving up a property does not mean giving up the mortgage on it. In the years 1991 and 1992 some homes lost 25% of their value. Suppose a buyer bought a house for £100,000 in 1990 paying £10,000 in cash and taking out a mortgage for £90,000. The property's value then fell to £75,000. The buyer still owes £90,000 even though the house is worth only £75,000. In the normal course of events, this matters little as house prices go up and down over the years anyway. The buyer would still live in the same house making the same mortgage payments; the value of the house would matter not. If the buyer simply stayed put, the property could be worth about £300,000 by 2006, so the problem would have solved itself with the buyer doing nothing at all.

A problem arises when a person needs to sell during negative equity. Suppose in the example two paragraphs above, the £300,000 house sold for only £180,000 (40% below its open market value). Not only has the buyer lost his home, *but he still owes £20,000* to the lender. This debt is not wiped out just because the home has gone. During 1991 and 1992, many people faced with debt and negative equity tried to 'walk away' by handing in the keys to their home. For many, it was an unpleasant shock to find that even giving away your home was not enough. An explanation of house prices is given on page 96.

Making some effort to prepare a home for sale will increase the price and result in a quicker sale. This may seem like the last advice needed by someone in serious debt facing eviction. However, a quick sale could mean the difference between selling it yourself and having £100,000 to start again, or letting the lender sell it and losing £100,000. For advice, see page 51.

A suspended possession order is usually only made when the proceeds of the home are sufficient to clear the arrears. It has been known for a suspension order to be made for three months, though this is generous.

Time order

If the mortgage is regulated by Consumer Credit Act 1974, it may be possible to obtain a time order.

This allows a debt to be cleared in such instalments as the court considers 'just'. This is considered in relation to the value in the property and the ability of the debtor to pay.

A time order is usually appropriate when:

- a debtor's troubles are temporary but are likely to improve; or
- the agreement was harsh, and the debtor was ignorant of the terms or was badly advised.

Sometimes applying for a time order can make the lender be more reasonable in agreeing a repayment plan.

Order for possession

If attempts to resolve the matter fail, the court will issue an order for possession, also known as an order for eviction. This usually takes effect from 28 days, though the court can extend this to 56 days (eight weeks) if there are special circumstances such as the debtor being seriously ill. The purpose of this time is to find alternative accommodation, probably from the local authority, not to make any further attempt to stay in the house.

A debtor or debt doctor should argue in court against a possession order if there are any grounds to do so. Such grounds include:

- being wrongly advised when taking out the mortgage, particularly if the bad advice came from the lender

- that legal action is being taken against a financial adviser in respect of the mortgage
- mortgage interest should be paid by Department of Work and Pensions (DWP) but has not been
- the mortgage is regulated by Consumer Credit Act 1974 but does not comply with the terms of the Act.

The order for possession states a date and time by which the occupant must leave the premises. The occupant can apply to the court to postpone the eviction.

If the person has not left, the lender applies for a **warrant of possession**. This states the exact time and date that the bailiffs will attend to evict.

Even at this late stage, it is still possible for a debt doctor to negotiate directly with the creditor. All lenders seek to avoid evicting people from their homes. Sometimes getting to this stage in the proceedings can be a useful reality check. Examples have been known of creditors agreeing terms with the debtor or representative after an eviction order has been issued.

Otherwise, the bailiffs will attend at the time stated. They have the right to smash down doors and forcibly remove anyone on the premises. If violent resistance is encountered, the bailiffs will call the police and stay until they arrive. If violent resistance is expected, the police may accompany the bailiffs. The police will not evict the person, but may intervene if anyone resists when the bailiffs evict.

The lender or his agent will usually be present in the background with a locksmith. Once the property is cleared, the agent will order the locks changed.

Any personal property still in the house still belongs to you, but the lender's duty is only to return the property to you. The lender is not obliged to provide any storage or transport. A lender is most unlikely to let you enter the premises to collect property. There is usually a two-week time limit.

Even after eviction, it is still possible to apply to the court to set aside a possession order, but this rarely succeeds. The only grounds likely to succeed are that the procedures have not been properly followed, such as not receiving the summons or other notices.

All the costs of the possession order and its enforcement are added to the debt.

If the sale of the property realizes more than the amount owed, the balance should be paid to the debtor as soon as reasonably possible. This is accompanied by an account of proceeds. Otherwise the lender is not required to give details of the sale.

If the sale of the property does not realize enough to clear the debt, the proceeds are applied first to the interest and then to the capital. The balance is known as a **mortgage shortfall** debt. This remains payable as an unsecured debt. Most lenders allow the debtor some time, typically one or two years, to recover before pursuing this debt. A debtor should never believe that the debt has been forgotten just because nothing has happened for several months. In general, the lender has six years to recover the debt (see page 188).

Possibly a bigger risk is that the lender will **sell the debt**. A debt is an asset just like a car or a bag of oranges, and can therefore be sold just like one. A debt for £10,000 may be sold by the bank for £2,000, writing off the other £8,000. The debt is now owed to a debt company who can pursue the debtor. In practice, these companies tend to be much tougher than the original lender.

It is possible to challenge a mortgage shortfall debt, though few such cases are brought in practice. The lender who has repossessed the property is known as the **mortgagee in possession,** and has certain legal responsibilities, breach of which could be actionable.

Possible examples to challenge a mortgage shortfall debt include:

- selling the property for well below its market price, particularly if there is reason to suspect that the sale was not in the open market
- failure to maintain the property, such as fixing a leaking pipe and mowing the lawn. The mortgagee in possession is not required to make any improvements to help the sale
- selling the property as soon as possible, and not delaying in the hope of getting a better price.

A mortgage shortfall debt is simply another unsecured debt. As such, it is treated in exactly the same way as other unsecured debts when preparing the financial statements.

Sometimes borrowers do not give their new address to the lender, hoping that they will not be found. Lenders can use tracing agents who manage to find about 50% of people who abscond, according to the Association of British Investigators.

Because lenders wish to lose mortgage shortfall debts from their books, they can be amenable to writing off the debt or accepting a lower amount in full and final settlement. Few debts can be sold for more than 20% of their value, so any offer around that level could be successful. You can point out that they may only get 25% in an individual voluntary arrangement (see page 224) or nothing in bankruptcy.

Mortgage indemnity guarantee

Many mortgages are sold with a mortgage indemnity guarantee. This is an insurance policy which the lender insists the borrower takes out because the loan is above the amount the lender would otherwise provide. It is usually sold for a single premium which is added to the amount lent and is repaid as part of the mortgage. As such, most borrowers do not really notice it.

This guarantee is for the benefit of the lender not the borrower. Even though the borrower pays the premium, the lender gets all the benefit. Suppose there is a mortgage shortfall debt of £20,000 which the policy covers. The insurance company will pay the £20,000 to the lender who can therefore bring no further claim against the lender. However, the insurer can. Under the principle known as **subrogation,** the insurance company will seek to recover the £20,000 from the borrower.

Mortgage rescue

Mortgage rescue is the name given to various schemes developed in 1992 which allow an indebted mortgagor to become a tenant in his home.

A local authority or housing association buys the home, allowing the mortgagor to clear his debts, and then lets him stay in the home as a tenant. A variant is the shared-ownership scheme where the mortgagor sells a part interest in the house, usually with a right to buy back that part. So a mortgagor could sell a 40% interest in the house and receive 40% of the proceeds of the house but then be liable to pay 40% of the normal rent for the property. When the house is sold, he gets 60% of the proceeds.

Such schemes are rarely available. In effect, mortgage rescue is similar to equity release.

Homelessness

A local authority has a statutory duty to provide advice and assistance to all who are homeless. In general, the law requires the local authority to accommodate anyone who is homeless unless they made themselves homeless.

A council is only legally required to provide accommodation to someone who is:

- eligible
- not intentionally homeless

- in priority need; and
- has a local connection.

These conditions are looked at individually.

To be eligible usually means either being a citizen of the UK or another European country or having the legal right to stay in the UK or having been granted political asylum.

To be **homeless** it is not necessary to be actually sleeping on the streets. A person is homeless if:

- facing eviction in the next 28 days
- they do not have permission to stay where they are living
- locked out of the home
- unable to stay at home because of violence
- accommodation is big enough for one person but not for others who live with the person
- the present accommodation is temporary (such as a friend's floor)
- the home has become uninhabitable or too unsafe
- unable to afford to stay in current home
- the person lives in a caravan or boat and cannot find a site or mooring.

If the council decides that a person is not homeless, the person has a right to appeal against that decision within 21 days. This obliges the council to reconsider the decision.

Having established that a person is homeless, the council next must decide whether the person is **intentionally homeless**. For this, all four of these conditions must apply:

- the person deliberately did or did not do something
- that something prompted the person to leave the accommodation
- if not done, the person could have stayed
- it would have been reasonable to have stayed.

Examples of behaviour that is likely to be regarded as intentional homelessness:

- not paying the rent or mortgage when able to do so
- being evicted for anti-social behaviour
- leaving the accommodation when it was reasonable to stay
- being subject to threats of violence which were unlikely to be carried out.

The following are *not* examples of intentional homelessness:

- only being able to pay the mortgage or rent by doing without other essentials such as food or heating

- leaving home because the person did not realize he could stay
- being wrongly advised to leave home
- the act or omission which prompted leaving was done by someone else in the household without the person's knowledge.

The last of these includes when a person believes that their husband, wife or other partner was paying the rent or mortgage but was not.

If the council decides that a person is intentionally homeless, it must give that decision in writing. The council can be required to reconsider this within 21 days.

Further guidance on homelessness can be found on the website of Shelter at http://england.shelter.org.uk/home/index.cfm.

Unlawful eviction and harassment

An attempt to evict a residential occupier from their home is a specific offence under Protection from Eviction Act 1977 s1(2). This states:

> ### Protection from Eviction Act 1977 s1(2)
>
> If any person unlawfully deprives the residential occupier of any premises of his occupation of the premises, or any part thereof, or attempts to do so, he shall be guilty of an offence unless he proves that he believed, and had reasonable cause to believe, that the residential occupier had ceased to reside in the premises.

A residential occupier is anyone whose home is there, regardless of what the legal arrangements are. So a residential occupier can include a partner, lodger or child. It does not include a visitor, hotel guest or squatter.

Eviction does not necessarily involve using or threatening force to get a resident off the premises. It is also eviction to:

- trick a resident into leaving; or
- use stealth to gain entry during the resident's absence.

The law does not limit the offence to the landlord or creditor. Anyone who attempts to evict or harass a residential occupier from their home can be found guilty.

There is a separate offence of harassing a residential occupier under s1(3) of the same Act. This states:

> ## Protection from Eviction Act 1977 s1(3)
>
> If any person with intent to cause the residential occupier of any premises –
>> (a) to give up the occupation of the premises or any part thereof, or
>> (b) to refrain from exercising any right or pursuing any remedy in respect of the premises thereof;
>
> does any act calculated to interfere with the peace or comfort of the residential occupier or members of his household, or persistently withdraws or withholds services reasonably required for the occupation of the premises as a residence, he shall be guilty of an offence.

Examples of harassment of a residential occupier include:

- intimidation and threats to occupants
- interference with the building, such as removing doors or windows ostensibly for replacement, but not replacing them
- disconnecting essential supplies such as water or gas
- failing to provide or pay for essential services.

It should be noted that a single act of interference with the resident's peace or comfort constitutes harassment, whereas withholding services must be 'persistent', which means that it must have continued for some time.

It is not necessary to show that the act of harassment itself is unlawful. The House of Lords has ruled that a landlord who disconnected a tenant's doorbell was guilty of harassment even though the tenant was not entitled to a doorbell under the tenancy agreement. This was an act which interfered with the residency and was intended to force the resident out, and was therefore caught by this Act.

Because section 1(3) requires proof of motive, which is difficult, section 1(3A) makes it an offence if a person believes or has reasonable cause to believe that his action has the effects described.

The Caravans Sites Act 1968 affords similar protection to residential caravans on protected sites.

If the police are called to a dispute relating to eviction or harassment of a tenant, their prime concern is to prevent a breach of the peace. If it appears to the police that there may be an offence committed, the first response is to explain the law to the parties. Whatever the outcome, the police report such incidents to the housing authority.

Harassment

In terms of debt, there are two different offences of harassment, one specific to debt collection and a general offence of harassment. A creditor is entitled to take reasonable steps to recover money owed, but does not have complete freedom of action to do whatever he likes. The separate offence of harassing a residential occupier is explained on page 118.

The specific offence of harassing a debtor is contained in the Administration of Justice Act 1970 s40. This makes it an offence to subject a person to 'alarm, distress or humiliation', because of their frequency or publicity or manner. It also makes it illegal to say that non-payment is a criminal offence, or to pretend that someone is a court official or court-sanctioned debt collector.

The section is reproduced below.

Administration of Justice Act 1970 s40

Punishment for unlawful harassment of debtors.

(1). A person commits an offence if, with the object of coercing a person to pay money claimed from the other as a debt due under a contract he:

(a) harasses the other with demands for payment which, in respect of their frequency, the manner or occasion of making any such demand, or of any threat or publicity by which any demand is accompanied, are calculated to subject him or his family or household to alarm, distress or humiliation

(b) falsely represents, in relation to the money claimed, that criminal proceedings lie for failure to pay for it

(c) utters a document falsely represented by him to have some official character, or purporting to have some official character which he knows it has not

(2). A person may be guilty of an offence by virtue of sub-section (1)(a) above if he concerts with others in the taking of such actions as is described in that paragraph, notwithstanding that his own course of conduct does not by itself amount to harassment.

Sub-section (3) goes on to say that it is not harassing a debtor to do anything which is reasonable and legal.

Someone is likely to be guilty of harassing a debtor if he:

- tells a neighbour or work colleague that you owe money
- parks a vehicle identifying himself as a debt collector outside the debtor's house

- discusses the debt in a voice loud enough for others to hear
- advertises that you owe money, such as pinning up details in a local shop
- calls at anti-social hours
- calls several times a day
- makes any kind of threat or violence or other action which is not legally justified
- calls at work unnecessarily
- tries to embarrass the debtor
- states that he is a court official or a court-sanctioned debt collector when he is not
- tells the debtor that he must pay additional charges when he does not have to
- sends documents which look like court documents
- pressures debtors to sell property to clear the debt
- falsely states that a court judgment or court order has been obtained.

All these are criminal offences. You have the right to order a person off your premises and may call the police.

The police do not usually prosecute harassment of debtors unless a more serious offence is also involved, such as blackmail, violence or fraud. The best approach is to do the following as appropriate:

- write to the creditor saying that such conduct is not acceptable and asking them to stop it (quoting the above section of the Act is often effective as it demonstrates that the writer knows his rights; it can help if you tell the creditor how he may contact you conveniently)
- write to the Trading Standards or Consumer Protection Department of the local council
- write to the Office of Fair Trading
- write to any trade association or professional body which has a Code of Practice.

The punishment for harassment is a £5,000 fine. Harassment can also lead to a revocation or non-renewal of a Consumer Credit Licence or private bailiff's certificate. A trade association or professional body may discipline a member.

It is also possible to bring a private prosecution in the magistrates' court, though this could be expensive and difficult. It is unlikely to be a viable option for a debtor.

The following actions are *not* likely to constitute harassment:

- calling you at a reasonable frequency on a telephone number you have provided or which is the only one the creditor knows
- sending statements and reminders

- saying that he will take action which the law allows him to take
- reporting your non-payment to a credit reference agency or sharing it with other suppliers
- refusing to supply you with any further goods or services.

There are some other laws which deal with harassment generally, which may also be relevant.

The Malicious Communications Act 1988 s1 makes it a criminal offence to send a letter or e-mail which is:

- 'indecent or grossly offensive' or threatening or contains information which the sender knows is false; and
- is for the purpose of causing distress or anxiety.

An offender can be fined in the magistrates' court. In practice, a letter has to be extremely bad to justify a prosecution. Writing a rude or angry letter is unlikely to be an offence.

The Criminal Justice and Public Order Act 1994 makes it a criminal offence to cause 'harassment, alarm or distress' with intent by using 'threatening, abusive or insulting words or behaviour' in a public place. Only the police may prosecute. News bulletins routinely show that they do not.

The Protection from Harassment Act 1997 makes it an offence if a person deliberately and unreasonably causes another person alarm or distress on at least two occasions. Section 4 contains a separate offence of causing fear of violence on at least two occasions. Only the police may prosecute. In addition to being fined, an offender can be made the subject of a restraining order. This Act was introduced to outlaw stalking, but has been used in many other contexts.

In addition to harassment, many such actions may be offences under other laws.

Any fear of violence is **assault** and any unlawful force is **battery**. Assault does not require any physical contact; it is the fear that violence is about to be used. So someone swinging a punch or threatening violence is guilty of assault even though there was no physical contact. In practice, threatening violence is more usually prosecuted under Public Order Act 1986. Battery does require physical contact but need not cause any pain. Holding someone's arm to stop them walking away is battery.

More serious cases of assault include **actual bodily harm** under Offences Against the Person Act 1861 s47. This requires an injury calculated to interfere with health or comfort in a more than trifling way. This can include psychiatric injury but not emotions such as fear, distress or panic. Section 20 of the same Act deals with the even more serious offence of **grievous bodily harm**. This generally requires wounding (breaking the skin) or very serious psychiatric injury. This offence can be committed indirectly, such as if a bailiff hammers on the door causing a person to jump from a window and break a leg.

Trespass itself is not a criminal offence. The occupier of the land may lawfully require a person to leave and give him reasonable time to do so. Failing that, the occupier may use reasonable force to remove the person. Other people may help the occupier. If a trespasser makes the slightest physical contact against the occupier, he commits the criminal offence of battery for which the police can be called.

In practice, removal of a trespasser or an altercation which escalates is more likely to constitute a **breach of the peace**. The offence of breach of peace is committed when harm is done or is *likely to be done*. So if a scene starts to escalate, the police should be called before the matter descends to more serious disorder. There are many other public order offences.

Where harassment or any other offence against a debtor is suspected, the debt doctor must record details and collect evidence. A contemporary record should be kept of all such instances. Such a record should note:

- the date, time and place of the incident
- the names or identities of the people involved
- details of the sequence of events
- where threatening words were used, the exact words or at least their meaning
- names of any witnesses.

8

Clearing the debt

General policy

Before looking at how to clear a debt, it is essential to understand what the words debit and credit mean, particularly as the word 'credit' in bookkeeping has the exact opposite meaning to everyday use. When you pay money into your bank, your account is debited, not credited. See page 14 for more explanation.

The policy for clearing debts involves these stages:

- identifying and quantifying the debts
- seeking to minimize each debt
- preparing a budget
- **preparing a financial statement**
- making repayment offers
- persuading creditors to accept the repayment offer
- implementing whatever is agreed.

The prime stage in this process is preparing the financial statement.

Once this statement is prepared, the debtor or debt adviser is in a powerful negotiating position. Preparing the statements can be difficult, frustrating and stressful. Once that period has passed, the debtor may be pleasantly surprised at how easy the remaining stages are.

The process of preparing these statements should be started immediately, even if there is scope for reducing a need or opportunity to reduce a debt. These statements are prepared on a **worst-case scenario** basis. It is not a problem to find later that the indebtedness is not as bad as first thought, nor that a debt may reduced. There can be a huge problem if it is later found that the debts are worse than believed.

Identifying debts

A debt doctor will usually need to conduct a thorough trawl of the debtor's correspondence and bank statements. It is quite normal for a debtor not to include all debts in any list he prepares.

In particular:

- check arrangements for payment of mortgage or rent
- check for evidence of hire purchase agreements, overdrafts, credit sales and similar
- list every credit card, charge card, store card, and other similar piece of plastic
- ask if any relations or friends have lent money
- ask to see *all* incoming mail (you are particularly interested in bills, reminders, credit card statements and bank statements).

It is common for a debtor only to regard something as a debt when he has trouble paying it. So if he has met all the repayments on a hire purchase agreement, that may not be included in any list provided to you. This is not deception; it is just not fully understanding what a debt is.

Similarly personal debts and disputed debts may be excluded. A debtor may say, 'my brother gave me £1,000, but he says I don't have to pay it back until I can afford to'. Perhaps so, but it is still a debt. Similarly a **disputed debt** is one where there is an argument on the amount owed or even if any money is owed at all. This can happen when a casual arrangement has been made for work done to a property; the builder can demand £500 when the owner says that only £300 is payable. The process for clearing debts can help resolve such disputes.

Financial statements

There are two elements to the financial statements:

- the debt statement
- the budget.

These are produced together, and are sent together to creditors.

The **debt statement** is simply a list of debts, distinguishing between priority debts and non-priority debts, as explained on page 77. This statement is also known as a **creditor sheet**, as it lists the creditors to whom the debts are owed.

The **budget** is a statement of expected income and expenditure for the debtor's normal everyday life. This should show a small excess of income over expenditure. That excess is used to clear the debts as listed in the debt statement.

Suppose a person produces a debt statement listing debts to creditors of £100,000. The same person produces a budget showing income of £30,000 a year and expenditure of £25,000 a year. That means that the person has £5,000 a year to repay the debts. It will take 20 years to clear the debt.

This does not mean that the debtor simply pays 5% of the balance to all creditors. The priority creditors will be paid more than 5% and non-priority creditors will receive less, at least at the start. In practice, the debts will be cleared much sooner than 20 years.

Suppose a non-priority creditor is owed £1,200, which the debtor is paying at the rate of £2 a month. This will take 50 years to clear. After three years, only £72 has been paid, so £1,128 is still owing. The creditor is probably bored with receiving these small payments. The processing costs and bank charges probably eat up most of each £2 anyway. The debtor then offers £400 to clear the balance. Although this means that the creditor is writing off almost two-thirds of what is owed to him, it is likely that the creditor will agree and be relieved to see the debt off its books. It has been known for an accounts department to buy cream doughnuts to celebrate the end of such a debt.

Common Financial Statement

There is no law which states how a financial statement must be presented. However, the British Bankers Association (BBA) and Money Advice Trust (MAT) have jointly produced a **Common Financial Statement (CFS)** (Figure 11). This document may be downloaded free from the BBA website at http://www.bba.org.uk/bba/jsp/polopoly. jsp?d=146&a=729. The BBA is the umbrella body for most UK banks; the MAT is a charity formed in 1991 to assist in debt recovery.

There is a single page format (reproduced here by permission of Money Advice Trust) and a longer five-page Budget Form. They each serve a similar purpose of stating a person's indebtedness, and identifying their current income and expenditure. Most banks, finance companies and an increasing number of other main creditors have agreed to use the CFS.

The first advantage of using the CFS is that it provides a standard layout which is readily understood by banks and creditors. A standard layout is easier to read as particular numbers appear in the same place on each form, making dealing with them much quicker and simpler. Also, a standard layout reduces ambiguity as there is no doubt about what a figure refers to.

The second advantage is that the CFS is part of a system based on trust between advisers and the banks. Generally, banks accept the repayment offers made on such a form. Most creditors will also accept offers made on a CFS.

There is also a fast-track system which uses **trigger figures**. These

Figure 11: Common Financial Statement.

Money Advice Trust	MAT/BBA Common Financial Statement [v3]	BRITISH BANKERS' ASSOCIATION

Client(s) name(s)	Dependants (Numbers & ages)
Address (inc. postcode)	Case ref no.
Date	Agency postcode

Income (All figures should represent MONTHLY amounts)	£
BF4 Wages/salary	
BF10 Other income	
BF18 Pensions	
BF31 Benefits	
BF32 Total income	

Please confirm that you have discussed the use of assets to make lump sum payments? **Yes** ☐

Expenditure (All figures should represent MONTHLY spend)	£
BF43 Rent	
BF44 Mortgage	
BF45 Other secured loans (2nd mortgage)	
BF46 Council tax	
BF55 Total other housing costs	
BF63 Total utilities	
BF64 Court fines	
BF65 Maintenance/child support	
BF66 Pension payments/AVCs	
BF67 Other life assurance	
BF68 HP/conditional sale	
BF69 TV licence	
BF70 Telephone	
BF71 Mobile phone	
BF85 Total travel	
BF95 Total housekeeping	
BF101 Total children	
BF105 Total health	
BF108 Total pets	
BF113 Total repairs & maintenance	
BF124 Total other expenditure	
BF125 Total expenditure	

Net income calculation	
BF32 Total monthly income	£
BF125 Total monthly expenditure	£
Available income per month	£

Creditor sheet 1 – Priority debts

Debt	Arrears £	Payment/offer £
Rent		
Mortgage		
Other secured loans		
Court fines		
Council tax		
Maintenance/child support		
Gas		
Electricity		
Other utilities		
Total		
Available income for other creditors		

Creditor sheet 2 – Other debts

Debt	Balance outstanding £	Court judgment? ✓ yes x no	Payment/offer £
Total			

See over for explanatory notes and space to provide additional information

Figure 11: Common Financial Statement (continued).

Explanatory notes to Common Financial Statement (CFS)

1. Trigger figures of expenditure are available for shaded items.
2. If you need to add any comments, please asterisk the relevant section and write comments in the space provided below. If necessary continue onto a separate sheet of paper and attach sheet to the CFS before sending to the creditor.
3. BF numbers relate to the Budget Forms which can be found at www.moneyadvicetrust.org, www.wiseradviser.org, www.fla.org.uk and www.bba.org.uk
4. BF85 (Total travel) relates to all expenditure relating to travel – fares and motoring.
5. BF95 (Total housekeeping) includes clothing and footwear.
6. BF124 (Total other expenditure) relates to items such as membership/professional subscriptions, postage, hairdressing/haircuts, TV/video/satellite/cable, other appliance rental, pub/outings, lottery, hobbies (e.g. gardening), religious and charitable giving, gifts (e.g. Christmas, birthdays, etc).
7. Banks will accept offers which are made via the CFS where the expenditure limits fall within the expenditure (trigger) figures set out in the CFS (provided there is no legal or regulatory impediment to doing so) unless the bank is aware of a history of fraud or other information which would raise concerns about the validity of the information in the CFS. In the latter case banks may request further information to establish the true financial position of their client.

If you have additional information relating to your client's expenditure, please give details here.

are average amounts of discretionary spending on areas such as entertainment. These trigger figures are known to professional advisers but are never disclosed to the debtor. A trigger figure is not a budget figure, so someone who spends less than average on food or clothing is not invited to spend more.

There are no triggers for mortgage, rent, hire purchase and similar expenditure, as these must be calculated on the facts of each case. There are no trigger figures for areas over which the debtor has no control, such as council tax, fines, pension payments, life assurance, TV licence, child support and secured loans.

The trigger figures are agreed with each creditor and revised every year. In general, expenditure which is equal to or less than the trigger figure is accepted without question. If expenditure exceeds the trigger figure, the adviser gives an explanation on the CFS. There are four sets of trigger figures depending on the nature of the household. There may be valid reasons such as having many children or being disabled. Creditors tend to accept such reasons on the CFS.

For the debtor and debt doctor, the advantages of using a CFS are:

- figures that fall within the trigger figure are accepted
- the CFS as a whole is accepted unless there is evidence of fraud or other grounds for suspicion
- debts which are sold remain subject to the CFS principles.

It is possible to negotiate a debt without using the CFS, though it helps to use a form and layout which is similar. A debt doctor must never pretend to be part of the CFS system if he is not.

Preparing a financial statement in CFS format or similar is an essential first step to negotiating the debt.

Creditors tend to attach considerable weight to who helped prepare the form. If prepared by a qualified accountant, the Citizens Advice Bureau or another recognized debt counsellor, a proposal is much more likely to be accepted than if sent by the debtor himself. This applies even if the adviser did no more than lay out the statement from information provided by the debtor.

Basis of the statement

Whatever statement is prepared, its basis must be stated. This must state:

- the reliability of the information
- whether the income is for the person or household
- whether income exceeds expenditure.

The **reliability** of the information is an important statement to protect the adviser. The debtor may not have told you the whole truth, either deliberately or inadvertently. It is normal for an adviser to include a statement saying something like:

> This statement has been prepared on the basis of documents made available to me and information provided by the debtor. I have not audited the accounts and cannot confirm whether this information is correct or complete.

This is not the same as saying 'I have no idea whether these figures are right or not'. There is a factual basis. If the debtor had told the adviser, 'actually I have another £10,000 salted away which I'm keeping quiet about', the adviser would not be able to issue the above statement. Similarly if the adviser found a letter demanding payment for £1,000 from a company, the adviser would investigate. Either this debt would be included in the statement, or the adviser would establish why the debt was not owed.

The **scope** of the statement must be stated. Creditors will want to know who else is a member of the debtor's household and what contribution they are making. The debts of one household member are not the debts of any other. However, a creditor will not look kindly upon an adult member of a household contributing nothing to the household income when capable of doing so.

A member of the household is simply someone who shares a home with the debtor. It includes a husband, wife, civil partner, adult child or other resident relative, live-in friend, lodger or any other adult who lives in the home. The nature of the relationship should be stated. A lodger is only required to contribute a reasonable sum for his lodging. A husband, wife or civil partner is legally required to support their partner. It is not necessary to give further details of the relationship, such as whether there is any sexual relationship with the other resident. (Note that a live-in girlfriend is *not* a 'common law wife'. A common law wife is a real wife but where the documents are missing – something which is now almost impossible.)

The third factor is the **balance** of income and expenditure. Efforts should already have been made to bring expenditure down to sensible levels, particularly if the debt arose because of extravagance in the first place. Any excess of income over expenditure is called **available income** because it is available to clear debts. If expenditure exceeds income, the available income is zero.

Practical problems

There are many practical problems which a debt doctor may encounter.

The first problem is the **mind your own business** attitude when asking details of personal expenditure and lifestyle. The response is that such details *are* the business of the debt adviser and a person's creditors. You are asking people to accept less than the amount they are legally owed, or at least to allow longer to be paid. The reason why they should accept this is very much their business.

The second problem is likely to be **quantifying** the figures. A debtor frequently goes into denial. A list of debts provided by a debtor is likely to be incomplete. A budget of income and expenditure is likely to be over-optimistic, assuming best-case scenario for income and probably assuming that expenditure is less than it is. Most people have little idea how they spend their money. It cannot be overstated that the budget must be the *worst-case scenario*. If the actuality proves to be better than budget, that will help the debt recovery programme as no creditor will refuse more than he expected. But if the actuality proves to be worse than budget, creditors can lose faith in the financial statements and take a much harder approach.

Sometimes the debtor simply does not know what the figures are. It may be necessary to demand to see *all* the debtor's mail and open it in his presence. The junk mail and few personal letters can easily be handed back. This way, the debt adviser is likely to find out about all significant debts, particularly if this is done for at least one month.

The budget

The budget must be:

- complete
- realistic
- prudent
- modest.

A budget is **complete** if it includes all income and expenditure of the debtor. No source of income should be omitted.

A debtor may be tempted to exclude child benefit, bank interest, money from family members, earnings from a hobby and other small items. They may similarly exclude expenditure to which that income is applied. For example, someone who plays in a band may decide that what they earn from music they will spend on music. This process of allocating income to expenditure is known as **hypothecation**. It has no place in a debtor's budget. *All* sources of income must be included, as must *all* items of spending. Any hint that income is being suppressed can be fatal to a debt recovery programme.

A budget is **realistic** if the figures contained in it are likely to be achieved. Income should be based on what may reasonably be achieved from normal working. It should not assume that overtime will always be available, that every week of trading will be a good week, or that some short-term benefit will continue indefinitely. Remember that no-one will object if a debtor manages to produce more income than the budget suggests, but they will object if a debtor produces less.

A budget is **prudent** if it errs on the side of caution, tending to understate income and overstate expenditure, rather than the other way round. This is an extension of the previous provision of being realistic. Prudence is one of the five **accounting concepts**. These are principles which are so fundamental to accounts that you may assume they apply unless the accounts specifically say they do not.

The general rule for a budget is that repayment offers should be low. No creditor will complain if you offer to pay £1 a month and then pay £2, but they will if you offer £2 and pay £1. The repayment period is almost irrelevant. In 2006, the Citizens Advice Bureau reported that many repayment schemes now exceed 70 years.

A budget is **modest** if it excludes extravagance. Large figures for entertainment, holidays, cigarettes, pets, clothes and hobbies will not be accepted by creditors. They will also question private education, expensive cars, building work and savings plans. Such things should be sacrificed to be fair to creditors before being indulgent to yourself and family. This does not mean that a debtor must live a bread-and-water lifestyle. A television, video, car, occasional modest holiday, children's toys, Christmas presents, and replacement clothing should be allowed for. More guidance is given on page 242 on what a trustee in bankruptcy is likely to accept.

Sorting out the debts

Debts are first sorted out between priority and non-priority debts. This is determined by the consequences of what will happen if the debt is not paid. Losing the home, having items repossessed, and incurring massive penalties are all factors which make something a priority debt. Further information on priority debts is given on page 77.

For priority debts, you offer the lowest amount you believe may be accepted. Remember that no creditor will negotiate a lower figure – they will only ever press for a higher figure. If you later realize that you can pay more, no-one will complain when you do, but you will have the advantage of deciding to use that extra money. It can be very effective in minimizing debts, as explained on page 140.

Non-priority debts

Non-priority debts must be paid in the most effective manner. The first consideration is to repay debts in a way which most reduces any charges still being incurred.

As explained on page 139, another part of this process is to stop interest and other charges being added. However, this is often only possible for the more serious debts and often only at a later stage of negotiation.

A good example of effective repayment is credit card debt. Suppose a debtor owes £4,000 as £1,000 each to four credit card companies. They respectively charge 2.5%, 2.0%, 1.5% and 1.0% interest on the balance every month. The minimum monthly repayment is the greater of 5% or £5. If this is not met, the company charges a late payment fee of £12. The debtor has £240 a month to clear these arrears.

Priority must be given to clearing the debt on the card charging the highest interest rate, but this must be balanced by avoiding late payment charges.

We consider three different strategies for clearing these four credit card debts:

(a) pay each card an equal amount;
(b) pay only the highest interest card and don't worry about any late payment fees on the rest; or
(c) pay off the minimum for each card and use the rest to pay off the balance on the highest interest card.

This means that in the first month, the debtor pays:

(a) £60 to each of the four cards;
(b) £240 to the card charging 2.5% a month, and nothing to the other three;
(c) 5% of the balance on each card, with the rest of the £240 to the 2.5% card.

The total amount of interest and charges paid under each of these strategies is:

(a) £792.12
(b) £1,013.84
(c) £617.18.

It can be seen that (c) is the best strategy as it incurs the least in charges.

Both (a) and (c) result in the balances being cleared in 20 months. Strategy (b) takes 21 months.

In practice, strategy (b) could not be followed as it means that no payments at all would be made on one card for 15 months, and the card company would have started recovery action long before then. Nevertheless, this does illustrate the advantage of using strategy (c).

A word about interest rates

Another practical problem is that the debtor probably does not know what interest rates are being charged on the cards. Every credit card statement must state the interest rate but this is often not on the first page. It can be buried in the small print on page 2.

There are also often different rates according to whether the card was used:

(a) to draw cash;
(b) to buy good or services; or
(c) as part of a promotion.

If the card was used for (c), there are some additional factors which need to be considered, as explained on page 252. (Basically, you do not use that card again until you have paid off the amount incurred in the promotion.)

As an example, an MBNA statement gives the interest rates in small print on page 2 where you are unlikely to notice it, even when looking for it. The monthly rates in January 2007 are 1.7366% for cash transactions, and 1.4566% for retail. The annual rates are not quoted. They are 22.95% and 18.95% respectively.

Barclaycard in the same month quoted annual rates of 27.9% and 14.9%, which are clearly stated on page 1 of the statement. Their rates are worse than MBNA for cash advances but better (or less bad) for purchases. The monthly rates are not stated, though they are 2.0718% and 1.0116% respectively.

In January 2007 the bank base rate was 5%, so these figures represent about five times the bank base rate. If you buy goods for £100 on a credit card and pay the full interest and perhaps one late payment charge, the bank's gross profit on that sale could be:

16% interest on £100 sale	£16.00
one late payment charge	£12.00
5% commission charged to shop	£5.00
	£23.00
less cost of lending £100	£5.00
Gross profit	£18.00

The expenses of administering the transaction are likely to be no more than £1, so the bank makes a cool £17 profit, or 17%, just from a person using their credit card. You can see why credit cards are so actively promoted.

Credit card statements will always show any interest figure as a separate item though it can often be difficult to see how it is calculated. In some cases it may be worth calling the credit card company to ask for an explanation of how the interest has been calculated.

The conversion of monthly interest rates to annual rates depends on how good your mathematics are. A rate of 2% a month does not mean an annual rate of 24% a year, as the rate is calculated using **compound interest**. This means that interest is not only added to the original sum, known as the **principal**, but each month interest is also added to the interest previously charged.

Suppose you borrow £100 at 2% a month. Over one year, the debt builds up as shown in Figure 12.

Figure 12: Effect of paying 2% a month on a £100 debt.

Month	Start	2% interest	New sum owed
1	100.00	2.00	102.00
2	102.00	2.04	104.04
3	104.04	2.08	106.12
4	106.12	2.12	108.24
5	108.24	2.16	110.40
6	110.40	2.21	112.61
7	112.61	2.25	114.86
8	114.86	2.30	117.16
9	117.16	2.34	119.50
10	119.50	2.39	121.89
11	121.89	2.44	124.33
12	124.33	2.49	126.82

Each month the interest comprises not just £2 interest on the principal but a further amount which is on the interest already charged. It starts as a low figure, just 4p in the second month, but soon starts building up.

Over a long period, compound interest can lead to massive increases. If this debt continued for 60 months (five years) it would grow to £328.10. If interest was only charged on the £100 principal (a process known as **simple interest**), the debt would be just £220 – that is, £100 plus £120 interest.

The formula for turning a monthly percentage M to an annual percentage A is:

$$A = 100[(1 + M/100)^{12} - 1]$$

So a monthly rate of 2% converts to an annual rate thus:

$$A = 100[1.02^{12} - 1]$$
$$A = 100[1.26824 - 1]$$
$$A = 26.824\%$$

In other words, £100 at 2% a month compound interest is the equivalent of £26.82 annual interest, as we saw in the table above.

Calculating 1.02^{12} is usually done with a calculator which has a button marked x^y. Usually, the keys to press are:

- 1.02
- x^y
- 12
- =

For those whose mathematics have already given up, Figure 13 is a table of annual equivalents to monthly interest rates.

Figure 13: Conversion of monthly interest rates to annual interest rates.

Month	Annual	Month	Annual	Month	Annual
1.0	12.683	1.7	22.420	2.4	32.923
1.1	14.029	1.8	23.872	2.5	34.489
1.2	15.389	1.9	25.340	2.6	36.072
1.3	16.765	2.0	26.824	2.7	37.672
1.4	18.156	2.1	28.324	2.8	39.289
1.5	19.562	2.2	29.841	2.9	40.924
1.6	20.893	2.3	31.373	3.0	42.576

To determine the monthly equivalent of an annual rate, the formula is:

$$M = 100[(1 + A/100)^{1/12} - 1]$$

Using a calculator, the process above is followed but the second stage uses a different button marked $x^{1/y}$. We can calculate that the monthly equivalent of an annual rate of 30% is 2.2104%.

Under English law, all rates must be quoted as the **annual percentage rate of charge** or APR. This is calculated as above. The APR must also reflect all charges such as documentation and arrangement fees. It is important to remember that the APR is intended *for comparison only*. It allows a person to compare rates from different sources. The APR is rarely used in any calculation.

Paying equal debts

Where debts are equal in terms of interest rate and other charges, the best policy may be to pay off the debts according to the debtor's convenience. It may be that one creditor is a supplier whom the debtor needs so that the debtor's business may continue. It may be that a creditor is himself someone having financial problems, or be a small business that cannot afford to bear a bad debt. So you pay the milkman and newsagent first. It may be that one creditor is being a particular nuisance in pressing for payment, and the debtor wants to 'get him off his back'.

In the absence of any such factor, the best policy is to pay off the smallest debts first as this reduces the number of creditors.

Suppose a person owes £10,000 in debts of £5,000; £2,000; £1,000; £600; £500, £400, £300 and £200. The debtor has eight creditors pressing him for payment.

Suppose the debtor can find £1,600. The **debt strategies** he may follow include:

(a) pay all creditors a pro rata amount
(b) split the payment equally between the creditors
(c) pay off the smallest creditors first.

These strategies will have the effect shown in Figure 14.

The number of creditors who will still be pressing for payment under each strategy is:

(a) 8
(b) 7
(c) 4

Strategy (c) has managed to halve the number of creditors pressing for payment. This makes negotiation simpler as there are fewer people with whom to negotiate. Also, the strategy leaves the large creditors with more of the debt owing, making it more likely that they will

Figure 14: Effect of different repayment strategies on equal status debts.

	Amount owed							
	5,000	2,000	1,000	600	500	400	300	200
Strategy (a) payments	800	320	160	96	80	64	48	32
Balance owing	4,200	1,680	840	504	420	336	252	168
Strategy (b) payments	200	200	200	200	200	200	200	200
Balance owing	4,800	1,800	800	400	300	200	100	–
Strategy (c) payments	–	–	–	200	500	400	300	200
Balance owing	5,000	2,000	1,000	400	–	–	–	–

negotiate the whole debt rather than harass the debtor for more small payments.

Smaller debts are often owed to smaller businesses who can be more of a nuisance to the debtor. Wasps are more annoying than elephants.

If the debtor becomes insolvent, strategy (a) must be followed by the insolvency practitioner, but by then the insolvency practitioner is protecting the debtor from his creditors anyway.

Working out a repayment schedule

Once the financial statements have been drawn up, the debtor and the debt doctor are in a powerful position. This in itself can have implications when the debtor has spent many months or even years feeling weak and vulnerable. A debtor can find it difficult to believe that at last he is 'in the driving seat'.

Basically, the debt doctor *tells* the creditors what they will receive. Legally, the creditors must agree to accept instalments or to waive any sum owed. In practice, the debt doctor gives them no real choice. The creditor can start legal proceedings and possibly even petition for bankruptcy, but in most cases this is unlikely to lead to any better result. The only real choice for the creditor is to negotiate – from a position of weakness.

A repayment schedule should try to offer every creditor something, however small. A token £1 a month can be good enough to start the process. If someone owes a creditor £5,000, repayments of £1 a month will take 417 years to clear, even with no interest added. Do not be distracted by the ludicrousness of such an offer. This is just the start of the negotiation process.

As soon as the financial statements have been prepared, they should be sent to all creditors. The points to make in the first communication are:

- the debtor cannot pay the whole amount when he should
- you want any interest and similar charges to be frozen immediately
- the debtor is paying what he can, as shown by the enclosed financial statements
- you are seeking the creditor's agreement to the repayment schedule
- if the debtor's circumstances improve, a better offer will be made automatically
- if there is any doubt about the amount of the debt, that should be stated
- the creditor may like to minimize the debt, such as by receiving back goods for a full credit or accepting a lesser sum in final settlement.

Sample letters can be found on the Motley Fool website at http://boards. fool.co.uk/Message.asp?mid=6576213.

It is essential that you ask for interest and charges to be frozen. The debt doctor is in a powerful position here. If the creditor sues for the debt, the summons automatically freezes any interest anyway.

The first payment is sent with the letter. You do not wait to get the creditor's agreement before starting to make payments. This is a key part of demonstrating the seriousness of the offer. The payment acknowledges the debt. If there is a dispute over whether any money is owed, no payment should be made though the other points should still be made and the financial statements sent. If the debt is acknowledged but the amount disputed, the creditor should be told that immediately and the first payment should still be made. Sending such a payment does not mean that you accept the creditor's figure of how much is owed.

On receipt of your letter, larger creditors will often pass the matter to a person trained in negotiating such matters. You must show equal competence when negotiating with such a person.

For a credit card company, it is effective to cut the card in half and send it with the letter. The credit card will be stopped as soon as the company receives the letter, so there is nothing to lose. Returning the card demonstrates that the account is closed in addition to removing a probable source of indebtedness.

Minimizing debts

A debt is minimized by getting the creditor to agree that the sum is less. This should always be considered in a debt recovery, but may not always be possible.

The main methods for **debt minimization** include:

- using a legal provision
- offering to return any goods to which the debt relates
- offering a smaller sum to avoid repayments.

These are considered in turn.

Not legally payable

The most effective is to establish that a debt is not legally payable at all. Common reasons include:

- the goods or service were faulty
- the goods or service were not ordered by the debtor nor by someone who has authority to act on his behalf
- using the rights to return goods under the Distance Selling Regulations (see page 49)
- a consumer credit sale where the requirements of the Consumer Credit Act have not been followed.

More information about legal rights are given in Chapter 9. There are other grounds which may make a debt legally unpayable, but the above are the most likely.

If such a claim is made, the creditor has to disprove it rather than the debtor having to prove it. Even if there is doubt on the legality, that may be sufficient to create useful negotiating points to help reduce the debt.

If a creditor states that he is owed £100 and the debtor says he owes nothing and there is a genuine doubt, the debtor and creditor may legally agree that the debt could be discharged for £60 (or any other figure they agree). Provided there is some basis for each side's claim, that is sufficient to create a 'consideration' for each side. This creates a new contract between the debtor and creditor. Once such an arrangement has been made, it is binding on each party. The debtor cannot then say he does not owe £60, nor can the creditor demand £100. More information on the law of contract is given on page 168.

Returning goods

Generally English law does not allow a customer to return goods for a full refund, or even a partial refund. If you find that the jumper does not fit, the paint does not match or your wife does not like the necklace, that is your hard luck. This legal principle is known as **caveat emptor**, which is Latin for 'the buyer beware'.

There is an exception if the seller agrees *before the sale is made* to take back goods. Usually there are conditions, such as a short time limit and the requirement that the goods are resaleable. Even if there is no such an agreement, nothing is lost by asking. The seller may agree. If a significant factor in the debt is extravagant spending, this is an equitable answer.

A company that has sold the debtor £2,000 worth of 'collectable' teapots is unlikely to be keen to take them back, and legally does not have to. Such items are probably worth between a half and a third of that figure to them, at most. The point to stress is that the debtor's finances are such that the alternative is that they will be lucky to receive £100. That is the only real argument in such a case. Despite what the company may say on the telephone, there is a figure below which they will realize it is in their interests to take the goods back.

Avoid agreeing to pay any handling charges or to refund the original postage and packing. Concentrate on establishing that they will accept the goods back. Once they have accepted that in principle, it is impossible in practice for them to demand any charges. It is probably appropriate to pay the postage to return the goods, but otherwise avoid anything less than a 100% refund.

The debt doctor should play hard to get. Rather than negotiate anything less than a full refund, it may be appropriate to end the discussion by saying that you will let them think about it and in the meantime you will continue paying £1 a month. Where there is any chance of returning goods, a repayment offer should be as low as possible. Confirm your offer in a polite letter. Then wait and try again. In three months' time they may be willing to accept back the collectable teapots in full settlement of a debt for £1,997.

Accepting a lesser amount rather than a repayment

A creditor may agree a lesser amount in full satisfaction rather than agree to an indefinite period of receiving small amounts, but may not agree immediately.

It is necessary to make the creditor realize that the whole amount of the debt cannot be paid immediately and that any legal action is likely to realize less than your offer. The financial statements are an essential element in this process. The actual amount of the lesser offer is a matter for negotiation. It can be advisable to establish the principle of accepting a lower figure before haggling over the exact amount.

Such an agreement is only legally binding if it can be shown that the alternative to a lump-sum settlement is repayments.

In terms of negotiation, some general advice is given on page 146. The figure should be a sum which is affordable within the debtor's resources. It may help by letting slip that similar offers are being made to other creditors and they will 'miss the boat' if they delay their decision while other creditors accept.

In terms of negotiating, it is probably reasonable to start the bidding at around one quarter or one third of the debt, showing great resistance to moving up. The creditor may say that he is agreeable to accepting a lesser amount but your and his figures are so far away that they cannot be negotiated. Do not be discouraged, simply say that you will make low repayments. Do not say that you will come back again later, even though you will.

After a few months, you can try again, assuming that the debtor has the resources to make the payment. If you make any further offers, make them for a *lower* figure. If you offer £600 towards a £2,000 debt after three months, offer perhaps £500 after six months. The creditor must never believe that he will get a better offer simply by holding out.

Responses to creditor objections

When you make offers to creditors, it is usual to find the offer resisted. Indeed, creditors are probably not doing their job properly if they do not resist your offer.

The important fact is to stress the reasonableness of your offer *from their point of view*.

All responses to creditor objections are variations on the one theme that this is the greatest amount you will receive. A person who is owed £1,000 will rightly object to being offered £400 in full settlement of that debt. But if the choice is to wait or sue and receive only £300, your offer *is* the correct option for the creditor.

The more experienced and professionally astute the creditor, the more likely they are to see this. Indeed, a common failing in small businesses is not realizing that reducing losses has exactly the same effect as maximizing profits.

Discussions with creditors can easily stray into irrelevance. Avoid long conversations about the state of the world and the meaning of life. Stick to the script:

- the debtor cannot pay any more
- nothing you do will make him pay any more
- my offer gives you the largest sum possible.

Some of the responses you may receive are noted below with possible responses.

It will open the floodgates, and no-one will pay

This is the **floodgates** argument. It may be extended to saying that an example must be made of non-payers to encourage other debtors to pay. 'It may cost us more than the debt to recover the money, but we are prepared to pay that. We don't want a reputation for being a soft touch in paying bills.'

The majority of customers do pay in full with little or no prompting. If they can pay but do not pay, there are effective means of forcing customers to pay. No company enhances its reputation by futile gestures, so that is just bluff.

The financial statements demonstrate how much the debtor can afford to pay. The response is simply to observe that this debtor cannot afford to pay more. Never be pressed into being more generous than you believe is appropriate. If negotiations stall, simply wait. Time is on your side.

We are a little company and cannot afford not to be paid. You should give us preference over big companies

The **little company** argument does have an element of truth in it. The local newsagent is less able to bear a loss than the bank. This matter is looked at on page 157.

Once it becomes clear that a debtor cannot pay all debts in full, or that debts can only be paid in instalments, different rules apply. The law requires that all creditors are treated equally. This generally means that every creditor should receive the same percentage of the debt every time a payment is made. If a debt can be cleared in 25 equal instalments, each creditor should receive 4% of the debt.

To favour one creditor over another is known as **preference**. This is not actionable in its own right until the debtor becomes bankrupt. If a debtor has shown preference to one creditor over another, the court may order that the position be restored to what it would have been if no preference had been shown.

You must decide how much preference it is appropriate to show the little company. Thereafter the response to the little company argument is, 'Are you asking me to show you improper preference?'

They had no intention of paying

This is sometimes called **won't pay, can't pay**. This may have an element of truth in it. Many debts are run up by people without thinking of how they will repay them. Had the person looked at the figures and asked how the bills would be paid, they should have realized that the bills were becoming unpayable. The reality is that the person did not look at the figures properly. This may mean that the person is silly, but it does not mean that the person is dishonest.

It is also possible that the debtor had followed some poor advice from a TV-advertised company and ran up a new loan to pay off old ones without realizing that this increased the total owed.

The debt doctor should avoid discussion on a debtor's past actions and what the motives were. However silly the debtor has been, that is history. Only the future can be changed. That future is being overseen by a proper debt adviser according to proper criteria.

We are not a charity

That is exactly why you expect them to accept an offer which is likely to maximize their income.

If a business is owed £500, it will quite properly resent being expected to accept £400 instead. In business, the **gross profit** is the excess of the sale less cost; the **net profit** is the gross profit minus the overheads. Typically the gross margin for a retailer ranges from around 25% for food and basic goods to 50% for jewellery and luxury items. Service suppliers, such as hire and professional services, have low costs, so their gross margin will often exceed 80%. The net margin depends on how efficient the business is, but any business with a net margin below 15–20% should seriously consider whether it should still be trading. If offering £400 for a £500 invoice, the debt doctor is probably confiscating the business's entire profit on that sale.

However, this is not the concern of the debt doctor. If any of the above explanations is offered (probably with lower percentages mentioned), the appropriate response is to note what the person says, but explain that the choice you are offering is not between £400 and £500, but between £400 and zero.

Junior staff may have more difficulty in understanding this than more senior staff. You can always try asking to speak to the accountant or accounts manager. Failing that, you can send a letter explaining how much they are likely to receive from bankruptcy and how long it will take them to receive it.

Our system cannot write off unpaid amounts

A common response is that the accounting system cannot handle the proposal.

Be clear that *every* accounting system can handle write-offs. What the person is saying is that *they* do not know how to write off an amount or may not be authorized to write it off. It is normal practice for write-offs to require authorization from someone senior.

There is no point in arguing the matter with a junior. The debt doctor should simply state that the offer is the best from the creditor's point of view and ask that it be referred to someone more senior.

If this gets you nowhere, do not perpetuate the argument but continue written representations. As the bill remains outstanding it will be referred to more senior people anyway. Any summons will be issued by the company secretary or similar legal officer, who will probably have a greater understanding of these matters.

The debtor should cut out expenditure

When a financial statement has been sent, a creditor may seize on some items of expenditure and say that these should be eliminated to realize more funds for paying creditors. Examples include such soft targets as cigarettes, pet food, cable or satellite television, entertainment and holidays. The use of trigger figures helps to avoid this challenge (see page 126).

In preparing the financial statement, such items should be pruned down already, but rarely can they be eliminated. A person probably should give up smoking 40 cigarettes a day, but it can be unreasonable to expect a person to cope with that stress at the same time as recovering from debt. Television is cheap relaxation which can help contain the stress and allow a person to work more efficiently and thus maximize income. Even in bankruptcy proceedings, televisions and videos are rarely seized. Similarly a reasonable level of entertainment and an occasional holiday maintain the correct lifestyle balance between work and rest which is essential to maximize future income.

It is best to avoid discussion on particular items of expenditure. The script is:

- I consider this to be within the scope of reasonable living expenses
- if you disagree, you can commence insolvency proceedings and argue the point with the insolvency practitioner.

Page 242 indicates the policy likely to be followed by an insolvency practitioner.

We have had too many bad debts already

This would indicate that their credit control is not very good.

A more diplomatic way of saying that is to note that you are not responsible for their credit control system nor for other debtors. The amount offered is the best that you can do. Your script is:

- I am offering you the best return you can hope for
- what other debtors offer is irrelevant.

This will only push up our prices

This is unlikely as most businesses allow for bad debts in their pricing.

Bad debts are an occupational hazard of business along with bad weather, bad sales figures, bad staff attendance and dozens of other risks. There are business disciplines of risk assessment and sensitivity analysis to quantify such problems. There are business services such as insurance and hedging to deal with them.

Your script is:

- the more of the debt you receive, the better for your business
- I am offering you the most you will receive of the debt.

Negotiation

Negotiation is a discipline in its own right. A debt doctor could be dealing with someone trained in this discipline.

The need for negotiation arises when:

- there are two or more parties
- there is an issue on which they are not agreed
- there is a mutual desire to resolve that issue
- they have both common interests and conflicting desires
- they intend to resolve the issue by discussion.

If any of these elements are missing, there is no scope for negotiation. For example, if one party refuses to negotiate, the process moves back one step. The other party must force the issue, commonly known as

upping the ante, to force the other person back to the negotiating table. Basically you must make the problem worse as a step to making it better. For a debt doctor, this is usually just leaving the situation to deteriorate.

Negotiation is likely to succeed when:

- those who negotiate have sufficient authority
- the desired objective is clearly understood
- there is a clear determination on both sides to negotiate
- neither side is trying to 'win' at the other's expense.

Negotiation specialists generally do not regard discussions just about price as negotiation. Such discussions are commonly known as **haggling** or **horse-trading**. Negotiating a debt is a form of haggling. Haggling can become proper negotiation if other factors are introduced.

There must first be agreement as to the medium of negotiation. The most effective in order are:

- face-to-face meeting
- telephone
- e-mail
- letter.

A face-to-face meeting tends to resolve issues of any kind more quickly, amicably and thoroughly than any other method. This is because of such factors as body language and the desire most people have of getting on with someone physically present. A face-to-face meeting tends to be time-consuming and expensive. Therefore the issue under negotiation must be sufficiently serious to justify this time and expense.

The process of negotiation is similar to playing a game like chess. You each make a series of moves designed to see what the other person will do and try to restrict his options in the manner you wish.

Unlike a game, you are not trying to score an obvious win. Indeed any hint of triumphalism is usually counter-productive. Most negotiators now follow the **Kennedy strategy** (named after the US president) of trying to find a way out for the other person as well as for yourself.

In debt negotiation, the simplest action is haggling. You each offer a figure and then progressively move towards each other. You offer £200, he asks for £600, and you then move 250, 500, 300, 450, 350, 400 agreed. The problem with simple haggling is that you both know you will end up in the middle, so each side will start with a more extreme position to get where they want. Methods such as pendulum arbitration have been developed to deal with this, but they are unlikely to be useful in debt negotiation.

Much of what may be called debt negotiation may actually be simply selling your debt recovery plan. This is salesmanship rather than negotiation. You are stressing why your scheme is superior and more cost-effective than any alternative. The process is broadly the same as selling a washing machine. You explain the benefits, answer the questions, and give the person time to assimilate the facts.

If you have a good logical argument, you use it on its merits. If your case is more based on hints and bits of argument, you say that your position is 'equitable in all the circumstances'.

Haggling can become negotiation when other factors are introduced by either side. This should usually be resisted by the debt doctor as time is on your side, and you usually have no need to 'muddy the water' by introducing other factors.

Other factors should only be introduced to help break a deadlock, assuming that the debt doctor *wants* to break the deadlock.

Factors a creditor may wish to introduce are:

- charging interest on the debt
- taking security for the debt
- converting debt into equity.

Usually they should all be resisted.

Charging interest is completely against the whole principle of debt negotiation. There is no point in reducing a debt down from £1,000 to £500 only to negotiate it back up again.

Security for the debt, known as **securitization**, should usually be resisted. This represents a loss of control. It may also comprise an improper preference for other creditors.

Converting debt into equity is usually only appropriate for a business that is or can become a limited company. A creditor may agree to convert a £100,000 debt for a 55% stake in the business. This means that the creditor owns more of the business than you do, and will receive most of the profits when the business becomes profitable again. In extreme circumstances this can be an equitable solution, but it represents a major restructuring of the business with implications requiring specialist skills beyond the scope of this book. It is a form of distress finance, explained on page 212.

Debt negotiation is more likely to concentrate on:

- how much is paid
- how soon it is paid.

Where instalments are agreed, the creditor may wish this to be backed up by a standing order or a series of postdated cheques. Agreeing to this should be part of the negotiation and not something given away for nothing by the debt doctor after the negotiation. Although cheques can be bounced and standing orders can be dishonoured or cancelled, this does provide the creditor with a measure of protection for reasons explained on page 171. This is one factor the debt doctor should be willing to negotiate, always ensuring that it can be met.

Factors that the debtor may wish to introduce include:

- further business
- payment in kind.

Further business is a difficult factor to promote as it begs the obvious question of how will the debtor pay for future supplies when he cannot pay for past supplies. Sometimes it *is* possible for a debtor to trade his way out of debt, but this is very difficult. A common example is a builder who asks for further building supplies so that he can complete a job and get paid (which rarely happens in practice). A creditor who agrees will probably want some arrangement to ensure that the trade or other activity is adequately supervised.

Payment in kind may be offered by any debtor, including a non-trader. This is simply **barter** – finding something that the creditor wants which the debtor has. This can be giving the creditor some goods, letting the creditor use machinery or vehicles or premises which the debtor does not need, or working for the creditor. Once the barter item has been identified, the negotiation is back to haggling in determining how much benefit should be provided for how much debt.

If negotiations stall, there are various methods to kick-start them back into life. These include:

- having a recess to reflect on offers and consider new factors
- setting a deadline to force the process to a conclusion
- delegating the matter to other people
- asking someone else to mediate or arbitrate.

As debt negotiation is such a simple form of negotiation, it is unlikely that any of these methods will be appropriate. If negotiations stall, the debt doctor's best strategy is usually to break off negotiations, revert to whatever was originally offered – and wait.

Time is on the debtor's side because it erodes resistance and not because it affects **decision-making** by the creditor. Making a decision is like putting weights on a balance. You identify the arguments for and against, quantify them and see which way the balance tilts. Once the arguments have been identified and evaluated there is no reason to allow time to pass. Putting the same weights on the same pans will give exactly the same answer in a week's time, a month's time or a year's time. Someone who wants to 'go away and think about it' is simply a poor decision-maker. That indecision gives you scope to press your case.

Whatever may be negotiated must be recorded in writing and agreed in writing by the other party. This may be by a memorandum which both parties sign, or by an exchange of letters. In the absence of such a record, it is possible for well-intentioned parties to go away and honestly believe they agreed different conclusions. The human mind tends to remember things as we would wish them to be rather than as they are. Any such difference is not only self-defeating but makes any further negotiation more difficult.

When agreement is reached

Once agreement has been reached, the debt doctor should ensure that the process is followed through. Undertakings must be honoured. Agreed payments must be sent as promised.

The process must be monitored in line with the budget. Debts may be minimized. The prudence concept may have overstated debt or expenditure or understated assets or income. All these can release more funds than expected. The debtor must resist the temptation to indulge himself with these funds rather than reduce the indebtedness. To withhold funds from creditors will reflect badly on the debtor in any further debt negotiation or insolvency.

The most effective use of such funds is to approach creditors being paid by instalments and make an offer of a single payment to clear the debt. The creditor may be told that if he declines the offer, the funds will be offered to another creditor.

If circumstances change significantly, the creditors should be informed. An informed creditor is more likely to remain content than a creditor who finds out.

If the situation deteriorates, creditors may be willing to agree some variations, but generally are unlikely to be sympathetic. Any attempt to reduce what has been agreed is likely to prompt a backlash.

If a creditor does decide to institute insolvency proceedings, all payments to creditors under the scheme cease, creditors are informed of what is happening, and the procedures outlined in Chapter 12 are followed.

Christian perspective

The idea of pressing people to accept less than their entitlement may seem to run contrary to Christian values that all debts are fully paid when due. The Christian should keep his word.

However, issues of right and wrong must not be decided on the basis of simplistic sentiment but on logical consideration of the alternatives. No-one is obliged to keep their word if circumstances make that impossible.

The principles outlined in this chapter have two honourable object-ives:

- to pay the creditors the maximum possible as soon as possible; and
- to release the debtor from problems as soon as possible.

It is difficult to see what is wrong with either objective or in the methods designed to achieve this.

It is appropriate to consider the parable of the unjust steward, commonly regarded as the most difficult of all Jesus' parables:

> [Jesus] said to his disciples, 'There was a rich man who had a steward, and he received complaints that this man was squandering the property. So he sent for him, and said, "What is this that I hear about you? Produce your accounts, for you cannot be steward any longer." The steward said to himself, "What am I to do now that my master is going to dismiss me from my post? I am not strong enough to dig, and I am too proud to beg. I know what I must do, to make sure that, when I am dismissed, there will be people who will take me into their homes." He summoned his master's debtors one by one. To the first he said, "How much do you owe my master?" He replied, "A hundred jars of olive oil." He said, "Here is your account. Sit down and make it fifty, and be quick about it." Then he said to another, "And you, how much do you owe?" He said, "A hundred measures of wheat," and was told, "Here is you account; make it eighty." And the master applauded the dishonest steward for acting so astutely. For in dealing with their own kind the children of this world are more astute than the children of light.'
>
> *Luke 16.1–8*

There is difficulty in justifying praise for a dishonest man. In the culture of the time, the steward would almost certainly have been fired on the spot (what we call summary dismissal) and would therefore not have the right of agency to negotiate anything with anyone on the master's behalf. It is probable that the steward relied on the fact that the debtors would not yet know that he had been fired, hence the urgency of reducing the debts.

Under the culture of the time, it is also likely that the steward was inflating the accounts and demanding more from the debtors than was due, and pocketing the excess for himself. Both the master and the steward were probably very unpopular with the debtors.

The consequence of the steward's action is to make both himself and the master popular. The master could have renounced the steward's action and demanded that the debts be paid in full, which would have made the steward's action counter-productive.

However, the steward knew his master. Under the law then, the steward could have been imprisoned immediately. The master chose not to do so, demonstrating his leniency. That is why the steward was praised for his 'astuteness' rather than his honesty. The steward showed sagacity in his decision, correctly predicting that the master would accept the arrangement. Once the master did accept the steward's actions, the debt reductions were ratified and so they were no longer dishonest.

The following verse contains the difficult words: 'use your worldly wealth to win friends for yourselves, so that when money is a thing of the past you may be received into an eternal home' (Luke 16.9). This seems to be suggesting that you *can* buy salvation and *should* buy friendship. A more credible explanation is that it is simply an exhortation to use money wisely and not let yourself be enslaved to it. Jesus is not praising the dishonesty of the steward, but praising the steward's ability to recognize his master's generosity.

All parables are stories which explain a fundamental Christian truth. This parable seeks to explain how to reconcile God's judgment with his mercy. However, the fact that a parable explains an abstract truth should not blind us to the fact that a parable also explains a literal truth. If we find ourselves in the situation of a person in a parable, we can take the story literally to guide our action. It is inconceivable for Jesus to explain Christian truth on the basis of literal sin.

The statement that 'the children of this world are more astute than the children of light' (Luke 16.8) shows that Christians often need humbly to acknowledge that, in financial matters, secular accountants are more likely to speak God's wisdom than Christian preachers – a view the author would endorse from his experience.

This parable is probably more applicable to debt reduction than may seem immediately obvious. Both involve reducing a debt without the creditor's permission, to create a situation which is more equitable for all parties.

If this matter still troubles you, it should be remembered that it remains perfectly legal for a debtor to pay any unpaid balance once restored to prosperity. A person can always write to a former creditor who wrote off, say, £1,000 and offer the money back ten years later with interest. The response will almost certainly be utter amazement, and probably a rejection of the offer on the grounds that the matter is settled. Legally and morally, the money is not owed and so such an offer is a voluntary donation. It is questionable whether the donation represents the wisest stewardship of funds, but the option should perhaps remain open for those who find difficulty salving their consciences in this matter.

9

Legal basis

Introduction

A knowledge of the legal basis of debt and its collection can be useful
as it can help set aside some debts, reduce others and moderate the
action taken by collectors. This book cannot be a treatise on all the law
a debt doctor may need to know, but it does aim to cover some of the
more important aspects of law. Some very basic points of general law
are included as many people lack knowledge in this area.

Types of law

English law applies in England and Wales. Northern Ireland has its own
system of law, which in practice closely follows English law. Scotland
has a completely separate system of Scots law.

Generally English law is divided into civil law and criminal law. **Civil
law** is concerned with the relationship between two people, such as
when X buys a car from Y. If X's cheque bounces or Y's car proves
faulty, the other can sue under civil law.

Criminal law is concerned with the relationship between the
individual and the state. So if you kill or steal, that is a criminal offence
as it affects your role as a citizen.

Some offences are both civil and criminal. If you hit someone, that is
the civil offence of trespass against the person, and the criminal offence
of assault. If you throw a brick through the window, the shopkeeper
can sue you for a replacement, and the police can prosecute you for
criminal damage. In practice, cases which are both criminal and civil
are usually tried as criminal cases only. If you are convicted of throwing
a brick through a shop window, you will probably be punished for the
criminal offence and ordered to pay compensation to the shopkeeper
at the same time.

A person is **sued** in a civil case, but **prosecuted** in a criminal case. In a
civil case, a **claimant** brings a case by suing the **defendant**. In a criminal

case, a state body (usually the Crown Prosecution Service) prosecutes the **accused**.

The standard of proof differs. In a civil case, a case is won on the **balance of probabilities**. The claimant must prove the case; the defendant does not have to disprove it. In a criminal case, the matter must be proved **beyond reasonable doubt**.

Sources of law

The two main sources of law are statutes and court cases.

A **statute** is an Act of Parliament. Its provisions are set out in numbered sections and Schedules. It may only be amended by a subsequent Act of Parliament. The Insolvency Act 1986 is a statute. It has been extensively amended by the Enterprise Act 2004.

Sometimes a statute is an **enabling Act** which delegates detailed provisions to someone else, usually a government minister. These provisions are then given in a **Statutory Instrument**. These are often indicated by a name or a number. For example, *The Insolvency Practitioners and Insolvency Services Account (Fees) (Amendment) Order 2007* is also known as SI 2007 No 133 or SI 2007/133. This amends a previous Statutory Instrument issued in 2003 by increasing a fee payable by insolvency practitioners.

The other main source of law is **court decisions**. These are indicated in a form like *John Henry Popely v Ronald Albert Popely [2004] EWCA Civ 463* (see page 236), which means that in 2004 John Henry sued Ronald Albert in the High Court. The letters and numbers at the end indicate where a copy of the judge's decision may be found in the court reports. Court decisions are also authoritatively published in *The Times* newspaper.

The judge's decision is a **binding precedent**. This broadly means that if the facts of that case are repeated, the judge is obliged to follow what the previous judge decided. Sometimes a judge's decision is a **persuasive precedent**, which means that it guides a subsequent judge but does not bind him.

Historically English law developed almost entirely from court decisions. This created **common law**, which is the collected wisdom of hundreds of judges' decisions. Although judges are now confined to clarifying law rather than creating it, there is still a large body of common law. Murder is a common law offence.

Courts

Generally, criminal cases are dealt with in separate courts from civil cases. The rules and procedures are different.

For **civil cases**, the commonest court is the **county court**. There are 220 county courts in England and Wales which hear nearly 2 million cases each year. Above the county court is the **High Court** which hears more serious claims. Appeals from the High Court lie to the Court of Appeal, and from there to the House of Lords.

The county court is intended to be a simple forum where debts may be recovered and disputes resolved. Almost any claim for up to £15,000 is started in the county court. Even for larger amounts, a claim should not now be started in the High Court unless:

- the amount claimed is in dispute; or
- the case is legally very complex; or
- the case has considerable public importance.

In practice, it is most unlikely that any of these factors will be present in normal debt problems, so the debt doctor will be dealing with the county court in practice.

It is recognized that many people resist paying debts until they have to. A county court summons is often an effective means of making someone pay.

A legal action can be started in the county court very easily. Forms may be obtained free from any court office or downloaded from the website. A claim for a fixed sum of money may even be started on-line at www.moneyclaim.gov.uk. Court staff will help a claimant complete the forms and will explain the procedure. Court staff will not comment on the merits of the claim. Anyone wishing to discuss the merits of the claim must see a solicitor, the Citizens Advice Bureau or another person or body able to give such advice.

A court fee is payable for issuing the summons, though this can be as little as £30. The person who issues this summons must pay the fee, unless the person can claim exemption. If using the on-line facility, the fee is paid by debit card or credit card. The court fee was once called the plaint fee, just as the claimant was once called the plaintiff.

There are several different types of summons which may be issued in the county court:

- recovery of a fixed amount of money
- for possession of goods under Consumer Credit Acts
- possession of land, such as possession of house by lender
- other claims, such as for recovery of goods.

Only the first of these may be started using the moneyclaim website. Each of these types of summons has a slightly different procedure.

The summons is sent to the defendant with a questionnaire to be completed. It should be remembered at this point that no independent person has considered the merits of the claim. Receiving a court summons for the first time is often an unpleasant shock, but it means little. Having a county court summons issued against you in itself proves nothing. It does not affect your credit rating, does not give you a criminal record nor cause any other problem. No-one even knows that the summons has been issued except you, the claimant and the court (and anyone you or the claimant decide to tell). There is no shame in issuing or receiving a summons; it simply means that you and another party are using the court to resolve a dispute just as you would go to the doctor to resolve a medical condition. Some people, particularly those in business, issue and receive summonses quite frequently.

Strictly speaking, there is no legal requirement for the claimant to make any effort to recover money before issuing a summons. In practice, the courts often take a dim view of someone who issues a summons without making some effort first. Such a claimant may find that the claim is struck out or full costs are not awarded. Normally a judge would expect to see:

- a claimant writing a letter asking for payment
- the defendant replying promptly, either acknowledging the debt or saying why they dispute it
- efforts at reasonable negotiation *before* issuing a summons.

If there is a genuine dispute, such as on the quality of goods, the courts will expect the claimant and defendant to have made some effort to resolve this. If arguing over whether a television set worked properly, the court will expect an attempt to have been made to agree an independent reputable person to look at the set and give an opinion. Such a person may be nominated by a relevant trade organization. There are also professional arbitrators and mediators who can hear disputes less formally. All such practices are encouraged by the courts.

'Without prejudice'

All such correspondence must be open and *not* marked 'without prejudice'. Many people make the mistake of believing that any letter written before possible legal action must have 'without prejudice' typed on it, without wondering what these words mean. The words mean 'without prejudice to my legal rights'.

Any letter marked 'without prejudice' cannot be shown to the judge (with one exception). Such a letter does not exist as far as any legal proceedings are concerned. If a creditor writes a letter demanding payment and marks it 'without prejudice', the creditor has made a big mistake. You can then write an open letter to the creditor explaining your position and ignoring this letter. The court will see your letter as the *first* communication, which will make you appear more responsible.

Generally, a letter marked 'without prejudice' requires a reply 'without prejudice'. If the 'without prejudice' letters are removed from the correspondence, there can be odd gaps and breaks in the dialogue if 'without prejudice' letters are answered in open letters. Conversely if an open letter is answered with a 'without prejudice' letter, it will appear to the court that the open letter has not been answered at all.

In normal debt negotiations, correspondence should *not* be marked 'without prejudice'. Such letters exist to allow an *alternative* negotiation to run in parallel with the legal action. A creditor may demand £1,000 in an open letter, plus interest and costs, and say that legal action will follow. The same envelope may contain another letter marked 'without prejudice' offering to settle for £900. You can reply to the creditor that you will defend the claim and are not prepared to pay a penny. In the same envelope you can send a 'without prejudice' letter saying that you will settle for £800.

This procedure may seem odd to those not experienced in such matters. In effect the two parties in the dispute are conducting two sets of negotiations in parallel on the same dispute. If the 'without prejudice' negotiations reach agreement, the matter is settled and the legal proceedings stop. If the 'without prejudice' negotiations fail, the legal proceedings continue and the court does not even know they ever happened.

The only time that 'without prejudice' letters *are* shown to the judge is *after* the matter has been settled and a claim for costs is made. These letters may then be shown to the judge for him to see how reasonable the parties have been in settling the matter.

Particulars of claim

The summons is accompanied by the **particulars of claim**. This is a concise statement of the facts prepared by the claimant. Particulars must give all the relevant facts and not assume that anyone already knows any details. The details are given in short numbered paragraphs. Particulars should avoid statements of opinion or law, and be expressed in polite and restrained language. It is not even necessary to say under what law the claim is being made.

No documents are sent to support the particulars of claim – yet.

Response to claim form

A defendant has 14 days to respond to the claim. In reality, a response can be made after 14 days unless the claimant has applied for default judgment.

The defendant is asked to complete a form and do one of the following:

- admit the whole claim and pay it
- admit the whole claim and offer to pay in instalments
- admit part of the claim, or admit the whole claim but make a counterclaim; or
- deny the claim.

If the claim is admitted, and the defendant pays the whole amount demanded, the case ends.

If the claim is admitted and an offer to pay in instalments is made, the claimant decides whether to accept this offer. If the claimant does, the case ends though further proceedings may be started if an instalment is missed. If the claimant does not, the case continues.

A claim may be partly admitted, such as when a person says 'I owe you for the jewellery I bought, but the amount we agreed was £500 not £600'. The claimant decides whether to accept the offer and end the case, or whether to reject the offer and let the case continue.

It is possible to make a **counterclaim,** to sue someone on their own summons. Care should be exercised before doing so. It can be tempting to invent a counterclaim, perhaps for harassment or consequential loss, in the hope that it will create a bargaining counter so you can say 'I'll drop my counterclaim if you drop or reduce your claim'. Most claimants and all judges can spot a frivolous counterclaim. It will not help you to look responsible. A counterclaim should only be considered if strong enough to support a legal action in its own right.

It is possible for a counterclaim to exceed the amount of claim. So someone could sue you for £2,000 and you admit the claim but counterclaim £3,000. If all this is accepted by the claimant or upheld by the court, the claimant can end up paying *you* money even though he sued you! This rarely happens. If, exceptionally, the balance of a counterclaim exceeds the maximum covered by the court fee, an additional court fee may be payable by the defendant.

If a counterclaim is made for a debt which is wholly or partly admitted, the matter is treated as a partly admitted debt.

If you deny the claim, you submit a defence. This is similar to the particulars of claim in that it is given in numbered paragraphs and should be free of opinion and comments.

Proceeding to trial

So far, no-one other than the claimant and defendant has looked at the claim. No judge has considered it. The county court has simply acted as a filing cabinet, keeping copies of documents which have passed between the claimant and defendant.

If the claimant and defendant are not able to resolve the matter, the court becomes involved. 'The court' in practice means the judge. You will receive a notice from the court telling you:

- the name of the judge
- the date, time and place of the pre-trial review
- a requirement to submit documents at least 14 days before the pre-trial review.

The **documents** comprise anything which may support the claim. Almost anything may be included. Typically they include photocopies of:

- documents relating to the matter which gives rises to the claim, such as agreements, receipts, invoices and statements
- correspondence between the claimant and defendant
- anything else which may be relevant, such as opinions by an independent expert, or statements from witnesses.

The documents are usually numbered. A list of documents is prepared saying to what each number refers.

Three sets of all documents are prepared: one for the claimant, one for the defendant, and one for the judge.

The defendant prepares three sets of his or her own batch of documents which are sent to the court and the claimant. Thus the claimant, defendant and judge all have identical sets of documents. Although documents submitted within the 14 days before the pre-trial review may be accepted by the court, a judge will take a dim view of this.

Documents must be a fair copy, with the original brought to court. It is not acceptable to take a photocopy with bits of the document blanked out. For this reason, care should be exercised when writing on original documents. If you write 'ignorant pig' on a document, the judge and the other party will see that. It is better to jot down such observations on a separate sheet of paper.

Sometimes evidence other than documents may be produced. This could include a video or audio recording, a computer program or even a tangible item such as a broken appliance. Where such evidence is to be produced, the court and other party should be notified in advance.

You should check with the court office that it has equipment to play any recording or program, or provide your own equipment.

Pre-trial review

The pre-trial review is heard in private, usually in a small room within the court building. The public is not admitted, and the permission of the judge is needed for anyone else to come in. There are no wigs or gowns, no oaths and few formalities. The parties sit round a table with the judge.

Here it is worth noting that the English legal system is completely different from the American system widely seen on British television. Although American law has much in common with English law (because that is where American law originated), the court procedures are completely different. No British judge would ever behave like Judge Judy. British judges are civil and patient, allow the parties to speak, listen to what they say and don't jump to conclusions.

The judge will already have read the papers, so there is no need for anyone to present their case. The arguments should have been put in writing. The judge chairs the meeting and will usually conduct it by asking questions to the parties. Although it is obviously in everyone's interest that the conversation is kept civil, you should not let the judge avoid an issue which is relevant, nor be misled in anyway. If necessary, you should ask the judge to allow you to make further comment. It is perfectly acceptable to say that you disagree with the judge, provided you do so respectfully. It is also acceptable to ask the judge to explain anything you do not understand.

Many people who have never attended a pre-trial review can be surprised at how informal and chatty it can all be. All this has a moderating effect on the parties, encouraging responsible behaviour and getting rid of frivolous and irrelevant material.

The judge will try to bring matters to a conclusion, such as striking out a claim or giving judgment for an amount. Either of these has the effect of ending the case.

If this is not possible, the judge will give **directions**. These are instructions telling one or both parties to do specific things, such as to produce more documents, produce a witness, calculate a figure, or let someone inspect an item. These directions must be followed before another pre-trial review or the trial itself is heard. Failure to follow a direction can compromise that party's position.

At any point until the judge gives his decision, the parties may settle a case on any terms they wish. It has often been noted that county courts settle more cases in the waiting room than in the court room.

If the case does go to trial, and very few do, this is heard in public by a robed judge. Evidence may be given under oath, and the judge may allow one party (or his lawyer) to question the other party.

Principles of trial

At both a pre-trial review and any trial, some principles of civil justice need to be understood.

First, it is the job of the claimant to prove his claim, not for the defendant to disprove it. If someone claims that you owe them £1,000, he must prove that you do. If at the end of the process, it is not obvious whether or not you owe the money, the claimant loses the case.

Second, the matter only needs to be proved on the balance of probabilities. If the evidence is not conclusive but clearly leans in the claimant's favour, the claimant wins. This is why it is so important in any civil action to behave well. If you can demonstrate that you responded promptly and completely to every issue raised by the claimant, he will have a difficult job persuading the judge that you ignored a particular letter. In all the conduct before the trial, you must make yourself look as reasonable, polite and honest as possible, and make the other party look the opposite. Such matters are of particular importance in deciding questions of costs.

Judgment

The case ends when the judge strikes it out, the parties settle or judgment is given.

Judgment is a statement by the court that an amount is owed by one person to another. In itself, it does not secure the payment, nor does it count as a black mark against the defendant in any way. If a judgment is given and the defendant pays promptly, the matter is finished. No record is kept on any available file. It does not affect the defendant's credit record.

If the judgment is not paid within 28 days, it is registered and will count against the defendant's credit record. If it is then paid, that will also be recorded. This reduces the severity of this black mark, but does not remove it.

Enforcement

Having obtained a judgment, the creditor must take **enforcement** action unless the debtor pays voluntarily. (As the court case has finished, we now refer to the claimant and defendant as creditor and debtor respectively.)

The choices open to the creditor are:

- warrant of execution
- charging order
- attachment of earnings order
- third party debt order
- order to attend court.

Insolvency proceedings are *not* a means of enforcement action, though their consequences can be similar (see page 217).

A warrant of execution allows a bailiff to seize goods belonging to the debtor. The powers of bailiffs are explained on page 187.

Charging orders

A **charging order** secures the sum against property owned by the defendant, usually the debtor's home if he owns it. In effect, a charging order turns an unsecured loan into a secured loan. When the property is sold, the amount owed (plus statutory interest) is paid from the proceeds *after* any outstanding mortgage and other secured debts. A charging order can be made against any property, and is sometimes made against shares or an interest in a trust. A charging order does not in itself force the debtor to sell the property, though it makes a sale more likely.

A charging order may only be made when judgment has been entered *and* the debtor has defaulted. If judgment is to pay by instalments, a charging order may only be made if a debtor has not kept up instalments, but it only needs one instalment to be missed by one day for an application to be made.

Such an order may appear to have little benefit to a creditor if the debtor is likely to carry on living in the same home for the next 20 years. Despite this, charging orders are popular with creditors. A charging order is registered with the Land Registry (where ownership of land is recorded). It can be a powerful incentive to force a debtor to pay.

A creditor first applies for an **interim charging order**, which is readily given by the court on evidence that a judgment has been obtained and the debtor has defaulted on it. The creditor usually also sends a **restriction** or notice to the Land Registry that an application is to be made for a charging order on the property. In effect, this blocks the sale of the property, which could interfere with other elements of a debt recovery package.

If a charging order is made against shares, a **stop order** comes into force. This stops the sale of shares or payments of dividends to the debtor.

The next stage is for the creditor to apply for a **final charging order**. The judge decides whether to make the interim charging order final or whether to discharge it. If the latter, all restrictions on the property or shares are removed. The debtor has the right to challenge a final charging order before a judge. Arguments which may prevent a final charging order include:

- that no payment has been missed, so there is no default
- a variation order has been agreed allowing for reduced instalments which have all been paid on time
- an application for redetermination has been made
- the charging order may unfairly prejudice other creditors
- the debtor is insolvent, so a charging order prejudices other creditors
- the debt is very small compared to the value of the property.

Conditions may be attached to charging orders, usually at the request of the *debtor*. Such conditions may restrict an order for sale (see below) until the youngest child has reached 18, for example.

After charging orders, the much more serious step is the **order for sale**. This is where the court orders the sale of the property or shares to realize the sum owed. Such applications are still rare, but their use is increasing. The judge has discretion whether to grant such an order. Usually it is only granted when it seems there is no other way that the creditor will receive payment.

A charging order may be made against a jointly owned property, though the order will only apply to the debtor's share. An order for sale may be made for jointly owned property, though the joint ownership creates further grounds for appeal.

If an order for sale is being considered, the debtor will almost certainly need specialist legal advice.

Attachment of earnings

An attachment of earnings order is a notice served on the debtor's employer which requires the employer to deduct money from the person's wages and pay it to the court, which passes it to the creditor. The employer has no choice but to comply with such an order, and can be penalized for any failure to do so. An attachment may only be made for an outstanding debt of at least £50. If the debt is just over £50 and a debtor fears an attachment, it is possible to make a payment to put the outstanding debt below £50 to prevent an attachment.

Obviously, attachments can only be used for debtors who are employed, and cannot be used for debtors who are self-employed or unemployed. A consequence of such an order is that the employer learns that the employee has financial difficulties. It is legal for the employer to question the integrity of the employee as a consequence of this. If the employee handles money, such as a bank clerk or security officer, the employee could be dismissed, though such a dismissal could be challenged.

The employer has the right to charge £1 for each deduction to cover his expenses.

Payments can be made from wages or salary, including overtime, bonuses and commission. They may also be made from pension payments or statutory sick pay. They cannot be paid from statutory maternity pay, statutory adoption pay, statutory paternity pay or tax credits. The court will check whether the person has any existing attachment orders. If so, the court may consolidate them into one larger order.

From 1 April 2005, attachments are made under the Courts Act 2003. The employer is told the total amount which is owed. The employer makes deductions until either this figure reaches zero or the employment ends. The employer is provided with a set of tables stating how much should be deducted according to the employee's net pay (after income tax and national insurance).

The latest tables applied from 1 October 1998. They are produced for daily, weekly and monthly payments. The monthly rates are given in Figure 15.

For example, if someone has net monthly earnings of £2,000, the amount attached is:

£1,480 at 17%	=	£251.60
£520 at 50%	=	£260.00
£2,000		£511.60

An attachment provides a discipline which ensures that debts are paid, but this is rarely to the benefit of the debtor who can see a large portion of earnings disappear at source. This reduces the scope to negotiate payment terms with creditors and agree better terms from the debtor's point of view. As other creditors could feel left out and have less money available for their debts, an attachment can make it more likely that other creditors will take tougher action, such as pressing for bankruptcy.

Figure 15: Rates of attachment of earnings for monthly earnings.

Net earnings	Deduction rate
up to £220	nil
£220.01 to £400	3%
£400.01 to £540	5%
£540.01 to £660	7%
£660.01 to £1,040	12%
£1,040.01 to £1,480	17%
above £1,480	17% on £1,480; 50% of balance

Attachment orders may be made for unpaid council tax. The rates and procedures are almost identical to attachments under the 2003 Act. Attachments may also be ordered by the magistrates' court under separate though similar rules. These are issued to pay fines or child maintenance.

Before the 2003 Act took effect, attachments were made under Attachment of Earnings Act 1971. Although no new orders are made under this Act, many existing orders continue. This has a system of priority and non-priority orders which determines what happens when there is more than one order against an employee. Such 1971 attachments state an amount to be deducted from each payslip and do not tell the employer how much is owed.

Third party debt order

A third party debt order orders someone who owes money to the debtor to pay it to the creditor instead. The commonest example is a bank which holds funds for the debtor. The court can order the bank to hand over the money. These orders were once called garnishee orders.

When a bank is served a notice, it must apply it to *all* accounts it holds for that person. An order cannot be made against a joint account unless the joint holder is also liable for the debt, such as when a husband and wife have defaulted on a mortgage.

An order may be made for funds to which the debtor will become entitled, such as when a policy matures.

A third party debt order is made in two stages. First an interim third party debt order is made when judgment has been obtained and has not been complied with. An interim order has the effect of freezing the account. The bank does not pay it to the court, but will not pay any to the debtor either.

A final order is made by a judge at a hearing where the creditor can be represented. The judge has discretion whether to grant a final order. If someone lives off savings, an objection could be raised that the order would deprive the person of the means of living and would unfairly prejudice other creditors.

If a debtor experiences difficulties because an account is frozen by an interim third party order, the debtor can apply to the court for a **hardship payment order**. This may only be sought for normal living expenses, and must be supported by financial statements. The court can grant an order for payments.

Only about 6,500 third party debt orders are granted each year.

Order to obtain information

An order to obtain information is when the debtor is summoned to court to be interviewed by a judge or (more usually now) a senior court officer on why a judgment has not been paid. Such an order was previously called an oral examination.

Strictly speaking, this is not a means of enforcing judgment but a means of obtaining information to help determine how to recover the debt. The debtor is given 14 days' notice and must attend bringing specified documents such as bank statements, rent books, credit agreements and anything else which relates to his or her finances.

There is a curious rule that the debtor may demand that the creditor pays his travelling expenses to attend. This amount is then added to the debt, so that the debtor should eventually pay it back. If the creditor refuses to pay, the debtor need not attend.

The debtor answers questions under oath, which means that any false answers are perjury, which is a serious criminal offence. The court officer asks questions to fill in the 12 pages of form EX140. The creditor may ask additional questions.

If the debtor fails to attend, refuses to take the oath, refuses to answer questions properly or to produce documents requested, the court usually makes a **suspended order**, which requires the person to attend a second hearing and comply. If the debtor does not do so, he is arrested and brought before the judge who may imprison him. A debtor will not be imprisoned if he co-operates fully.

The information order is followed by some means of enforcement. About 32,000 information orders are made each year.

Debt

There is no law of debt as such. A debt only arises because of a legal process, usually one of:

- contract
- tort
- statute.

If you sneeze in a shop so loudly that a nervous man standing nearby drops a valuable ornament, the man or shopkeeper may consider that you are liable. Almost certainly, a court will not.

A contract is a legally enforceable agreement between two people. In general, two adults are free to agree whatever they wish, even if it is a bad bargain between two people. Some contracts, particularly consumer credit contracts, are subject to legal restrictions.

A tort is when one person causes loss to another for which the person is liable, such as through negligence.

Statute is a law which creates a particular liability, such as for tax.

If being pressed for a debt, it can be profitable to see if there is any legal liability at all.

Contract

A contract is a legally enforceable agreement between two or more parties, where a 'party' can be an individual, company, local authority, government body or almost any other form of recognizable entity. Although contract law arises from the long-established unwritten common law, there are now many Acts of Parliament which impose requirements on particular forms of contract.

It should be appreciated that contract law, like most branches of law, is a vast subject with many detailed provisions. The following notes do no more than give a brief understanding and point out some implications most likely to be relevant to someone in financial difficulties. If seeking to set aside a contract, it may be advisable to get professional advice.

A contract may be made in writing, verbally, or assumed from the conduct of the parties. Suppose you walk into a shop, pick up a loaf of bread and give the shopkeeper the advertised price which he puts in his till. No words have been written or spoken, but it is obvious what you are both doing.

A contract is made when one party accepts an offer from the other. It does not matter whether John offers to sell his car for £1,000 which Susan accepts, or if Susan offers to buy John's car which he accepts.

The contract is made at the point of acceptance. Suppose John offers to sell his car for £1,000 but Susan says she will only pay £500. There is no contract as there is no offer which has been accepted; there are only negotiations. If they haggle, a contract is only made when they have agreed the price. Price tickets and catalogues do not constitute an offer to sell. The offer is made when a person offers to buy the item; the contract is made when the seller agrees to sell it.

The conditions for a contract to be legally valid are that:

- the parties have capacity to contract
- the contract is legal, moral and possible
- there is an intention to create legal relations
- the contract is entered into freely and voluntarily
- there must be an offer and an acceptance
- each side provides a consideration to the other
- the parties are in agreement on the substance of the contract
- any formalities for particular contracts must have been followed.

If any of these conditions are not met, the contract may be void, voidable or unenforceable – the legal consequences of which are different.

The **capacity to contract** simply means that the person has a legal right to make a contract. There are some restrictions on children, bankrupts, and war enemies. A contract can only be made while a person is sane and sober.

A person cannot make a valid contract while drunk, under the influence of drugs, or suffering from a mental problem. Such a contract is void, which means there is no contract at all. The test is whether the person knew what they were doing. A contract cannot be set aside just because a person has had a few drinks or has a mental problem, if they were sufficiently lucid to understand what they were doing. A mentally ill person may have lucid periods when they are able to contract normally. A debt doctor may be able to avoid payment completely on a contract if the other party took advantage of the client's intoxication or mental disability.

For further comments on mental capacity, see page 178.

Emotions which fall short of mental illness do not void a contract. Someone who has lost his temper or who is totally exasperated and shouts 'OK I'll give you £2,000 for the wretched car' may find that he has made a valid contract.

Contracts with minors

Someone under the age of 18, legally a **minor**, may only make a contract for **necessaries** at a reasonable price. Necessaries are 'goods suitable to the condition in life of a minor and his [or her] actual requirements at the time of sale and delivery'.

Nature of contract

A contract must be **legal, moral and possible** or it is void. A contract designed to evade tax is illegal so there is no enforcement where you 'pay us in cash, guv, and we'll not charge VAT'. There are also some Acts of Parliament which restrict certain types of contract, such as price-fixing by suppliers. A contract can also be illegal because it contravenes public policy, such as by obstructing justice or prejudicing good relations with other countries.

For contract purposes, a contract is immoral if it is for gambling or prostitution.

Legal relations

There must be an **intention to create legal relations**, in other words there must have been an understanding to make a contract. A contract may be made informally by people who are related or close friends; what matters is their understanding of what they were agreeing.

This condition is most relevant in family agreements such as 'come and live with us for a while' where the existence of any contract depends on exactly what was agreed.

Influence

A contract must be made freely and voluntarily. If someone points a gun at your head, that is **duress** and voids the contract. The courts will also accept **undue influence** as voiding a contract. Broadly, if there is a **fiduciary relationship** between the parties, the **dominant person** must prove there was *not* undue influence; otherwise the other party must prove that there *was* undue influence. A fiduciary relationship is one where one should trust the other, such as parent and child, doctor and patient, solicitor and client, or priest and parishioner. In debt counselling, a common issue is the fiduciary relationship between a husband and wife. Undue influence by a husband to force his wife to allow their home to be used for a secured debt can prevent the lender taking the home (see page 195).

Offer and acceptance

The rules on **offer and acceptance** lie at the heart of the contract. An offer must be absolute and unconditional. The fact that something has been agreed in principle with only details still to be settled means that there is no contract. Any agreement 'subject to contract' is also just a negotiation. Negotiations may be broken off at any time without either side being liable to the other. In the case *Walford v Mills [1992]*, the House of Lords ruled that you cannot contract to make a contract, so an agreement to continue negotiations was not in itself a contract. The contract is made for whatever the parties agree. You cannot get out of a contract just because it is a bad bargain.

Consideration

Each party must provide a **consideration** to the other. This is basically a benefit provided or a detriment suffered. In most contracts one party provides the consideration of money, while the other provides goods or services. A gift therefore cannot be a contract unless it is made under deed. A contract may be to sell something for a nominal sum, such as to sell your house for £1. The consideration must not be past. If someone has already supplied you with goods, you cannot make a contract to buy them. You may voluntarily agree to pay for them, but there is no contract.

Being 'ad idem'

The parties must be in agreement on what they are doing; they must be **ad idem**. A contract to buy 'my car' is not valid if I own two cars and the buyer thinks he is getting the other one. A contract can be valid even though one or both parties was mistaken on some aspect of it.

If one party deliberately or carelessly makes a false statement, that is **misrepresentation** which could compromise the contract. For example, a car salesman who falsely says that a car can travel at 150 mph and does 50 miles to the gallon could invalidate any contract to buy that car.

Setting aside a contract

If a debtor is being chased for payment for goods or services, it may be worthwhile checking the contractual arrangements. Some examples are given below.

The condition was made after acceptance

A contract is made at the time that one party has accepted the other's offer. Suppose you buy goods by telephone and then receive a confirmation of your order giving all sorts of conditions, such as charging you interest for late payment. Those conditions are not valid. The contract was made when the company agreed to supply you the goods. They cannot impose new conditions *after* the contract has been made. An attempt to enforce any post-acceptance condition can legally be resisted. It would be different if the company said it was accepting your order only on its standard conditions or pointed out the conditions during the telephone call. Many cancellation charges and late payment charges are not payable for this reason.

The goods are faulty

If you buy goods from someone who sells them in the course of a business (such as from a shop or mail order company), the goods must be 'of satisfactory quality' under Sale of Goods Act 1979 s14 (2). This means fit for the purpose for which it is intended, unless defects have been pointed out, the customer first examined the goods, or they were sold on a 'sold as seen' basis, such as selling broken equipment for spare parts.

If the goods are faulty, the buyer's remedy is usually to allow the seller to repair or replace them. The buyer need not pay for goods not yet supplied in working condition. A supplier is not obliged to offer a refund nor to exchange satisfactory goods which prove unsuitable (such as clothes that do not fit) unless the supplier agreed this at the time of the sale. In practice, a supplier will often agree to refund money rather than trying to satisfy a customer by repair or replacement.

A cheque is a separate contract

When a cheque is issued a new contract is made between the parties. If the cheque is stopped, it is possible to 'sue on the cheque'. There must be a good reason to stop a cheque.

In the House of Lords case *Nova (Jersey) Knit Ltd v Kammgarn Spinnerei [1977]*, Lord Wilberforce said that a cheque is the equivalent of cash. A cheque may only be countermanded for 'such limited defences as those based on fraud, duress or failure to provide consideration'.

Once a cheque has been issued, it is no longer possible to argue that the goods were faulty, the price was too much, a discount should have been allowed, a longer payment period should be allowed, or any other such argument.

Interest on late payment

Interest may be charged on late payment of goods only if either:

- the debt is a commercial debt; or
- interest is specifically allowed for in the contract.

A **commercial debt** is one which arises under a contract between two businesses for the supply of goods or services. Such a contract attracts statutory interest under Late Payment of Commercial Debts (Interest) Act 1998. Section 2 of this Act defines a business as including a profession, so a doctor or accountant who buys goods or services from a commercial supplier can be within the scope of the Act. These provisions do not apply to contracts other than for goods or services, so they do not apply to contracts of employment or credit agreements. Similarly, the provisions do not apply to sums owed otherwise than from a contract, such as compensation or a refund.

This Act was introduced in three stages:

- 1 November 1998: small businesses may claim from large businesses;
- 1 November 2000: small businesses may claim from all businesses;
- 7 August 2002: any business may claim from any other.

A small business is one with 50 or fewer employees; a large business is one with more than 50 employees.

The interest rate is the bank base rate plus 8 percentage points. So if the base rate is 4.75%, the interest rate is 12.75%. This is calculated on a simple interest basis at a daily rate. From 7 August 2002, the interest rate is fixed for six months at a time using the base rate for the previous 30 June or 31 December.

From 7 August 2002, a creditor is also entitled to statutory compensation for late payment depending on the amount owed:

Amount owed	Statutory compensation
less than £1,000	£40
£1,000 but less than £10,000	£70
£10,000 or more	£100

All these provisions apply equally to all parts of the UK. The devolved authorities in Scotland, Wales and Northern Ireland each have powers to vary the Act but have not done so. A contract with a body outside the UK is bound by the Act if the contract was made under English or Scots law.

Statutory interest and compensation only start running from when the sum should have been paid. This is when the period allowed on the invoice has ended, or when the period otherwise agreed (such as by long-established custom and practice) has expired. If no period is agreed, the law assumes 30 days.

The parties may agree other rates of interest and compensation, but these must be 'substantial'. The law does not allow a big company to pressure a small supplier into accepting inadequate rates. The court will strike down any provision and substitute the statutory rates where there is evidence of this.

The charging of interest and compensation is not compulsory. The aim of the Act is to encourage prompt payment, not to increase debtors' costs. In practice, most creditors apply the Act in this spirit. Many suppliers do not bother with the Act at all. Those who do usually use it as a threat to encourage prompt payment and give a warning before imposing the charge, though a supplier is not obliged to give a warning.

If the goods bear VAT (or any other tax or duty), interest applies to the VAT-inclusive sum. VAT is not charged on the interest.

If the provisions of the Act are invoked against you, they can be expensive. Suppose you owe £100 to one company and £10,000 to another, you should have paid the invoices within 30 days but still owe the money after 180 days, and the relevant bank base rate is 4.75%. The interest is calculated as 150/365 x 12.75% of the sum. This can increase the amount owed significantly, as shown below:

Sum owed	Interest	Compensation	Total owed
£100	£5.24	£40	£145.2
£10,000	£523.97	£100	£10,623.97

If a supplier is threatening you with this Act, it is probably time to pay the invoice.

Consumer Credit Act

Consumer Credit Act 1974 regulates most forms of hire purchase, credit cards and similar forms of credit arranged by individuals in the course of their everyday lives. This includes hire purchase, credit cards, personal loans, overdrafts, budget accounts, conditional sale agreements, credit sale agreements, mail order, interest-free period agreements, pawnbrokers and trading vouchers. The Act does not apply to credit arranged in the course of business.

The Act was passed to provide much-needed protection to consumers. Before the Act a person could sign a hire purchase agreement to buy a washing machine, for example. This was held to be two separate contracts, one with the supplier and one with the finance company. The supplier could go bust and not supply a machine yet the consumer could still be liable to pay all the hire purchase instalments for a machine not provided. The Act makes the finance company liable for the goods supplied using its credit. This includes a credit card, so if goods bought by card prove faulty and the supplier has gone, a claim may be made against the card company, even if the credit card bill has been paid.

This Act has now been amended by Consumer Credit Act 2006, which progressively comes into force between 2006 and 2008. Its main provisions are to extend the powers of the regulatory authority. It also changes some terms and definitions. The original aims of the 1974 Act are unchanged.

The Act applies to any **regulated agreement**, which covers almost all credit agreements. These are any agreement on a sum between £50 and £25,000 (£15,000 if made before 1 May 1998). The upper limit is expected to be removed for new personal agreements made from 6 April 2008.

The supplier must have a consumer credit licence and comply with detailed regulations, particularly on what information must be given to the consumer. The exact scope of what must be included has changed over the years. For an agreement made after 30 May 2005, the following information must be given in this order:

(a) a heading describing the nature of the agreement;
(b) names and addresses of the creditor and client;
(c) key financial information, namely:
    a. amount of credit or credit limit;
    b. total amount payable in fixed interest rate agreements;
    c. repayment details; and
    d. the APR;
(d) other financial information, namely
    a. description of goods;
    b. cash price;
    c. advance payment;
    d. total charge for credit; and
    e. details of interest rates, including whether fixed or variable;
(e) key information, namely
    a. description of security supplied;
    b. list of default charges;
    c. a statement that the agreement is not cancellable (if so);
    d. examples of amounts to settle early;
    e. statement of consumer protection and remedies;

(f) signature box;

(g) cancellation box.

In some cases, some of these items may not be relevant.

For agreements made before 31 May 2005, some of these items are not strictly required.

A copy of the agreement must be made at the time the customer signs, if present. In all circumstances, a copy must be sent to the customer within seven days. The customer has five days **cooling off period** in which he may cancel the agreement without penalty and receive back the full amount of any deposit.

If the agreement is not made face-to-face, it is a **distance agreement**. This includes agreements made on-line or by telephone. From 1 October 2004, basic information must still be given when the agreement is made, a written agreement (which includes e-mail) must be sent giving the prescribed information *before the agreement takes effect*. The customer has a cooling off period of *14 days*.

The creditor is responsible for ensuring compliance. If a creditor fails to include any details, he may only enforce the agreement with the consent of the court. The court will consider what disadvantage the customer has suffered and how blameworthy the creditor has been. The court can set aside an entire agreement or allow enforcement of only a lesser sum.

Before 6 April 2007, any lack of client's signature or lack of notice about cancellation rights is fatal. The agreement is totally unenforceable. This strict rule is relaxed from 6 April 2007, giving the court discretion.

The 1974 Act allowed agreements to be set aside for **extortionate credit**. In practice, this proved difficult to enforce. From 6 April 2007, this provision is replaced by the **unfair relationships** test which is wider in scope. It includes **linked transactions** such as extended warranties. These do not become illegal, but must meet new tests of fairness.

The 2006 Act imposes a new requirement for the creditor to provide annual statements. This is expected to apply for new *and existing* personal agreements made from 6 April 2008. Once an agreement is in arrears by two payments, an **arrears notice** must be issued within 14 days and then at six-monthly intervals until the arrears are cleared. From this date there are new provisions regarding arrears.

It should be understood that the whole area of consumer credit is very detailed and complex. If it is believed that an agreement may not comply, it is essential to get proper legal advice on the matter.

Guarantors

A **guarantor** is someone who promises to pay someone else's debt. This arrangement is known as a **guarantee**, though that word has other legal meanings. Guarantees are often sought in respect of rented property. A landlord may ask a parent to act as guarantor of the rent owed by the son or daughter. The son or daughter is fully liable to pay the rent on exactly the same basis as any other tenant. If the son or daughter fails to pay the rent, the landlord can take action as for any other tenant. The guarantee gives the landlord an *extra* right of taking action against the guarantor. In practice, a landlord is likely to do this if he believes the parent has more money than the student.

Individuals should always be wary of signing any guarantees. There have been many instances where individuals have signed guarantees thinking they were like references and that they were simply saying they know the person and consider him or her to be honest. The guarantor does not realize that he or she could be liable to pay the person's bill if the person fails to.

A guarantee must be in writing and signed by the guarantor. There must be no doubt that the document is a guarantee.

Sometimes the person who makes the contract is known as the **first purchaser** and the guarantor is known as the **second purchaser**. It should be appreciated that the contract is for the benefit of the first purchaser. A second purchaser usually receives no benefit from the contract.

The guarantor must only sign for an amount he or she is prepared to lose. A guarantor should always try to limit the amount of guarantee. For example, a guarantee for rent should be limited to six months or one year, and not for an indefinite period. It would be exceptional for a person to act as a guarantor for anyone other than a close family member or a close friend.

A guarantee may be for payments under a hire purchase or similar agreement. If the guarantee is for a transaction that comes within the scope of the Consumer Credit Act 1974, the guarantor must be treated the same as the first purchaser. This means, for example, that the guarantor must sign the relevant consumer credit forms and be provided with a copy of the agreement.

A guarantee is not valid if the guarantor was misled or pressured into agreeing. A creditor who relies on a guarantee must have taken reasonable steps to satisfy himself that the person understands what a guarantee is. This can be done either by recommending that the person sees a solicitor, or the creditor can explain the matter himself. It is not enough that the creditor simply knows that the guarantor has seen a solicitor – the creditor must know that the guarantor has seen a solicitor to explain the liability under the guarantee.

A guarantee is not valid if a person was unreasonably pressured into signing. Normal persuasion and even cajolery is usually insufficient, but any misrepresentation is usually enough to set aside a guarantee.

The particular circumstances of a husband or wife acting as a guarantor for the other are explained on page 195.

In summary, a claim under a guarantee may be set aside on any of the grounds that:

- it was not in writing
- the written document was not signed
- the guarantor was misled about the nature of the document
- it is within the scope of the Consumer Credit Act but does not comply with its requirements; or
- unreasonable pressure was put on the person to sign.

Personal capacity

The law assumes that all people over 18 have full capacity to deal with their affairs, unless there is a specific provision which assumes otherwise.

Where someone has a **physical disability,** such as an inability to write, someone may sign on their behalf. A signature should be witnessed by someone who can confirm that the signed document was understood by the person and represents their intentions.

It is possible to sign a **power of attorney.** This allows someone (called the **attorney**) to act for another person (usually known as the **donor,** or sometimes as the principal or constituent). The power may be limited in time or scope, and may never be used for the attorney's personal benefit. Such a power may be signed when someone is absent for a long period, or when they are about to have extensive medical treatment. The law is the Powers of Attorney Act 1971. The power is effected by signing a deed in front of two witnesses. Legal advice should be taken in drafting the deed. The attorney then has the power to act as if he were the donor.

It is possible to make an **enduring power of attorney (EPA).** This allows someone to act on the principal's behalf now or at a future time. Unlike a normal power of attorney, an EPA may continue into or start from a period of mental incapacity, when the donor cannot act for himself or herself. This power is similar to choosing an executor in a will. There is a prescribed form for an EPA.

When an enduring power is signed, the procedure is:

- the attorney registers the enduring power with the Public Guardianship Office (see page 180) at the first sign of mental incapacity (evidence of mental incapacity is only required if the EPA requires it)

- the attorney then has limited powers to act for the donor, such as in safeguarding property and maintaining the donor
- a copy of the registration is then sent to the donor and to the three closest relatives as defined by law
- once the notices have been filed, the attorney may apply for registration, which takes 35 days so that the PGO can consider the matter, including any objections
- if an objection is received, the attorney is allowed to comment (if the matter cannot be resolved by correspondence, there is a hearing before the Court of Protection)
- once registered the attorney may act for the donor.

Mental incapacity

Mental incapacity is the state where a person suffers such defect of mind or brain that they cannot administer their affairs properly. Mental incapacity may arise from mental illness (such as schizophrenia), age (as in dementia), accident (as with brain injury) or handicap (serious learning difficulties). The law is basically the same in all cases.

Such a person still has the same rights as everyone else; they are just unable to exercise them in the same way.

About one person in six in the UK suffers from a mental health problem at some point in life. A person with a mental health problem is three times as likely to have financial difficulties. Worry about financial difficulties can exacerbate many types of mental problem.

For the debt doctor, the most relevant factors about a debtor with mental incapacity are:

- some contracts may be void
- the debtor is entitled to special consideration in debt collection
- someone may need to be appointed to act for the debtor.

The scope of **mental incapacity** is defined more closely since the implementation of the Mental Capacity Act 2005 in April 2007. The general principles of the Act are:

- a person is assumed to have capacity unless it can be established that they do not
- a person lacks capacity if at the time of making the contract, they are unable to make a decision for themselves because of a temporary or permanent disturbance in the functioning of the mind or brain
- someone is not treated as incapable of making a decision just because they make an unwise decision.

A person is regarded as incapable of decision-making if he cannot:

- understand the information relevant to the decision or its reasonably foreseeable consequences
- retain that information, even for a short period
- use or weigh that information as part of the decision-making process; or
- communicate that decision by any means (including sign language).

It is also a condition that the other party knew or should have known of the person's incapacity.

This does not mean that someone with any mental problem or learning difficulty cannot make a contract. Some conditions permit lucid intervals, and some contracts are easier to understand than others. A person may be capable of buying a sandwich but not of taking out a mortgage.

The Finance and Leasing Association has a Code of Practice which specifically covers mental health issues. Even if the lender is not a member of the Association, a debt doctor may still quote it as an example of good practice. This Code requires the lender to:

- take particular care for sufferers of any relevant health problems
- refer the debt collection to staff trained to deal with sufferers of mental health problems
- be sensitive to a person's condition, and 'respond appropriately' to the person or someone acting on their behalf.

The Code says that a lender may require evidence of a person's health problem, but will restrict the number of times that evidence is required, and will accept reasonable evidence. However, the Code makes clear that the sensitivity based on a debtor's physical or mental health must start as soon as it becomes apparent that there is a health issue.

Guidance has been produced by the British Bankers' Association (BBA) and the Money Advice Liaison Group (MALG) on what should happen when it is realized that a debtor suffers from mental incapacity. The creditor should:

- not sell the debt nor pass it to a credit reference agency, but deal with it in-house
- use specially trained staff to deal with the debtor
- take a more lenient view on interest and charges
- be prepared to write off debts for long-term conditions which are not expected to improve
- seek to negotiate a settlement with the debtor or their adviser
- give additional consideration before taking any legal action; and
- not seek payment from disability benefits.

MALG formally introduced its recommendations in November 2006.

It should be understood that if the contract was valid, the debt remains payable even if the person has a serious mental problem. In serious cases, such as where large amounts are involved, the lender may reasonably expect to see the affairs dealt with by a person acting on behalf of the patient.

The **Public Guardianship Office (PGO)** is set up to deal with the affairs of people mentally unable to act for themselves. Their address is given in Appendix 2. They share premises with the **Court of Protection**.

Under PGO arrangements, a debtor with mental incapacity is referred to as the **client**. The Court of Protection may appoint a **receiver** to act for the client if the client:

- has not made an enduring power of attorney (see page 177)
- is mentally incapable of administering their own affairs; and
- has assets needed to maintain the client.

(Note that the word 'receiver' has other legal meanings.)

An order appointing a receiver is usually made by the Court when:

- there are assets of at least £16,000
- property needs to be sold; or
- the level of income is such that an appointment is desirable.

In other cases, the court may make a short order, explained below.

An application to be appointed receiver is made on forms available from the court, which may be downloaded from its website. The application is considered by reviewing the prospective receiver's suitability, notifying the client's relations, and inspecting medical evidence. The Court has limited power to allow emergency action to be taken without completing this process first.

An application may be made by a relation, friend or anyone concerned about the client's situation. Applications are usually made by a close relation or close friend.

A **short order** is an alternative to receivership. It can allow a person to:

- receive trust income and pension income from any source
- receive money in bank and similar accounts
- pay personal expenses of the client, such as nursing fees, accommodation, debts and legal fees
- take custody of legal documents and other property.

Credit reference

Consumer debt is largely regulated by Consumer Credit Act 1974, as amended, and by regulations issued under this Act. Knowing the law can greatly assist in the process of debt recovery.

A first sign of debt problems may be problems in obtaining credit. This can be an outright refusal, such as when an application for a loan, mortgage or credit card is refused. Another sign is if credit is offered at a higher rate than quoted.

In such a case, there is no right to demand from the company why they have refused credit or quoted a higher rate. Although there is no law to stop a company telling you why, it is most unlikely that any company will do so. However, the company must tell you what credit reference agency it has used (Consumer Credit Act 1974 s157) and you can demand a copy of your file from that agency (s158). Sometimes a company may use more than one agency, in which case it must give details of all agencies.

There are only three credit reference agencies in the UK:

- Experian
- Equifax
- Creditcall.

Their addresses are given in Appendix 2.

To obtain a copy of your file, you write to the company enclosing a payment of £2 and ask for your file. All three agencies now allow individuals to obtain their credit file from their websites. From October 2004, the file only includes your details and those of someone with whom you have a 'financial association', such as a joint mortgage or joint bank account. Previously the file contained details of everyone with the same surname at the address.

In general, the companies have a good record in replying promptly with a full copy of your file. They also usually provide explanatory material to help you understand it. You cannot obtain a copy of anyone else's credit file unless you have registered with the agency and comply with their conditions of use. If the agency has no file on you, it must notify you of this, but does not refund the £2 fee.

The file notes:

- whether you are on an electoral roll for voting purposes
- what county court judgments and other court penalties are registered
- whether you have been declared bankrupt
- what credit cards you have, and the balances allowed
- your record in repaying credit cards

- what loans you have, and your payment record
- how many searches have been made of your record.

Records are kept on file for the duration of what is being reported, plus six years. So if a debt incurred on 1 January 2007 was finally paid on 1 February 2008, this fact will be on the credit file until 31 January 2014.

No record is entered just because you have a county court judgment (or any other court judgment) entered against you. The court may have been used to settle a genuine dispute. Provided the judgment is paid within one month, it is not entered on the file. Once it has been entered, it stays there for six years, though a separate record should be made when it has been paid.

The payment record is indicated as a series of digits indicating how long you took to pay each month's instalments. 0 means paid on time, 1 is one month late, 2 is two months late, and so on. Guidance from the Information Commissioner states that a person should not be recorded as in default until a payment is at least three months late.

The credit reference agency does not say whether someone should have credit or not. The agency simply provides raw factual information and lets the lender decide whether to give credit. Each lender decides its own policy. This may be done by credit scoring.

In many cases, it may be quite obvious from the record why you have been refused. For example, many companies will refuse to lend to anyone with a recent county court judgment, who has been bankrupted, or where there is a poor history of repayment. Most lenders expect to see a line of 0s by a loan, though the occasional 1 will be ignored as most people can slip up occasionally. A single 2 or higher can lead to credit problems.

On receipt of a credit file, the subject should check the accuracy of the details. Any errors, such as a wrong address, should be notified to the agency promptly.

It may be that the credit file is correct but gives a misleading picture. It is possible that a person took three months to pay a debt because there was a genuine dispute. For example, a credit card company can be liable to refund the charge for faulty goods, though the companies resist this strongly and can still register you as in default.

There are two ways to deal with this. The former is to contact the company which put this information on the file and ask the company to correct this. In practice, they are unlikely to agree. The alternative is to use the procedure in Consumer Credit Act 1974 s159. This procedure is as follows:

- the objector notifies the credit reference agency of what entries should be deleted or corrected

- within 28 days, the agency must respond confirming that the entry has been deleted or amended, or stating that it has not amended the file
- within 28 days of receiving such notice, the objector may serve a further notice requiring up to 200 words of explanation to be added to the file
- within 28 days, the agency must either notify the objector that it is adding the words as requested or give a reason for refusing to add them
- either the agency or the objector may appeal against a decision to the Data Protection Commissioner, who decides what words may be added.

An agency may refuse to publish words of explanation, if the agency believes the words are:

- incorrect
- unjustly defamatory of another person
- frivolous
- scandalous; or
- otherwise unsuitable for publication.

For this reason, any explanation should be kept factual and should avoid any abusive or intemperate remarks. An example may be: 'This account was not paid because the goods purchased were faulty. The credit card company was notified immediately but failed to respond in time. It took them four months before they acknowledged their liability.' Provided this is true, there should be no objection to adding such words.

While that is the law, what happens in practice can often be different. Most credit reference agencies suggest suitable wording as soon as they know of an objection. The agency then contacts the party which provided the disputed reference and asks for their agreement to the amendment or to the additional words. If the reference provider does not agree, the agency rules may require the parties to submit evidence to determine the matter. In practice, the reference provider often cannot be bothered to spend time, money and effort in a matter which brings itself no benefit, and therefore agrees to delete the offending entry from the file. A credit card company does not want a file telling the world that it took four months to deal with a claim for faulty goods. However, it is dangerous to assume that a credit provider will always do this.

Some businesses offer the services of a **credit repair agency** to improve a person's credit rating. Such an agency charges a fee to do what the individual can easily do for himself. The steps to improving your credit reference are:

- ensure that you are on the electoral roll held by your local authority
- pay any unpaid bills
- check any other names listed with yours; if they have a bad record, ask for the file to be amended accordingly – a former partner or a lodger could be damaging your credit record
- check the factual accuracy of all statements, and correct any mistakes
- use the section 159 procedure if necessary.

If none of this is sufficient to repair the credit file, the only alternative is to behave from now on. As time passes, old records become less relevant and some disappear after six years. Eventually, the record will look better.

Credit scoring

While a company using a credit reference agency may simply look at a credit file and make its decision, most lenders automate this process by using credit scoring. This takes information from the credit file with information provided by the individual on an application form.

Various factors believed to influence someone's creditworthiness are then given a score in the form of a number. These numbers are added (or sometimes subtracted) to give an overall score. The company sets a 'pass mark' at or above which it gives credit. The score may also determine the rate of interest it is prepared to charge.

Each company makes up its own rules and sets its own pass mark, so a person refused credit by one company may be offered credit by another. Some companies are much more willing to lend to people with a poor credit record, perhaps by charging more interest, taking security or having tougher collection procedures.

The credit score will largely be based on credit history. Records of prompt payments on cards and loans count in your favour. That is better than having no record at all, so a better record is established by having credit cards and paying them promptly than by not having cards at all. Poor records count against. A bad record of payment cannot usually be compensated by other factors.

You can check your credit score by logging on to www.moneyforums. co.uk/credit_score_calculator.php. It should be noted that this is just one calculator, and that different companies will use different criteria and attach different degrees of importance to each criterion. The advantage of a credit score calculator is that you can see how your score changes if your circumstances change.

For example, we take a person who is 50, married with children, a house owner who has lived at that address in postcode area KT

(Kingston) for 10 years, owns the house, is on the electoral register, has been with a present employer (or self-employment) for more than 5 years, has had the same bank for up to 10 years, has a landline telephone, has three credit cards with a total limit of £25,000 with no debts other than mortgage and always pays on time, has a current account and has no county court judgments. He scores 941 (or thereabouts) out of 1000, which is excellent.

Figure 16: How circumstances may affect credit score.

Age: compared with age 50:
−5% at 25; −4% at 30; −2.5% at 40
can increase by up to 2% to age 70

Married: −2.5% for being single
−2% for being divorced

Children: −3% for having no children

Property: −4% for owning a flat rather than a house
−7.5% for living in rented accommodation
−8.5% for living with parents

Postcode: changes of up to 1% according to area

Residence: compared with living at address for 10 years
−4% for living at address for less than 1 year
−2% for living at address for 5 years
no increase for more than 10 years

Voting: −13% if not on electoral register

Landline: −2.5% for no landline telephone

Income: compared to income of £40,000 a year:
−15% for £10,000 year
−10% for £20,000 a year
−5% for £30,000 a year
+4.5% for £50,000 a year
+6% for £100,000 a year

Employment: compared with 5 years in current job:
−7% less than six months
−5% six to 12 months
−2.5% for 2 years
−5% if retired
−16% if unemployed

Credit cards:	compared with owning three cards: –3% for only one card –1% for just two cards +0.5% for four cards +3% for five cards +0% for six cards –1.5% for seven cards –7% for ten cards
Total credit:	compared with a total of £25,000: +3% for only £5,000 +4% for £10,000 +3% for £20,000 –6% for £40,000 –12% for £50,000
Debts:	compared with owing nothing: –2.5% for owing £1,000 –1.5% for £2,000 to £5,000 –1% for owing £10,000 to £20,000
Bank account:	–5% for not having a current account
CCJ:	–14% for court judgments in last six years
Payments:	–5% for sometimes being late –13% for missing some payments –18% for being in arrears on any card –24% for regularly missing payments –16% for having no credit cards

Please see text for comments on this table.

The percentages in Figure 16 may change significantly in other circumstances, and other calculators may use different factors. Some will reduce credit scores for having several children or being divorced. Some will want to know how long ago you last defaulted on a payment. It should also be remembered that credit scoring factors change almost daily, so these figures should be seen as an indication only.

It is also noticeable that Figure 16 is based on prejudice or generalization. Why should someone who is divorced be a worse credit risk than someone who is married? Why is someone who owns a flat less creditworthy than someone who owns a house? Credit scoring cannot consider factors covered by discrimination law, such as a person's sex or race. But it must make assumptions about people, and credit scoring is at least an attempt to base it on experience.

It should also be noted that those who do not use credit cards or loans at all have a lower credit rating that those who use credit facilities responsibly. The most creditworthy borrower on the above calculator is a person who has five credit cards with a total borrowing limit of £10,000. It may seem unusual that a person who borrows money can be seen as a better risk than someone who manages without borrowing. But remember that a credit score is not attempting to evaluate your honesty or prudence but how well you can handle credit. Someone who shows they handle debt well is a better risk than a person who has not handled it at all.

To get a good credit rating, you do need to borrow money. This can be done simply by acquiring five credit cards and using each sparingly, repaying them in full. This creates a shiny white credit record, allowing a person to borrow larger sums at lower rates.

Bailiffs

A bailiff is a court officer who acts under the authority of the sheriff. The term is also now used for **private bailiffs**. A private bailiff must be licensed by the county court and either deposit £10,000 as a bond or have indemnity insurance for that amount. These days, the authorities prefer to use terms such as **enforcement officers** or **enforcement agents**.

Bailiffs and Enforcement Officers are people authorized to remove and sell your possessions in order to pay the money you owe to a person or an organization, conduct evictions, and arrest people.

County court bailiffs are employed by the county courts and are responsible for enforcing court orders by recovering money owed under a county court judgment. They can seize and sell your goods to recover the amount of the debt. They also effect and supervise the possession of property and the return of goods under hire purchase agreements, and serve court documents.

Enforcement Officers are responsible for enforcing court orders by recovering money owed under a High Court judgment, or a county court judgment transferred to the High Court. They can seize and sell your goods to cover the amount of the debt. They also effect and supervise the possession of property and the return of goods.

Certificated bailiffs enforce a variety of debts on behalf of organizations such as local authorities. They can seize and sell your goods to cover the amount of the debt you owe. They also hold a certificate which enables them, and them alone, to levy distress for rent, road traffic debts, council tax and non-domestic rates. They cannot enforce the collection of money due under High Court or county court orders.

Non-certificated bailiffs are entitled to recover the money owed for a variety of debts by seizing and selling your goods but cannot levy distress for rent, road traffic debts, council tax or non-domestic rates, or enforce the collection of money due under High Court or county court orders.

- They can seize and sell your goods to cover the amount of a debt and costs you owe (this is called **levying distress**).
- They may, initially, contact you by telephone or by letter to give you the opportunity to pay the debt. If you do not respond, or you do not agree to pay the debt, they will visit your premises to seize your goods but will not do so if you pay what is owed. You may be able to arrange to pay the debt by instalments. You can discuss this with them.
- If they seize your goods, they may take them straightaway or leave them at your premises. If they leave the goods with you, this is called walking possession. This means that unless you keep to the arrangement to pay, they have the right to return to your premises at any time to remove the goods and sell them at public auction. Once they have taken **walking possession** you cannot dispose of the goods seized until the warrant is withdrawn.
- They will try to obtain the best price for your goods if they are selling them at public auction. This price includes the fees that they are entitled to charge, the cost of removing the goods and the cost of selling them.

For a debtor, the bailiff is the person who seizes property to sell to recover money owed. Certain legal terms are used in connection with bailiffs. These terms should be clearly understood as their legal meanings can be significantly different from their everyday meanings.

Distress is the legal process of removing goods to force the owner to do what the law requires. Someone who does this is said to **levy distress**. The process of levying distress is known as **distraint**.

Execution is the enforcement of civil court judgments by seizing and selling goods. For more on bailiffs, see pages 99–105.

Limitation

The law has rules known as **limitation of actions**, which mean that there are time limits for *starting* a legal action. The main law is the Limitation Act 1980.

For most contracts and torts, the period is six years from the cause of the action. So if a debt arose on 1 April 2007, the creditor has until 31 March 2013 to start a legal action. For a mortgage, the time starts running from each missed payment, not when the mortgage started. If a subsequent acknowledgment is made of the debt, such as paying part of it, the six years runs from the date of the acknowledgment. A payment can restart the six-year limitation period, but not revive any duty to pay interest. This does not apply if the acknowledgment is made after the limitation period has expired. In other words, an acknowledgment cannot revive a debt once statute-barred.

Once started, there is no limit on how long the matter may take. However, unreasonable delays in legal action can lead a court to strike out an action on other grounds. If no action is taken to recover a debt within six years, the debt is not extinguished but becomes **statute-barred**. This means that it may be possible to recover the money by some other means, but the lender cannot sue in the courts for it.

A judgment debt is never statute-barred. So a judgment given by a court in 1998 could be enforced in 2007. However, any statutory interest on such a debt is limited to the last six years.

For actions relating to land, or to contracts made under deed (which are very rare), the limitation period is 12 years. For claims relating to personal injury, the limitation period is three years.

In some cases, the start of the limitation period may be deferred. For example, if fraud is discovered, the limitation period runs from the date of discovery.

Other limitation periods apply in other circumstances.

A debtor must specifically claim that a debt is statute-barred when judgment is sought, otherwise judgment will be given.

Legal tender and receipts

It is sometimes wrongly said that if payment is offered in legal tender (such as in a huge bag of coins) and refused, the debt is extinguished. This is not so.

In England and Wales, legal tender is as defined by law, particularly Currency and Bank Notes Act 1954 and Decimal Currency Act 1971 as amended by Currency Act 1983. Legal tender comprises all current Bank of England notes to any value, and coins from the Royal Mint up to £10, except 5p and 10p which are legal to £5, and coppers which are legal to 20p. Some coins not in general circulation are also legal tender. These include gold coins minted from 1837 and commemorative £5 coins.

In settlement of a debt, a creditor is not obliged to:

- accept other notes such as Scottish or Irish bank notes
- accept cheques or cards
- give change.

In practice, most creditors will accept payment other than by demanding legal tender. Should this be refused, the debtor can pay the money into court. The debtor then has a good defence against any action from the creditor, and the debt stops carrying interest.

Proof of payment may be evidence by receipt, but this is not conclusive either way. Other reliable evidence, such as a witness statement, may be given to confirm that payment was made. Conversely, it can be argued that a receipt was obtained dishonestly. Under the Cheques Act 1957 s3, a cheque which appears to have been cleared to the creditor's account is a receipt.

Particular circumstances

Students

Introduction

Students often get into serious debt trouble, and most universities report horror stories. The problem is exacerbated by:

- receiving funds and loans at the start of the academic year, giving a false sense of wealth
- inexperience in budgeting, particularly when from a home where parents pay for everything
- temptations to indulge in expensive night life.

The particular issue for students is to be disciplined in spending. The first year is critical; a student who has no financial problems in the first year will probably have none in future years.

Students have the advantage that they are surrounded by colleagues in the same position. There can be a certain common bond, and even fun, in the collective frugal lifestyle.

Income

A university student spends about £6,000 a year in 2006, broken down thus:

- £1,000 university fees
- £2,500 accommodation
- £2,500 food, recreation and other living expenses.

In the UK, universities are now able to set their own fees, which can be as much as £3,070 a year. Scottish students studying in Scotland do not have to pay this fee. Other than for overseas students, the rest of the cost of university education is paid by the state.

All students are eligible for a student loan of at least 75% of the maximum. In 2007, the maximum is:

- £6,315 if living in London
- £4,735 if living outside London
- £3,445 if living outside London at home.

The latest figures can be found at the University and Higher Education section of the website www.direct.gov.uk.

The loan is repayable from earnings at the rate of 9% of income above £15,000. So if you earn £25,000 a year, you will have £900 a year deducted from your pay at source until the loan is repaid. Any loan outstanding after 25 years is written off.

Grants, which are not repaid, are now strictly limited. In England, there are 10,000 bursary grants of £2,700 a year (in 2007). To qualify:

- the student must be under 21 at the start of the course
- the family must have little or no income
- the student must live in 'a designated area'.

The school is most likely to know if a pupil could qualify.

There are similar learning grants in Wales and bursaries in Northern Ireland, each with its own rules. Scottish students who study outside Scotland may qualify for a Young Students Outside Scotland Bursary of up to £520 a year.

It is also possible to receive funds from the university itself from its Hardship Fund (Financial Contingency Fund in Wales). Priority is given to students:

- suffering severe financial difficulties
- with disabilities; or
- leaving care.

Qualifications in medicine and similar disciplines are often supported by the National Health Service, which pays fees and provides a bursary. In any event, no fees are charged after four years of study. In some instances, it may be possible to obtain finance from industry.

Expenditure

Care should be taken with accommodation, even when on a university recommended list. The tenancy agreement should be read and understood. In particular, you need to know what bills are charged in addition to the rent: does the rent include insurance, electricity, gas, water, television, TV licence, breakages? Do you have to pay rent during the holidays?

Course fees and accommodation can usually be paid in instalments, which can help with budgeting. If the course includes field trips, their cost must be budgeted for.

Joining the National Union of Students provides a card which gives discounts on travel, stores, cinemas and restaurants. Union bars and facilities are often much cheaper than similar commercial facilities.

A new student should resist the temptation to join every organization promoted at a freshers' fair. Many students find they only regularly attend two or three bodies. They can all be joined later in the year.

Books, computers and social life need careful budgeting. Often, expensive books may not be needed or a second-hand book may be just as good. It is better for private study to be in college premises: the heat and light is free, and there is no temptation to raid the fridge.

A particular problem is social spending. A good discipline is only to take cash when going out. If you can allow yourself £10 for a night out, just take £10 and you will not overspend. If going out, work out how you will get back; a bus there is cheap, a taxi back is dear.

Ration how frequently you enjoy the night life, and find less expensive alternatives for other evenings. Eating, drinking and generally socializing at each others' homes is much less expensive than going to the pub.

As explained in Chapter 3, there are considerable savings for a student who cooks rather than microwaving ready meals. Cooking meals for groups is more cost-effective than cooking for one, such as a group of four taking it in turns to cook for each other. Preparing sandwiches for lunch is particularly cost-effective. Drink bought at a supermarket is cheaper than drink bought at the bar.

Insurance for personal property such as music systems, computers and bicycles can usually be added to the parents' home and contents policy, which is usually the cheapest option.

Credit Action provides a free Money Manual for Students which goes into these areas in much greater detail.

Young people

For young people who are no longer at university, money can be very tight from a combination of student debt, large mortgage and low earnings. There can be a temptation to overspend on luxuries, such as clothing, holidays and socializing.

Provided the person is not over-committed on rent or mortgage, this period should be affordable. Problems at this point often arise from a lack of budgeting. The key is often in attitude and lifestyle. Socializing need not be expensive. There may be plenty of room to economize by preparing your own food (see page 28).

Another problem is the 'I'm free' syndrome if the person has had repressive parents. If someone believes they have been deprived in childhood, there can be a tendency like a released spring to over-indulge. A budget is the obvious way to contain this.

Parents will often find that children still need some financial support into their twenties or even later. There is nothing wrong with this, provided the help is to assist into a financially secure independent life and not to subsidize an extravagant lifestyle.

It is advisable to start a **pension** young, no later than 25. Very roughly, every ten years' delay halves the final pension. So a pension started at 45 is worth only a quarter of what it would be worth if started earlier. In the long term, pensions outperform most other investments. They qualify for tax relief and typically grow at about 6.5% a year compared with perhaps 4% in a deposit account. The difference is that £1,000 earnings before tax over 40 years will grow to £12,400 in a pension fund but only to £3,700 in a deposit account.

Parenthood

Having a child imposes a financial strain on a couple at an emotional time. It can mean a change from feeding two mouths on two incomes to feeding three mouths on one income. This needs careful budgeting. There are many expenses of parenthood – look at the price of children's shoes, for example.

It is dangerous to rely on the wife going back to work soon after childbirth. This is not always possible nor desirable. Child-minding expenses can eat up much of the mother's income. Such expenses are not tax-deductible and so must come out of after-tax income. An employer may provide childcare vouchers of up to £55 a week free of tax and national insurance, but does not have to do so.

A woman is entitled to nine months' paid maternity leave followed by three months' unpaid leave. Generally, during maternity leave a woman receives **statutory maternity pay** (SMP) of 90% of her normal wages for the first six weeks and a fixed rate (£108.85 a week for 2006/07) for the next period of up to 33 weeks. If a woman has low earnings, she may be entitled to the social security benefit of **maternity allowance** instead. The father is entitled to two weeks' statutory paternity pay at the same fixed rate. The government has promised to increase the paid maternity leave to 12 months by 2010. An employer may pay occupational maternity pay on top of SMP; this should be checked.

A woman does not have to take the whole nine months or 12 months leave. She may return to work at any time from two weeks after the birth (four weeks if she works in a factory). However, it is risky to rely on this. There may be complications for either the mother or baby which make a return to work impossible. A new-born baby is very demanding and tiring. Breast-feeding is the healthiest way of bringing up a baby, but is not readily compatible with full-time work. Similarly the father cannot assume that he can work extra hours to make up any shortfall. The father is needed to give emotional and practical support which means that he cannot be permanently absent from home.

Becoming a parent is one of the most wonderful and sacred moments in life. Being involved in the creation of a life is probably the nearest we come to God this side of death. Don't let financial strains ruin the moment.

Husband and wife

Marriage is the voluntary union for life of one man and one woman to the exclusion of all others. It is, among other things, a contract of mutual support between one man and one woman. The Christian church believes that marriage is much more than a contract between two people, but most of the financial consequences of marriage flow from this contract element.

It must be understood that the legal rights and duties of marriage only apply to couples who have completed the necessary formalities required by law. The term **common law wife** (or husband) means a real wife or husband who has difficulties in proving their marriage. Such a situation, which is now almost unknown, can be resolved by a court confirming that they are married. A cohabiting girlfriend is *not* a common law wife and does not acquire the rights and duties of a wife. There are some situations where cohabitees are treated in a similar manner to a married couple, but this arises because of specific regulations. For example, many social security benefits can be restricted where a couple are **living together as husband and wife** (commonly abbreviated to LTAHAW).

The husband and wife remain as two individuals, each capable of owning property in his/her own right. A husband and wife have a legal duty to support each other. How they arrange this is a matter for them to agree. In Victorian times, it was fairly common for an impoverished wife to buy food from a grocer on the basis that the husband had to pay the bill. This is still the law, though it is unlikely that any modern supermarket would allow someone to acquire goods without immediate payment. Prosecutions for not supporting a husband or wife are occasionally brought by the social security authorities. In practice, it is now more likely that the marriage would end in divorce.

A husband or wife may act as a guarantor for the other. Guarantors are explained on page 176. Because of the emotional link within marriage, there is much more opportunity for **undue influence** to be exercised. A husband could press his wife to sign a document on the grounds that 'we will lose the house' or 'if my business does not get this money, the children will suffer'. (Although the law is exactly the same if a wife pressures her husband, all the court decisions are when the husband has pressured the wife.) A wife who is so pressured may be able to have the guarantee set aside. This can be of vital importance if the wife has signed a secured loan for their home which a company is now seeking to repossess.

The fact that a bank or other lender may have a solid case against the husband allowing them to seize his home does not mean that the bank has a solid case to seize the home from the wife who signed the paperwork at her husband's bidding.

There have been many court cases on this point, including appeals to the House of Lords. There have been some subtle shifts in emphasis between these decisions. For example, between 1983 and 1985 it was accepted that a wife was only bound if the bank knew that the wife had received independent legal advice. That is no longer so.

The present law is generally as stated by the House of Lords, the highest court in the country, in the case *Barclays Bank plc v O'Brien [1994]*. This held that a wife (or cohabiting girlfriend) must be treated as a special class of guarantor because of the emotional involvement. Unless the guarantee is fully explained to the wife and understood by her, the guarantee is void.

The bank is regarded as having **constructive notice** that there may be undue pressure. Constructive notice means that the bank knows this without having to be told. A bank must have ensured that the wife has understood the nature of the guarantee, either by explaining it to her themselves or if she has obtained independent legal advice. Usually the bank will want evidence of this, such as the wife signing a statement that she has received legal advice.

The situation is different if the loan is made *jointly* to the husband and wife, rather than to the husband or wife alone with the other acting as guarantor. On the same day that the Lords gave their ruling in the *O'Brien* case, they gave a different ruling in *CIBC Mortgages plc v Pitt [1994]*. Here the wife was bound, even though she had been pressured by her husband into signing away their home. The difference is that the wife derived some benefit from the guarantee as the loan was partly made to her.

Details of exactly what a solicitor must say to a husband or wife guaranteeing the other's debt was spelled out by the Court of Appeal in the case *Royal Bank of Scotland plc v Etridge (No 2) [1998]*. That case held that the wife is bound only if:

- she is told that she is free not to sign
- the solicitor is satisfied that she was not subject to undue influence
- the guarantee is one which she would want to make if there were no undue influence
- she is specifically told that she is liable for debts already incurred, if that is the case
- she is specifically told that she is liable for unlimited amounts of future debt, if that is the case; and
- she is advised that a limited guarantee is more acceptable than unlimited guarantee.

The law is the same if the wife presses a husband to sign.

Cases continue to be heard frequently on whether a couple's home may be seized when the wife has signed forms at her husband's prompting. Because of the seriousness of the matter and the complexity of the legal rulings, a debt doctor should usually seek professional legal advice.

From 21 December 2005, two people of the same sex may make a **civil partnership**. The rights and duties within a civil partnership are similar to those of a marriage. It is therefore assumed that the provisions relating to a husband and wife apply equally to civil partners.

In some other countries, two people of the same sex may marry. Such a relationship is recognized as a civil partnership in the UK. In some states, it is permissible for a man to have more than one wife (known as **polygamy**) or, more rarely, for a woman to have more than one husband (known as **polyandry**). To contract a second or subsequent marriage while the former is still in effect is the crime of **bigamy**. However, if a polygamous marriage was legal in the country where made, it will usually be recognized in the UK.

Financial arrangements always change on divorce, separation or annulment. **Annulment** is when the marriage is set aside because it was found to be illegal or because it was not consummated. **Separation** is when the marriage remains in force but the couple formally live apart. **Divorce** is when the marriage is legally ended, and the law allows the parties to remarry. Sometimes individuals seek to protect their property on marriage by signing a **prenuptial agreement** which determines what happens if the marriage ends. Such agreements are usually of little practical effect. In reality, when a marriage ends, the division of property is a matter for negotiation between the two people, and their solicitors.

The elderly: pensions

Being old need not mean being poor. Many people now retire on good pensions with savings and other income, with the mortgage paid off and a comfortable but not expensive lifestyle. That should be everyone's aim.

The state retirement pension is (from 2010) payable to everyone who has paid national insurance for at least 30 whole tax years. It is paid from the age of 65, with lower ages for women who retire before 2020.

It is most unlikely that anyone can live comfortably on the state retirement pension. The rate for 2006/2007 is only £84.25 a week for a single person and £134.75 for a couple. Council tax can take away almost half of that. Someone who has been employed since 1978 may have contributed to a government scheme called **SERPS** or (from 2002) **State Second Pension**. These can provide significant additional amounts of pension.

It is always worth knowing what the state will provide. This can be found out by completing a **State Pension Forecast**. This can be obtained on-line from the website of the Department of Work and Pensions at http://www.thepensionservice.gov.uk/atoz/atozdetailed/rpforecast.asp. A form may be printed out from the same website and posted. Details can be given by telephone on 0845 300 0168, or you can write to Future Pension Centre, The Pension Service, Tyneview Park, Whitley Road, Newcastle upon Tyne NE98 1BA. It takes about three weeks to receive the estimate. The service is free. The report may also highlight missing national insurance years which can be plugged by paying Class 3 national insurance contributions.

If at any time during a person's working life they were in an occupational pension scheme, a pension is payable (unless the person left within two years and chose to have a refund of contributions). For jobs where a person left before retirement, the pension is either **deferred** or was transferred into the pension scheme of the next job. In the public sector, changing jobs often does *not* mean changing pension scheme. Someone moving from one local authority to another, or from one NHS hospital to another, has not changed jobs as far as the pension is concerned.

A deferred scheme means that no more contributions are added to the fund, but it still grows by a small percentage each year. It is possible that a person may have a deferred pension from a job they left 30 years earlier. Even if the company is no longer trading, the pension fund should still be there.

Deferred pensions can be traced by calling 0845 6002 537 or writing to **Pension Tracing Service**, The Pension Service, Tyneview Park, Whitley Road, Newcastle upon Tyne NE98 1BA.

Occupational pension schemes are either **defined benefit** (also known as final salary) schemes, or **defined contribution** (also known as money purchase) schemes. The former are usually the more generous, and are now largely confined to larger employers. If fortunate enough to be in a defined benefit scheme, the person should rarely consider leaving it. Public sector workers and Church of England clergy have very generous defined benefit schemes. On request, the pension scheme should provide an estimate of the benefit it is projected to provide.

The third source of pensions is the **private pension**. These have been available since 1988, before which a person could take out a similar **retirement annuity**. Most of the restrictions on pensions were relaxed from 6 April 2006 when a simpler regime was introduced. It is now possible to have as many pensions as you like (or can afford), and to receive a pension from an employer while still working for them.

For most pensions, there is a choice of when to start receiving the pension. A private pension must usually start between the ages of 55 and 75. Every year that a person can afford to wait before starting to take the pension gives a *double* increase to the amount payable. A man of 66 will expect to live about one year less long than a man of 65, so the amount of pension (known as the **annuity rate**) is more. The pension company pays more because they expect to pay it for a shorter time. Secondly, the pension fund will have had one more year to earn interest and so grow in size.

Using quoted rates from 2007, a man with £100,000 in a pension fund could expect to receive a pension of £593 a month for the rest of his life if he retired at 65. If he is able to wait just one more year to 66, this rises to £648, an increase of 9.3%. Tables of the latest annuity rates with explanations can be found at the website of the Financial Services Authority at http://www.fsa.gov.uk/tables/.

The elderly: other aspects

It is possible to continue working beyond the age of 65. In the 1980s there was a fashion for **early retirement** and a tendency to regard anyone beyond the age of 50 as unemployable. Mercifully, that attitude has now largely gone as it is appreciated that older people can still have years or even decades of working life in them. Ronald Reagan was president of the USA at the age of 77, and Sir Winston Churchill was prime minister at the age of 81. And few people from the swinging sixties probably expected the Rolling Stones still to be performing past the age of 60.

From 1 October 2006, **age discrimination** is illegal in the UK. An employer cannot set a retirement age below 65 unless that can be objectively justified. An employer must give an employee six months' notice of retirement. If this notice is not given, the employee may work for six months from when it is given, even if this is past his retirement age. An employee who wishes to work past the age of 65 has the right to ask to continue working and to request flexible working hours. An employer must properly consider such a request. Any such agreement extends the employment by six months. These agreements may be repeated indefinitely if the employer and employee agree.

It is also illegal to discriminate against employees in the provision of benefits and opportunities. A person cannot be refused training because he is too old.

Working past retirement age no longer affects entitlement to the state pension or any other pension. There is a small amount of additional tax relief for the elderly which can add about £9 a week to pay. You stop paying all national insurance once you reach retirement age, though the employer continues to pay it.

Moving from full-time work to the enforced idleness of full-time retirement can be a shock. It can be better to fade out more gradually by moving to part-time work and then reducing hours. Many companies now offer pre-retirement planning.

Many benefits are now provided to the elderly, such as winter fuel allowances, free prescriptions, bus passes and reduced charges for many public facilities. There are charities such as Help the Aged which can provide much advice and practical help for the elderly. This includes financial advice on their website at http://www.helptheaged.org.uk/en-gb/AdviceSupport/.

Elderly people should deal with debt problems by:

- ensuring that all claimable pensions are received
- checking entitlement to other state benefits
- if still working, ensuring that they get the age allowance for income tax and are not paying any national insurance
- looking for suppliers, such as hairdressers, that offer lower rates for senior citizens
- if any relative lives with them, checking that their payments are reasonable and sufficient to cover expenses
- seeing if there is any local charity able to provide assistance.

This is additional to the general budgeting advice given in Chapter 2.

Finally, it is possible to consider moving to a smaller house to release capital from a home which is now too big (see page 51) or to consider an equity release scheme (see page 55).

Death

It is possible for a person to die insolvent. Debts are not extinguished on death but should be paid from the estate of the deceased.

The estate is administered by the **personal representative** (PR) of the deceased. If the deceased left a will, the PR is an **executor** who obtains **probate** and administers the estate according to the will. If the deceased did not leave a will (known as intestacy), the PR is an **administrator** who obtains **letters of administration** and administers the estate according to the intestacy rules.

For the death of an insolvent person, the debts must first be paid in the ranking for insolvency (see page 219). Only if all the debts are paid do the beneficiaries of the deceased receive anything.

Any debts that cannot be paid from the estate are extinguished. There is no legal or moral obligation on the beneficiaries or family to pay the debts themselves. The OFT guidelines prohibit a creditor seeking payment from someone not liable to pay it.

Possible exceptions to this rule are:

- if there was joint and several liability by the debtor and someone else, such as a joint mortgage, the creditor may proceed against the surviving debtor
- if property has already been passed to beneficiaries which should have been available for creditors, the PR can be made personally liable for the value of such property
- a mortgage on a property remains
- if a tenancy automatically passes on death, any arrears of rent also pass
- the surviving partner of a marriage or other relationship is liable for the deceased's council tax for the year of death.

It cannot be too strongly stressed that every individual should have a valid will, which should be reviewed each ten years or so. The will should be properly drawn up by a solicitor, rather than trying to write a home-made will or using a form provided by a stationery shop or charity.

Business debts

Introduction

One of the commonest forms of serious debt comes from a failed business venture. Too many entrepreneurs grimly hang on to a business activity long after it has ceased to be commercially viable, usually with the consequence of more serious debt.

Common mistakes made by small businesses include:

- not having a proper business plan
- regarding turnover (rather than profit) as income
- not setting aside sums to replace assets
- delegating all financial control
- over-dependence on one supplier or customer
- being caught out by tax.

A **business plan** is a strategy for running a business. It considers four aspects:

- you, or your management team
- the product or service you will provide (how is it better than every-one else's?)
- how the business will be financed, including providing income while the business builds up
- how you will market your product or service.

If someone seeks finance from any source, the first question will be 'Where is your business plan?' If a businessman does not know how he will succeed, how can he expect anyone else to know?

Producing such a written document need not be a long or complex process. If a business has been properly thought through, the business plan is little more than documenting those thoughts. The discipline of putting the plan into writing is a good discipline. Often the process highlights areas which have not been properly considered.

The television programme *Dragons' Den* has shown just how dreamy-eyed some would-be entrepreneurs are. Howlers from the author's experience include:

- seeking a loan on the basis of projected accounts which do not include any provision to repay the loan
- forgetting to include wages
- forgetting about tax
- forgetting other overheads such as business rates and insurance
- assuming that a shop will be open for 365 days a year
- assuming that staff will work for 24 hours a day
- arithmetical errors in the projected accounts
- ignoring legal requirements such as health and safety.

A proper business plan will also look at the risks to the business. A simple method is the **SWOT analysis**, which simply lists Strengths, Weaknesses, Opportunities and Threats to the business. More sophisticated methods include risk analysis and sensitivity analysis.

Risk is an unavoidable part of any business. The proprietor should not try to eliminate or avoid all risk, but should identify the risks and then:

- minimize the likelihood of the risk
- minimize its consequences
- have plans to address those consequences.

To take a simple example of the premises and stock catching fire. The three steps against the risk will be:

- follow fire precautions such as having no naked flames
- have fire extinguishers and fire doors to contain any fire
- have insurance to cover loss caused by fire.

There are many other risks which need to be identified. For example, back in 1988 one couple remortgaged their home to raise funds for a business selling exotic perfumes which they blended. The business started well, and then in one year interest rates doubled from 7½% to 15%. There were three consequences:

- their debt repayments became unpayable
- their business dried up as their customers also had much larger mortgage and debt repayments and so cut back on luxuries
- the value of their home fell and became worth less than its mortgages.

The business failed, the home was repossessed and they were bankrupt and homeless. They were vulnerable to interest rate rises three times over.

Turnover and profit

Suppose you run a business manufacturing bird tables. Your accounts may show:

Turnover:	£100,000
less Cost of sales:	£40,000
Gross profit	£60,000
less Overheads	£50,000
Net profit	£10,000

The accounts are likely to be much more complicated than this, but somewhere on the profit and loss account, those figures above should be seen.

Turnover is the amount a business receives during the year. **Cost of sales** is the direct cost of producing what is sold, such as materials and labour. **Gross profit** is the margin made on the sales. **Overheads** or expenses are the amounts paid for being in business rather than for the trade. It includes such items as insurance, rates, bank charges, stationery and accountancy fees. **Net profit** is the amount the business contributes to the owners.

ONLY NET PROFIT IS INCOME

A common mistake made by small businesses is to confuse turnover with profit. Someone with the accounts above could boast that 'I make £100,000 a year'. The obvious problem with the business above is that overheads are out of control, a very common failing for a small business.

Also remember that assets need replacing. A driving instructor will soon need a new car. This is an expense which must be allowed for, or the business will fail when the old car wears out.

Financial control must never be wholly delegated. The entrepreneur who says 'I leave it all to my accountant' (or more likely to his friend 'who is good with figures') is heading for a fall. The financial success of most businesses depends on keeping a close eye on:

- sales – are you selling your product or service?
- cashflow – are your customers paying you promptly?
- expenses – are your expenses under control?

If the management of the business is left to others, ensure that there are routine reports to you, and keep hold of the cheque book yourself.

Problems from delegation of control can arise because the manager:

- is dishonest
- does not work as hard as you; or
- does not understand the business.

A company called Red Letter Days, offering 'experiences' for special occasions, traded successfully for 16 years. By June 2005, the company was worth an estimated £25 million and was about to be listed on the Alternative Investment Market (a junior Stock Exchange). Two months later it collapsed into administration, worth nothing and owing £8 million. The proprietor Rachel Elnaugh told *The Daily Telegraph* that 'In 2002 I made the mistake of stepping back from the business and putting in a chief executive from a corporate background who didn't understand the entrepreneurial culture and wanted to put in lots of overheads and structures. I should have stayed in control.'

Over-dependence is when a business relies heavily on one supplier or one customer. If you lose that supplier or customer, your business can easily fail. Usually when a big business fails, it takes many small businesses with it.

This commonly happens in a **monopsony**, when a business is dependent on one customer. If that customer becomes insolvent, it can bring down other companies. It is not even necessary for there to be a direct trading relationship. When there have been closures of coal mines, steel works and car plants, the knock-on effect has been felt by local traders starved of the trade from former employees. The monopsony risk is one which should be considered in the business plan (see page 202).

Profit is the most important 'expense' of any business. If you cannot make a profit, you do not go into business at all. It is wrong to have the attitude that you will do the best you can and hope there is some profit left over for you. If a business stops making a profit, it should be closed down. There is an exception if the losses are temporary, but many business owners are too keen to see a permanent decline as a temporary blip.

As with all aspects of debt management, the sooner you face up to the problem, the easier is the solution.

Tax catches out many small businesses. Basically a company pays corporation tax on its profits, whereas a sole trader or partnership pays income tax.

A particular problem arises from income tax on business. Once the business is established, tax is paid on the profits of the *previous* year. The exact interval between earning profits and paying tax on it depends on the date in the year to which the accounts are made up. For month ends, the longest interval comes from using 30 April; the shortest from using 31 May.

This can be demonstrated by assuming that a business has seen its taxable profits fall from £400,000 in year 1 to £250,000 in year 2 and pays income tax at 40%. In year 2 it will pay tax of £160,000 (which is 40% of £400,000) out of profits of £250,000. This is an effective tax rate of 64%. Unfortunately the UK income tax system hits shrinking businesses very hard.

No tax computation is as simple as the above, as there are personal allowances, capital allowances, lower tax bands and other complications. However, the principle outlined above remains valid.

A further problem of the income tax system is that the statements from HMRC are frequently full of figures laid out in an unhelpful manner. Sometimes it is impossible to work out how much tax is owed from a statement.

At its simplest, a business's income tax for one year is paid in three instalments. By 31 January it pays half its expected taxable profit for that tax year. By 31 July it pays the other half of its expected taxable profit for the same tax year which has now ended (on 5 April). By the following 31 January it pays the balance now that it knows its actual taxable profit. On that date the first instalment is also due for the following year. If the first two instalments have overpaid the tax due, the third instalment is actually a rebate which is offset against the first instalment for the following tax year.

The expected taxable profit is assumed to be the same figure as for the year before. However, if you know that this figure will be less, you may write to HMRC asking for the figure to be reduced. You will be asked to complete form *SA 303 Application to Reduce Payments on Account*. The form asks for a simple explanation of the reason why. For declining profits, you simply tick a box. In practice, HMRC usually accepts whatever is stated on the form. Completing this form does not reduce the total amount of tax paid; it will simply reduce the first two instalments and increase the third (or reduce the overpayment).

When a business goes wrong

If a business starts to fail, the business must be finished off. This is not a pleasant experience, as you are being asked to kill 'your baby'. Vain optimism is not a business asset. Ask a trusted accountant for an honest opinion on your business prospects and listen to what he or she says.

The steps to follow when a business goes wrong are:

- keep calm
- stop the bleeding
- generate cash

- slash expenditure
- negotiate with creditors
- inform staff.

Keep calm

One of the biggest problems in dealing with debt recovery for a business is to keep the business owner rational. Avoid court cases wherever possible. Concentrate on what is important. Keep level-headed and objective.

At the same time, look after yourself so you do not collapse with exhaustion or have a breakdown. Also, look after those closest to you. A husband who spends 16 hours a day struggling to keep a sinking business afloat can find problems from an ignored wife. At times like this, you may find out who your real friends are.

Do not drown in a sea of despair, but concentrate on what is important. Set yourself attainable targets. Do not be afraid to ask for help or advice. Always be honest to yourself.

Here churches often have a poor track record. There is often a lack of sympathy for the member who gets into commercial difficulty. People who will earnestly pray about your hernia will completely ignore your failing business or financial problems. The author knows of church leaders who have taken the view that 'it serves you right for trying to make money'. Try to find someone in the church who also runs a business. They are likely to be more sympathetic.

Also the UK has a less sympathetic approach to business failure than more commercial countries like the USA, where a few failures are more readily accepted as management experience.

Stop the bleeding

In all First Aid, the first step is to stop the problem getting worse. Only then do you consider how to make it better. The same is true when bleeding money – the first priority is to stop the bleeding.

Debt collection

The easiest way for most businesses to generate cash is to chase up its debtors.

In business, most debtors are also creditors. You should press your own debtors to settle their accounts. In this, the debtor is now 'on the other side of the fence'. You will gain experience of what it is like to be on the other end of the calls you receive.

The rules for effective collection of debts are:

- send out regular statements and reminder letters
- have reliable records of what is owed and what for
- record all conversations
- chase up using the telephone
- use the three Ps: persistent, patient and polite
- don't take 'no' for an answer
- ask specific questions to counter fob-offs
- use county court summonses if necessary.

Persistent means that you ring every day until you are paid. Don't apologize for ringing up – you are simply seeking to recover what is rightfully yours. Most businesses will soon tire of 'it's him again' and pay you to stop the calls.

Be patient and note down whatever you are told. Whatever excuse is proffered ask them for a solution – when will your director return? who else may sign a cheque? when will you have the funds? Never give a debtor time when you will let up the persistent calls. Say 'I'll call you tomorrow anyway to see if things have improved'.

Don't take no for an answer. Press the person for all the details you can think of, record them, and be ready to quote them back. A common fob-off is 'the cheque is in the post'. As untruths go, this is second only to 'of course I love you'. Ask for the cheque number. The answer is completely irrelevant, but it forces the person to admit that 'well, we haven't actually written the cheque yet but it will be in the post'. You then ring the following day to see if they did manage this great feat.

Politeness is essential as any rudeness gives them an excuse not to speak to you.

Cash generation

Other forms of generating cash are:

- debt factoring
- distress sales
- distress financing
- distress equity.

Debt factoring

Debt factoring is a commercial arrangement with a bank or other financial institution. They will lend you money against your invoices. Typically they will pay 75% to 90% of the value of the invoice within a day or two of issuing the invoice. The actual percentage paid depends on the nature of the business. The following attributes will lead to a higher percentage being paid:

- your business has a good credit record
- the business is straightforward
- there is little scope for disputes over bills.

The debt factor becomes responsible for recovering the debt. This can be an advantage to a business which finds credit control difficult as debt factors are much more experienced in debt recovery. Debtors may be less willing to string along a big finance company than a small business.

The debt factor will usually want to see some evidence of a business plan and want to review your trading record. The factor will usually want security, at least over all the debts. This means that all the company's debts belong to the debt factor to whom all money must be paid; it is not usually possible to retain the right to invoice good customers and farm out the slow payers to the debt factor. For small businesses with a higher risk, the factor may want personal guarantees. This means that you become personally liable to pay any outstanding charges to the debt factor if they cannot otherwise be recovered.

There is a charge for using a debt factor. Typically this has three elements:

- an invoice charge – typically 1.25% to 1.5%
- an interest charge – typically 1.5% to 3% above base rate for the time it takes to recover the debt, calculated on a daily basis
- outstanding balance charge – typically 0.3% a week on the total of invoices outstanding.

Suppose a customer owes you £100 (including any VAT). Your debt factor provides 80% of funds on issue of invoice and charges you 2%, 2.5% and 0.3% for the three elements listed above. The base rate is 4.5%. The customer takes three months to pay.

As soon as the invoice is issued, the debt factor pays you £80. The charges levied are:

invoice charge of 2%	£2.00
interest charge of 7% for three months	£1.75
outstanding balance charge of 0.3% for three months	£0.90
TOTAL CHARGE	£4.65

This is deducted from the balance of £20, so three months after the invoice, you receive £15.35. In practice, you will find that the total factoring charge is around 4% to 6%.

Debt factoring is most effective when:

- the business lacks in-house credit control facilities
- most of the customers are small businesses
- the business is solvent and growing steadily
- there is a good profit margin on the goods or services provided.

Manufacturers of goods can often find debt factoring useful. A service company (such as a consultancy) should never need to use a debt factor. Only a growing business should consider debt factoring. Debt factoring is not usually available for consumer sales to private individuals.

The last point is particularly important. Suppose your business's profit and loss account looks like this:

	£
Turnover:	100,000
Cost of sales:	55,000
Gross profit	45,000
Expenses	35,000
Net profit	10,000

The net profit (which is the figure that really matters) is just 10% of turnover. If you are paying a debt factor 5%, you are giving half your net profit away and should probably consider an alternative. However, if your profit and loss account looks like the above, a more pressing need is to cut down on expenses.

The factoring described is the common form of **recourse factoring**. This means that the debt factor pays the balance only when the debtor pays the invoice.

Non-recourse factoring is where the balance is paid after a fixed period regardless of whether the invoice has been paid. Obviously there is a higher charge for this service, typically equal to another 0.5% to 2% of turnover.

Full-service factoring is where the debt factor takes over the whole management of your sales ledger. This may be used for recourse or non-recourse factoring.

Invoice discounting is a form of secured lending against debts. It is simpler but more expensive. It is usually only used for large amounts and for international debts. You continue to run the sales ledger. The customer does not know of the arrangement, unlike debt factoring where the customer is told to pay the debt factor direct.

On starting such an arrangement, the debt factor is unlikely to accept:

- stale debts – usually those more than 90 days old
- excess debts – where the customer is already above his credit limit
- disputed debts – where the customer maintains that the amount (or some of it) is not owed.

The debts which are accepted are known as **approved debts**.

Once your finances are established you can discontinue debt factoring, but most factors want between three and 12 months' notice.

Further information is available from the Association of British Factors and Discounters, telephone 0207 930 9112 or their website at www.thefda.org.uk.

Sometimes a business can be both debtor and creditor. A business in difficulty may find that its customers are also in difficulty. In such circumstances, the most constructive approach is to work with the customer. There may be other ways to discharge the debt and other opportunities to co-operate. Helping the customer can both help you and help him to pay his debt. If the customer will not co-operate, the only choice is to get heavy.

Distress sales

Funds can be realized by selling whatever you do not need. Many businesses have more assets than they realize. Some shopkeepers in freehold premises struggling to get by would earn much more by selling the premises and investing the proceeds than by struggling to make a living selling gifts or whatever.

Assets can include intangibles. There may be copyrights and patents which can be exploited. Mailing lists and sales contacts are saleable. Even experience can be a valuable commodity which may be exploited by books, conferences and consultancy.

Every problem is an opportunity looked at the wrong way. Other businesses in a similar line, possibly your competitors, may look at your business like vultures. It is easy to take the attitude 'I would not let *them* have it on principle'. What principle? Surely the principle which matters is to recover from business failure.

Stock may be sold off at a heavily discounted price to generate cashflow. Many 'stock clearance sales' are really distress sales. After all, if a sofa or music centre was good enough to sell six months ago, why has it suddenly become unsaleable now?

Borrowing

Borrowing to recover from debt is almost always inadvisable. The business has got into debt because of its inability to pay its way. A loan may clear the business debts but at the expense of creating a loan to repay which will give the business another expense, probably a heavy one, making it even less likely that the business can recover.

Lenders are willing to fund an expansion of a business or a takeover of another business, but are unlikely to provide funds to prop up a failing business. Lenders always look cynically at any request for funding for 'business expansion' to see what the expansion is. If a business is trading profitably, it should be generating its own profits to fund its own growth, known as **organic growth**.

This does not mean that loans will not be forthcoming. Lenders will always lend money if they can be reasonably sure it will be repaid and they will earn a profit. You may be able to obtain **distress finance** to bail out a business. The price is a hefty interest rate – perhaps eight percentage points above base rate, and security such as over your home.

Distress-financed businesses rarely recover. More usually they simply drag out the inevitable business closure and leave the owners with even bigger personal debts.

Distress equity

Distress financing does not necessarily mean borrowing money. There are many ways a business may obtain funding, but they are all variations on one of two themes: debt and equity.

Debt finance means that the business simply borrows the money, repays the loan with interest and keeps whatever is left as profit. **Equity finance** mean that part of the business is sold to someone. The money provided is not repaid like a loan, but the person is entitled to a share of the profits. Debt finance comprises such financial instruments as loans, debentures, preference shares. Equity finance usually comprises ordinary shares or a partnership holding. Many businesses use both forms of finance, often with debt finance providing funds for short-term expansion and equity finance for long-term growth.

In terms of distress financing, debt finance is distress borrowing as explained above. There is an equity-based alternative which we can call distress equity. This is where an outside investor provides finance for a share of the profits. Such an outside investor can be found through accountancy firms or through specialist firms that seek to match investors with businesses. In the colourful terminology of private finance, such a firm is known as a **dating agency**. An individual who invests is known as an **angel**.

A debt financier is likely to be a demanding angel. Almost certainly, the angel will want a majority stake in the business, although there could be an **earn-out** arrangement whereby particularly good profits could be used to buy out some of that stake. In practice, it is unlikely that distress equity will work.

Business rates

Businesses pay **unified business rate (UBR)** on their premises, rather than council tax.

Unpaid UBR is recovered by a liability order from the magistrates' court which can then be enforced by seizing goods. Unlike most other forms of debt recovery, there is no exemption for tools, books or goods, so seizure of goods can easily force a business to close. Depending on what is kept at the premises, unpaid UBR can be a priority debt.

When a business has ceased to trade, no UBR is payable for three months. After that half UBR is payable until the premises are used again for business.

A local authority has the power to write off arrears in the case of hardship. This should always be sought.

Romalpa clause

Goods may be supplied on the basis that ownership does not pass until the invoice has been paid. This is known as **reservation of title**, or **retention of title**. It is also known as a **Romalpa clause** from the leading case *Aluminium Industrie BV v Romalpa Aluminium Ltd [1976]*.

Aluminium supplied £85,000 worth of aluminium foil to Romalpa under a contract with such a clause. Aluminium claimed that it still owned the foil and was therefore entitled to the whole of its return, rather than have it included as part of the stock from which it would receive little or no payment.

If the foil has been used to make other products, the right to reclaim can be 'traced' to those goods, which may be taken, though most such claims fail in practice. If the goods have been sold, a Romalpa clause does not allow a reclaim of the proceeds.

While Romalpa clauses are widely used, they are rarely enforced. For a company to claim back their unpaid supplies, they would usually need a right to enter premises and to know where it is kept. The goods must be specifically identifiable as from the supplier – it does not allow a supplier to take identical goods from another supplier.

The practice is that the insolvency practitioner takes possession of all goods which appear to belong to the business, and awaits any Romalpa challenge from a supplier, who needs to move quickly to have any chance of success.

Although a Romalpa clause may be used in a contract with a consumer, it is very rare for such a clause to be enforced.

Slash expenditure

Expenditure must be cut dramatically. The approach must not be 'What may I cut?' but 'What must I keep?'

This can mean laying off staff as they are often the biggest overhead in any business. This is always unpleasant. It is possible that church people will complain that 'you are putting profits before people' and lament the lay-offs after loyal service. That is one half of the story. The other half is that a business laden with unnecessary staff is more likely to fail. A business which takes the necessary medicine, however unpalatable, is more likely to recover and be able to re-engage staff.

If faced with a difficult situation, bring the staff into your confidence. You may be surprised how many are willing to accept a cut in pay, accept deferred wages or even to work for no pay. Indeed you could fall foul of UK employment law if you make staff redundant without offering them choices. Walt Disney was bankrupted before becoming the successful cartoon film mogul. When working on *Snow White*, his studio ran out of money. He brought the staff into his confidence. They shared his vision and agreed to work for deferred pay.

Here is an example:

A computer service company was in financial difficulties and was considering increasing prices, offering new services and cutting existing services.

A look at the accounts quickly showed that the company was stuffed with overheads. The owner could not say what his staff did or when, nor how much they earned. Nor could the owner explain why he maintained premises for the staff. His profits were being used to pay for a social club for them.

He was eventually persuaded to put the staff on to 'as required' contracts and to give up the premises. Despite his fears, the staff and landlord simply accepted this without demur. The company quickly returned to profitability.

Whatever the business decides to do should be shared with staff and professional advisers.

Business insolvency

Chapter 12 explains insolvency for individuals. The rules for businesses depend on how the business is set up.

If the business is a sole trader, partnership or unincorporated association, the rules for insolvency are the same as for a business. The law makes no distinction between the business and the person running it.

If the business is a company or a limited liability partnership (LLP), the rules are different. This is because the company (which for these purposes includes an LLP) is regarded as a separate 'legal person'. This legal person can sue and be sued in its own name independent of those who own it. The legal person can live and die independently of those who own it.

A company may compound for debts in the same way as an individual (see page 218). A company may also make a **company voluntary arrangement** (CVA), which is similar to an IVA (see page 224). In practice, the main requirements for a CVA are:

- a business which is fundamentally sound
- acceptance that the company management must be changed
- a realistic structure for paying debts
- (usually) introduction of working capital
- acceptance that a period of hard work for low reward is necessary.

If compounding or CVA cannot address the problem, the choices in increasing severity are basically:

- administration
- receivership
- liquidation.

These are usually instituted by the company's creditors though they can be instituted by the company itself.

Administration means that the company is run by someone else. This is suitable for a business which is basically sound but badly run.

Receivership is when the company cannot be successfully run as it is, though bits of it may be viable. A receiver is generally allowed to run successful parts with a view to sale, and to shut down other parts.

Liquidation is when the company is wound up (i.e. killed) after selling whatever can be realized.

The administrator, receiver or liquidator is usually a qualified accountant with specialist training in insolvency work.

It should be remembered that a company can be wound up without any need for liquidation. You simply ask Companies House to remove the name from its register. This provides no protection should a creditor subsequently wish to bring proceedings as a company can in some circumstances be restored to the register.

12

Insolvency

Introduction

The ultimate option for someone with serious debt problems is one of the forms of insolvency procedure. This last resort is a serious step, which should only be considered when all other options are failed. It is the equivalent of amputation – a drastic measure, but one which may be necessary.

The word **insolvency** just means owing more than you own. It is a *financial* status which, in itself, carries no legal implications at all. If someone can keep their creditors content while sorting themselves out, they incur no legal restrictions while doing so. In contrast, **bankruptcy** is a *legal* status with serious consequences.

It should be noted that bankruptcy only applies to individuals; companies may go into administration, receivership or liquidation (see page 215).

All forms of insolvency procedure involve paying less than the full amount owed, with a view to being forgiven the rest. All of the procedures are designed to pay the creditors what can reasonably be paid, and then wipe the slate clean to give the insolvent person a second chance in life.

For many of the insolvency procedures, a trustee is appointed. Their duties are broadly marshalling, realizing and distributing. **Marshalling** assets simply means finding them and taking possession. **Realizing** assets means turning them into cash, usually by selling them. **Distributing** means making proportionate payments to creditors.

Although the general principle of bankruptcy law has remained unchanged for over 100 years, there have been considerable changes in procedure. The present law is the Insolvency Act 1986 as amended by the Enterprise Act 2002, and applies from 1 April 2004.

Insolvency work is overseen by the Insolvency Service, which is an executive agency of the Department of Trade and Industry. The Official Receiver is a government official employed by the Insolvency Service. Details of this department can be found on its website, www.insolvency.gov.uk.

Types of insolvency procedure

A person who is insolvent may make an *informal* arrangement with creditors known as a debt management plan. If such an arrangement can be negotiated, there is no need for a formal procedure.

If the informal procedure of a debt management plan cannot be concluded, the alternative is to use one of the three formal procedures.

This gives a choice of four insolvency procedures. In order of increasing severity, they are:

1 debt management plan
2 administration order
3 individual voluntary agreements (IVAs)
4 bankruptcy.

Normally the choices should be considered in this order.

It should be noted that the first two on this list only apply in England and Wales. The separate procedures which apply in Scotland are explained on page 247.

A debt management plan is any arrangement (including a formal arrangement) whereby a creditor agrees to accept less than the amount owed in full settlement of the debt, such as when a creditor is owed £100 but agrees to accept £70 in full settlement. Such an arrangement is known as **compounding**. A creditor may be willing to accept £70 now rather than wait for a long period and risk receiving much less or nothing. Further details are given on page 148. A debt management plan may be arranged by the Consumer Credit Counselling Service, whose address is in Appendix 2.

An **administration order** may only be used when the total indebtedness does not exceed £5,000. A sum is paid to the court each month. The court distributes this to the creditors in the proportion of their claim.

Individual voluntary agreements (IVAs) are formal arrangements where the creditors who are owed 75% or more of the debt can agree a plan to receive regular payments of their claim. An IVA binds all creditors, including those who did not support the IVA.

Bankruptcy is the process whereby a person's possessions are taken and sold. The proceeds are shared between the creditors. The bankrupt is under serious restrictions until discharged.

Ranks of debt

For IVAs and bankruptcy, there are **ranks** of debt. The basic principle is that the whole of one rank must be cleared before paying any of the next rank.

In practice, there are five ranks:

- pre-preferential debts
- preferential debts
- secured debts
- unsecured debts
- deferred debts.

Within each rank, there are sub-ranks which further determine priority.

A **pre-preferential debt** comprises the fees and expenses of the insolvency practitioner administering the IVA or bankruptcy. The insolvency practitioner is paid before all creditors.

A **preferential debt** is one which the law has determined should be given priority over other debts. The only preferential debt which now remains is unpaid wages, up to a limit. Before 1 April 2004, certain taxes also ranked as preferential debts, but all taxes now rank as unsecured debts.

The limit for wages is £800 per employee, or the four months' wages before the insolvency if less. Wages includes all normal pay, bonuses, commission, guaranteed pay and statutory sick pay. If an employee is owed more than the limit, the balance ranks as an unsecured debt. So if an employee is owed £2,000, this comprises £800 preferential debt and £1,200 unsecured debt.

If an employee does not receive full payment, a claim may be made to the Department of Trade and Industry on form IP2. The maximum amount which may be claimed is eight times the figure for **a week's pay** as used to calculate redundancy pay. This figure changes each year on 1 February. The week's pay is £310 from 1 February 2007, and £290 for the year before. Latest figures can be accessed from the DTI website at http://www.redundancyhelp.co.uk/PayWeek.htm.

A **secured debt** is one where the creditor has rights over specific assets. Mortgages, bank loans and debentures are common examples of secured loans. If a secured debt is not paid, the creditor has the right to seize the asset to obtain payment before other creditors. A common example is a mortgage. This is a loan secured on your home. If you fail to pay the mortgage, there comes a point when whoever lent you the money can take your house from you and sell it to recover the debt (see page 107).

It was once the case that the secured debts usually took all the assets in any insolvency, leaving nothing for other creditors. From 1 April 2004, the law is amended so that some of the assets must be reserved to pay unsecured debts. The amount which must be so reserved depends on the value of realized assets:

Realized assets	Reserved for unsecured debts
up to £10,000	half
over £10,000	£5,000, plus 20% of the excess to a maximum of £600,000
£2,985,000 or more	£600,000

So if someone has realizable assets of £100,000, the amount reserved for unsecured debts is £5,000 plus 20% of £90,000. This is £23,000. The secured creditor can take £77,000. For the other £23,000, he ranks on the same basis as an unsecured creditor.

An **unsecured debt** ranks after secured debts with the exception that not all assets may be used to pay secured debts.

A **deferred debt** is one which is specifically agreed to rank after unsecured debts, such as loans from close relations. If a deferred debt is paid, the person is not insolvent at all.

Suppose a debtor owes £100,000 as:

- £10,000 preferential and pre-preferential
- £40,000 secured debt – £30,000 to creditor A and £10,000 to creditor B; and
- £50,000 unsecured debt, including £5,000 to creditor C and £1,000 to creditor D.

The trustee first realizes £22,000. He pays all the preferential and pre-preferential debts of £10,000. This leaves £12,000, which he pays in proportion to the secured creditors. So creditor A receives £9,000 and creditor B receives £3,000.

The debt is now reduced to £78,000, of which £28,000 is the rest of the secured debt, and £50,000 is the whole of the unsecured debt.

The trustee then realizes another £33,000. This is enough to pay all the £28,000 owed to secured creditors. So creditor A receives £21,000 and creditor B receives £7,000 and they are owed no more money. There is just £5,000 left to start paying the unsecured creditors. As £5,000 is one tenth of the total of £50,000, each creditor receives one tenth of what is owed. So creditor C receives £500 and creditor D receives £100.

The legal term for paying debts proportionately is **pari passu**. This is Latin for 'with equal step'.

If all debts can be paid in full and there is money left over, the balance is returned to the debtor. Such situations do happen, though rarely. Perhaps an antique or painting proves to be particularly valuable. In practice, the trustee will simply pay all creditors in full and apply to the court to end the bankruptcy or other insolvency procedure.

Administration order

An administration order may be made by a county court when a person's total debts do not exceed £5,000. This low limit, set in 1991, makes administration orders of very limited value in practice. Only 60,000 or so are made each year. Every administration order is registered at the Registry Trust. This information is accessed by the credit reference agencies, so an administration order is likely to be a serious blow to a person's credit rating.

An order may only be requested by the debtor, not by a creditor. The debtor must have at least one county court judgment or High Court judgment against them.

No fee is charged by the court for making the order, but costs are added later at the rate of 10p for every £1 paid to creditors.

An administration order is requested on form N92 available from the county court. This requires the debtor to list all their debts, including any arrears of:

- rent or mortgage
- council tax
- maintenance payments
- hire purchase
- credit card and other consumer credit debts.

Sometimes a person may have joint and several liability for a debt. The whole amount of such a debt must be disclosed, with one possible exception. This is where the debt is jointly owed by another party who seeks an administration order at the same time. This commonly happens when a couple becomes insolvent.

The list of debts does not include any arrears of Social Fund loans nor of benefit overpayments if the debtor is still receiving any benefit from which the overpayment may be deducted.

If the debtor is employed, the court will make an attachment of earnings order (see page 163).

Once the administration order is made, the debtor makes a single payment to the court each month. The court distributes this to the creditors in proportion to the amount owed. These distribution orders are made every three months.

The court tells each creditor how much they will each receive and how long it will take to clear the debt. An administration order needs the approval of a district judge if the period is more than 'a reasonable time'. This is not defined in any regulation, but court guidance suggests that this is usually three years.

The judge may make such an order without a hearing. If the judge does order a hearing, the debtor and creditors are notified of the amounts listed as owing to them and the suggested terms of the order. The creditors have 14 days to confirm or amend the amount owed, and to say whether they object to the terms of the order. If no objections are received, a **final order** is made and the administration order comes into effect. If there are objections, the judge orders a hearing and determines the matter. If there is a hearing, the creditors may attend, but rarely do so in practice.

An administration order is often used where a debtor can clear the arrears, given enough time. If the debtor has no realistic prospect of clearing arrears within three years, a **composition order** may be made which allows for only part of the debt to be repaid.

The proposal for a composition order is worked out by the debtor (or the debt doctor). The steps are:

(a) determine the total debts
(b) determine a reasonable figure of monthly payment
(c) multiply (b) by 36
(d) subtract 10% court fee from this figure
(e) divide (d) by (a).

For example, a man has £4,000 in debts, and just £80 a month available to clear them.

The above steps give these figures:

(a) £4,000
(b) £80
(c) £2,880
(d) £2,592
(e) 64.8%

Under the proposal, each creditor will receive 64.8%, nearly two-thirds, of the payment within three years. If one creditor is owed £1,000, which is one quarter of the debt, that creditor will receive one quarter of the monthly payment of £80 less the court's 10%. This is £18. The court will make a quarterly payment of £54 every three months. After 12 quarterly payments of £54 over three years, the creditor will have received £648 in total, which is 64.8% of the £1,000 owed. The other £352 is written off.

In practice, administration orders are not usually opposed, but composition orders usually are. This is because an administration order simply requires a creditor to wait for his money; a composition order requires a creditor to give up part of the claim also. The higher the percentage offered, the more likely it is that a creditor will accept the composition order.

A court may refuse to grant an administration order if it considers that this will unreasonably deny a creditor the opportunity to pursue another remedy. An administration order is regarded as a concession to the debtor, so any false statement by the debtor could result in the court refusing to grant an order, forcing the debtor to consider the more serious options of IVA or bankruptcy.

Once an administration order is granted, all interest is frozen on all debts. No creditor may take action against the debtor for the debt. This applies even if the creditor already has an attachment of earnings order for the debt. A local authority may object to including council tax arrears in an administration order on the grounds that it already has a council tax attachment of earnings order. A court case in 1997 established that an administration order may be made and include council tax arrears. The administration order in effect then supersedes the council tax attachment of earnings order.

An administration order may be reviewed by the court at any time on an application from the debtor, from any creditor or by the court itself. Sometimes an administration order may include provisions for periodic review. The commonest reason for a review is a change in the debtor's circumstances, such as a significant decrease in the amount available to pay creditors. Such a request should be accompanied by a financial statement. On a review, the court may:

- reduce the payments
- suspend all payments for a defined period
- vary a composition order, including reducing it to 0%
- reinstate a revoked order; or
- make an attachment of earnings order.

Once an administration order is made, further creditors may be added if they apply to the court. There is no provision for the debtor to add further creditors. Further creditors may be added to an existing order, even if this pushes the total amount owed to more than £5,000. The court always has a discretion to cancel an administration order. In practice, this only happens if the court believes that the process is being abused, such as by a debtor deliberately excluding some creditors from the initial order to keep below the £5,000 limit.

If the debtor misses two consecutive payments or persistently fails to make payments on time, the court sends a notice to the debtor. If this is ignored, the administration order is revoked after 14 days, though the court has discretion subsequently to reinstate a revoked order. If the order is revoked, the creditors are informed of this by the court. The creditors must then pursue payment of the debts by other means.

In practice, most creditors regard an administration order as a reason to write off the debt. Any payments made under the order are regarded as bunce. If an order is revoked, creditors do not usually bother to contact the debtor nor to seek any other method of recovering the debt. This means that, in practice, a debtor can avoid paying debts simply by including them in an administration order and then not making any payments. Such a policy is immoral but legal.

A debtor has the right of appeal to a circuit judge against a decision of a district judge on a point of law only. This must mean that the district judge wrongly decided a legal issue or that there was a serious procedural irregularity. An appeal cannot be made simply on the basis that the debtor does not like the district judge's decision and wants a second bite at the cherry, such as to agree a lower figure for monthly repayments.

Individual voluntary arrangements (IVAs)

An **individual voluntary arrangement (IVA)** is a formal arrangement between the debtor and creditors. General advice on whether an IVA is appropriate may be found on the website www.r3.org.uk. IVAs have been marketed on television as a 'loophole' or 'a little known provision'. They are not a loophole, but a deliberate piece of law which is well known to accountants and those who should know.

An IVA is only made for one individual. If a couple conclude that they both need an IVA, they each need to make an IVA. Once made the two IVAs may be considered together, though they remain separate IVAs and can have different repayment terms and different conditions.

An IVA allows for:

- extra time for the debts to be paid; or
- payment of less than the full amount of the debt.

In reality, an IVA usually provides for both. An IVA has a finite life, typically five years.

There is no upper or lower limit to the amount of debt which may be included in an IVA, so it is usually the first consideration for an insolvent debtor with debts over £5,000. In practice, because of the costs, an IVA is usually only considered for debts of at least £15,000 unless there are other reasons favouring bankruptcy.

An IVA is more serious than an administration order but less serious in consequence than bankruptcy. However, there are circumstances when bankruptcy may still be a preferable option. It is possible for someone who is already bankrupt to set up an IVA. Conversely, the failure of an IVA can lead to bankruptcy.

An IVA is made at the behest of the debtor. In any application for bankruptcy, a court is required to consider whether an IVA is more appropriate.

A debtor wishing to set up an IVA must first appoint an **insolvency practitioner** (IP). An insolvency practitioner is usually an accountant who specializes in that area of work. A debtor may choose any IP he wishes, and may find the IP any way he likes. In practice, the choice of insolvency practitioner is usually:

- suggested by the debt adviser
- suggested by the office of the local official receiver, which keeps lists of local IPs recommended on a rota basis; or
- selected from a list kept by the Association of Business Recovery Professionals (address in Appendix 2).

In practice, it is essential for there to be a personal relationship between the debtor and IP. The debtor must meet the IP in person and must be able to communicate readily and easily by telephone. The debtor should not deal with different individuals every time he contacts the IP. An arrangement whereby everything is done by post tends not to lead to a successful or equitable IVA.

The IP charges a fee for this service, which is typically £3,000, though a higher fee may be charged for particularly complex cases. The IP usually charges an up-front fee, though some IPs are prepared to be paid during the period of the IVA. A common practice is to charge:

- a nominee fee (perhaps £1,000 to £3,000); and
- a supervisor fee (perhaps £500 to £1,000 a year).

This fee is paid by the creditors, not the debtor, though the creditors pay it out of the money provided by the debtor.

The IP draws up an **IVA proposal** to be submitted to the court and to the creditors. In drawing up the proposal, the IP must balance the rights of the creditors with the needs of the debtor. In reality, the IP draws up a proposal which is the least amount of repayment he believes the creditors and court will accept.

The debtor must provide the following information to the IP:

- why an IVA seems appropriate
- likely income during the life of the IVA
- details of assets which can be realized (such as property which can be sold)
- details of contributions made by any third parties, such as payments by relatives to help the debtor avoid bankruptcy
- details of any charges on property, such as mortgages or secured loans
- full details of all debts.

Often, other information may be requested by the IP. It is an offence for a debtor to give false information to an IP.

Once the IP has drawn up the IVA proposal, the IP is required to endorse the proposal. The endorsement confirms that the IP is prepared to act for the debtor. From this moment on, the IP is known as the **nominee**. An IP is unlikely to endorse a proposal unless he believes that it has a realistic chance of acceptance.

A **statement of affairs** must be prepared by the debtor, though the IP usually assists.

Within 14 days of endorsing the IVA proposal, the nominee must file a report at the court saying that the proposal is viable, and stating when and where the creditors' meeting is to take place. (It is theoretically possible for the nominee to file a report saying that a proposal is not viable, or that there will be no meeting of creditors, but this is unlikely in practice.) The meeting is usually at the offices of the nominee.

The nominee also files at the court a copy of the proposal, the statement of affairs and the court fee. Other documents may sometimes also need to be filed.

The court is the county court for the area where the debtor lives, unless the debtor is an undischarged bankrupt. Then the court is the one overseeing the bankruptcy.

Although not strictly necessary, it is usual for the nominee also to apply for an **interim order**. The protection of an IVA does not take effect until the IVA has been approved. An interim order protects the debtor until approval. It prevents a creditor instituting bankruptcy proceedings, exercising a landlord's right of peaceful re-entry, or exercising any other legal procedure for debt recovery, such as distress. A further court fee is payable for an interim order. A court may **stay** any other legal proceedings to recover the debt. This means that those legal proceedings are temporarily stopped.

A court may make an interim order only if:

- the IP has indicated his willingness to act as nominee
- the court is satisfied that the IVA proposal is serious and viable
- the debtor has not made an application for an interim order in the previous 12 months; and
- the debtor is either an undischarged bankrupt or could petition for his own bankruptcy.

Provided the court is satisfied that the IVA proposal is worth being put to creditors, it will endorse the recommendation and extend any interim order to seven weeks after the proposed date of the meeting. Where all these matters are dealt with together, the order is known as a **concertina order**.

The **creditors' meeting** is where the creditors decide whether to accept the IVA. The alternative is usually bankruptcy.

An IVA must be approved by creditors representing at least 75% of the total debt. Suppose a person has debts of £100,000 owed to four creditors thus:

A £40,000
B £30,000
C £20,000
D £10,000.

Approval must be obtained from creditors who are owed at least £75,000 worth of debt. In this case, A and B must accept the proposal, as must *either* C or D. Provided that 75% is obtained, all creditors are bound. So if A, B and D accept the proposal but C does not, the proposal is approved and C is still bound by it. In this instance, A and B each have a veto on the IVA.

Every creditor must be included in the IVA, including unpaid milk bills and loans from family members. The IVA documents specifically require the debtor to sign a statement saying that all creditors have been included. If another creditor is discovered later, this can be sufficient to cause the IVA to fail which could mean the debtor becomes bankrupt. If the new creditor is for a small amount, it may be acceptable to the existing creditors to add it to the list. If the new debt reduces payments to existing creditors by more than 10%, the permission of the existing creditors is needed.

An IVA is intended to pay unsecured creditors. A creditor who has a preferential or secured debt (see page 219) is only bound by an IVA if the creditor so agrees. In reality, such creditors do agree to an IVA which may reflect the preference they would receive in a bankruptcy.

If a debtor owes money to friends and family members, these must be included. It is illegal to exclude them, and it is an offence to pay them in full when not paying other creditors in full. As creditors, they will have the same voting rights as other creditors. This is usually to the debtor's advantage as they will usually favour the IVA. Once the IVA has been adopted, non-commercial loans from friends and family members are unlikely to be included in the IVA. The loan must be paid outside the IVA, often when the IVA has finished.

If a bank is included as a creditor in an IVA, it is usually advisable to open an account with another bank first. Remember that some banks operate under more than one name, such as HSBC and First Direct, and Halifax and Bank of Scotland. A bank will usually freeze an overdrawn account as soon as it learns of an IVA. If the debtor also has a deposit account with the same bank, it can help itself to the deposit to reduce the overdraft on another account. It is prudent to withdraw the deposit before notifying the bank.

Overall, about one third of IVAs are rejected by creditors. However, many of these are rejected because the proposals have not been drawn up properly. If the figures are accurate and the proposals are reasonable, the success rate can be much higher.

If an IVA *is* rejected, it is possible to prepare another IVA proposal. In reality, a second IVA proposal has to be significantly better to be accepted. And if a better IVA proposal is put forward, the creditors will reasonably ask why this better offer was not made in the first place. In practice, if an IVA is rejected, the alternative is another scheme of debt recovery, usually bankruptcy.

The process of identifying creditors and the amounts owed to them is often not simple in any insolvency. It is common for subsequent creditors to be identified. Such creditors are bound by the IVA unless they successfully challenge it in the court within 28 days of the IVA being made. A challenge may only be made on procedural grounds, such as false information on the financial statement or the proposal unfairly prejudicing their rights against other creditors.

An IVA takes effect immediately it is approved by creditors. Once adopted it immediately freezes the debts so that no more interest or charges may be added.

It is perfectly proper for the nominee to have private discussions with creditors before the meeting to establish what they are likely to accept. Usually, the largest creditors are banks and the tax authorities. It is their usual practice to vote at these meetings. HMRC (the tax authority) will often be a creditor. Notifying HMRC about an IVA is likely to lead to an inspection of tax returns, so a debtor should be sure that all tax returns and accounts are up to date. Tax returns should still be submitted even if the amounts cannot be paid.

Advice from the specialist firm Thomas Charles & Co Ltd (*IVA Bankruptcy and Other Debt Solutions* by James Falla, Blue Sky Publishing) suggests that a minimum of £300 a month is needed for debts up to £32,000. For larger sums, a correspondingly larger minimum sum is needed unless there is a lump sum which can be found such as by selling a house. However, the important aspect is to work out the maximum sum which can be afforded and to offer that.

It is unlikely that an IVA will be agreed for a person on income support. Although there is no legal restriction, creditors are unlikely in practice to agree.

If the creditors approve the IVA, they must also approve the appointment of the **supervisor** who oversees it. In practice, the supervisor is usually the nominee who thus has a further change of title.

It is possible for the creditors not to agree an IVA or to vary the terms of any proposal. If an IVA cannot be agreed, the usual consequence is that the debtor is bankrupted.

Contents of IVA

An IVA will always include details of assets, liabilities and income of the debtor. This will include what assets the debtor is allowed to keep for his own use.

Where the debtor does not wholly own but has an interest in any property, such as in a family home or a business, the IVA will include specific proposals on that interest.

It is usual to include a **windfall clause**. This means that if the debtor receives any unbudgeted income during the period, such as a prize, bonus or inheritance, that windfall is added to the income for the benefit of the creditors.

An IVA will often include provisions for amending payments if the debtor's circumstances change, for the better or the worse. A common provision is to allow a longer period for the repayment of debts if the debtor's income falls.

Where the debtor has any kind of partner, the IVA does not affect that partner directly. So if the debtor and his wife jointly own property, or the debtor and a business partner jointly own a business, the IVA does not restrict the creditors pursuing the wife or business partner for the debt. In reality, the position of any partner is considered when making the IVA.

An IVA usually includes the provision that if the debtor fails to comply with its terms, the supervisor may petition to make the debtor bankrupt.

Operation of IVA

The supervisor is responsible for ensuring that the provisions of an IVA are carried out. So if the proposal includes the debtor paying £1,000 a month to creditors, the supervisor is responsible for ensuring that this happens. The supervisor may always apply to the court for directions.

If the debtor's circumstances change, the IVA may include provisions on how its terms are to be amended. If the change is outside the scope of any such provision, the supervisor may call another meeting of creditors.

If the debtor owns a house or other property, an IVA will usually expect a person to raise money against the property. This is known as **IVA equity release**. This is usually done in the fourth or fifth year of the IVA, which is much later than for bankruptcy. This is usually arranged by a specialist mortgage adviser. If it is possible to realize a large amount of equity, this may be arranged earlier to end the IVA earlier, but this should be checked with the insolvency practitioner.

Otherwise, the equity release often takes the form of a new mortgage, provided that the repayments do not exceed the monthly amount being paid under the IVA. So if the debtor was paying £300 a month to creditors under the IVA, the maximum mortgage would be £300. If a 25-year mortgage can be agreed at a rate of 5.25%, this would create an equity release of about £50,000. If the debtor does not want to take on a new mortgage or increase an existing mortgage, it is acceptable for a family member to provide the same amount of money for an interest in the property. The creditors' objective is to secure their money, not to inconvenience or punish the debtor.

Provided the debtor complies with the terms of an IVA, when it finishes, any debts which remain unpaid are extinguished. The debtor has wiped the slate clean and may start again.

Bankruptcy

The last and most serious form of insolvency procedure is bankruptcy. The debtor's assets (or most of them) are taken and sold to raise funds to pay the debts.

The purpose of bankruptcy is not to punish the debtor but to pay the creditors as much as possible while allowing the bankrupt a second chance in life. The possessions of the bankrupt are not taken from him as a punishment, but purely for the money their sale can realize. If a possession will not realize any money, it will not be taken.

A common scenario for bankruptcy is a home-owner whose debts are so great that they cannot afford the repayments required by any other form of insolvency procedure. Losing their home is the only solution. They have no choice.

For those who do not own property, bankruptcy can be an attractive prospect as there is little to lose.

A close relative, such as a parent in a home, may suggest that he or she borrows the money to clear their son's or daughter's debts and then the parent declares bankruptcy where the consequences are much less severe. Such an idea will not work. The money given to the bankrupt will be seized by a court order and the debtor is back in the original position.

The bankrupt is under severe restrictions for a period when he is known as an **undischarged bankrupt**. When this period is over, any outstanding debts are wiped out. The debtor is then said to be a **discharged bankrupt**. Although the debts are gone, the record and stigma remain. Credit reference agencies hold details of the bankruptcy for at least six years. In practice, a discharged bankrupt can still find life tough.

About 30,000 people a year were declared bankrupt until 2004 when the number exceeded 46,000. This large increase was due to the relaxation of restrictions introduced that year.

Scope of debts

Bankruptcy is intended to wipe out a person's debts. However, some debts are not wiped out by bankruptcy and remain payable. These are:

- student loans
- court fines
- maintenance orders and Child Support Agency orders
- repayments due to the Social Fund or of certain social security benefits.

If most of a person's debt comprises debts in the classes above, it is unlikely that bankruptcy will achieve anything.

Consequences of bankruptcy

It cannot be stressed too much that bankruptcy is an extreme step which must be carefully considered with proper independent advice. In particular, a debtor should consider whether an IVA is more appropriate.

The consequences of bankruptcy are:

- the bankrupt loses most of his possessions and money permanently
- a bankrupt is barred from being a company director, or involved in the administration of a company or charity
- a bankrupt cannot hold any public office, such as councillor or school governor
- a bankrupt cannot obtain credit for more than £500 without disclosing that he is an undischarged bankrupt (which will almost certainly mean that he will not be given credit)
- a bankrupt cannot open a bank account without disclosing that he is an undischarged bankrupt (which usually means that he cannot open an account at all)
- there are certain professions, particularly accountant and solicitor, which cannot be practised while bankrupt
- some contracts, such as tenancy agreements, have automatic termination clauses
- there is still some stigma attached to being bankrupt

- even after discharge, there is a record of the bankruptcy readily available for six years which can seriously compromise the person's ability to obtain credit afterwards
- utility companies (gas, electricity, water etc.) may require security or insist on a pre-payment meter after bankruptcy. They cannot, though, make future supply conditional on paying pre-bankruptcy debts.

Comparison of IVA and bankruptcy

Both IVA and bankruptcy have their advantages and disadvantages. The advantages of an IVA over bankruptcy are:

- the debtor does not lose all his possessions and money, only those which are agreed as part of the IVA
- the debtor is not under any restrictions with regard to being a director, seeking credit, holding public office, or opening a bank account
- there is no equivalent to a bankruptcy restriction order, which can last for up to 17 years after the insolvency
- a student loan is included in an IVA but not in bankruptcy
- there are not the same difficulties about practising law or finance
- an IVA does not stop someone from working in the police or armed forces
- an IVA does not automatically trigger any termination clause in a tenancy agreement
- an IVA can allow a trader to keep stock, so a retail or manufacturing trade can continue
- an IVA does not have the same stigma as bankruptcy
- any property owned by a bankrupt debtor must generally be sold immediately or after one year
- an IVA is not advertised in a local newspaper, so there is less chance of neighbours, friends, relations and employers finding out.

The advantages of bankruptcy over an IVA are:

- the restrictions usually last for just one year whereas an IVA typically lasts for five years
- payments from income to creditors are typically required for three years, rather than five years for an IVA
- bankruptcy usually has a clear end date, whereas an IVA is more easily extended
- an IVA involves a long and possibly difficult process of negotiation with creditors, whereas bankruptcy follows laid-down rules
- bankruptcy has lower costs, particularly if the creditors present the petition.

In terms of the stress and other impact on the debtor, the two methods each have advantages and disadvantages. Bankruptcy has the advantages of certainty and (probably) a shorter period of restriction, whereas an IVA has less stigma and more privacy. If the debtor is reluctant to face reality and still nurtures unrealistic hopes, bankruptcy is more likely to bring him to his senses, albeit brutally.

It should always be remembered that a debtor may not have a choice. If creditors are determined to bankrupt the debtor, little can be done to stop them.

Bankruptcy initiated by creditors is most likely when:

- there is more than one large debt (such as loans from different lenders and credit card companies)
- there are insufficient assets to cover the debts
- the debtor has a low income
- the debtor has been irresponsible in managing his finance; or
- there is no real prospect of any significant improvement in the debtor's finances.

Process of bankruptcy

The process of bankruptcy starts with a petition which must be presented by one of:

- the debtor himself
- creditors who are owed at least £750; or
- the supervisor of a failed IVA (see page 229).

Two or more creditors may jointly present a petition. So if a debtor owes £400 to each of five creditors, any two of them may jointly present a petition.

Bankruptcy is not a form of enforcing judgments obtained in the courts (see page 161). A court is unlikely to grant a petition simply where the debtor has assets to satisfy the judgment but the creditor is having difficulty getting paid. Bankruptcy is a procedure intended to balance the competing needs between giving creditors as much of what is owed to them as is possible and allowing the debtor a second chance in life.

A person may be made bankrupt if they are domiciled in England and Wales, or if they are a member of another state in the European Union (other than Denmark and some recent members) and have lived in England and Wales or have run a business here in the previous three years. **Domicile** is a legal term which describes the country a person regards as his natural home. A person may only have one domicile even if he has dual nationality or is resident in more than one country. A domicile is normally the country in which you are born, but it can change where there are clear indications that you have adopted another country.

Whoever presents the petition must pay court fees. In 2007, this comprised a court fee of £140 and a deposit of £310. The court has limited discretion to waive the fee, but not the deposit. If a debtor cannot raise the deposit, the only choice is to wait for a creditor to present the petition.

The petition must be accompanied by a **statement of affairs**. This is a form provided by the court. It has 13 sections as follows:

- personal details
- details of self-employment
- assets and their value
- secured and unsecured creditors
- bank accounts and credit cards
- employment and other income
- household expenditure and other outgoings
- property owned
- property disposed of in the previous five years
- details of household members and dependants
- causes of bankruptcy
- declaration
- continuation sheet.

Each section asks a series of questions. These must be answered as honestly and as comprehensively as possible. For some questions, it may be necessary to make an estimate, such as in how much a house is worth. The fact that an estimate subsequently proves to be wrong does not make the statement dishonest, provided the answers were reasonable given what the debtor knew at the time.

A copy of this form should be kept by the debtor. If the debtor does become bankrupt, many of the questions will be asked again by the Official Receiver (see page 238).

Some points are worth noting about this form.

Asset values must be based on what they could be sold for. This is likely to be much less than the amount paid for the asset. Looking at the prices fetched for equivalent items on a website like eBay can give a pretty good idea. The asset value is much less than the value for which it is insured or the 'net book value' at which it may appear in any accounts. A car is valued at what is known as 'bottom book value'. However, many assets may not be seized at all (see page 242).

Bankruptcy is no respecter of **sentimental value** or family **heirlooms**.

If assets belong to a bankrupt, they can be seized and sold to realize funds for the creditors. If a family wishes to keep heirlooms, this should be arranged by a family member promptly, making clear that they will buy the heirloom for a sum *greater than its realizable value*. The IP is obliged to accept the best price.

If it is impossible to value an asset, it must still be disclosed and the words 'unsure of value' written in the box.

Income refers only to regular income. This normally includes all income coming into the household even if that income does not belong to the debtor. Income includes social security benefits.

Expenditure requires just one figure for household expenditure. It is not necessary to give separate figures for food, petrol, newspapers etc. Although the form lists the most usual forms of expenditure, all details must be given, including any unusual expenditure.

Property must be disclosed if it is owned or rented by the debtor. Property must be listed even if the debtor does not own a property, such as where an insolvent man lives in a house owned by his solvent wife. The law may still regard the debtor as having a financial interest in the property, which can come as a most unpleasant shock to the wife. Where the debtor rents property, there is unlikely to be any issue for the landlord, but such property details must be disclosed.

Section 9 requires details of any **property disposed** of during the previous five years. Property includes anything of value, and is not limited to land and buildings. It can include jewellery, household goods or even intangible rights such as a copyright.

This section includes property which is sold as well as property given away. This is intended to stop people who know they face bankruptcy from frustrating their creditors by first giving away or selling their property to friends and family. If a man gives away his home to his wife three years before going bankrupt, the trustee in bankruptcy will simply demand that the home be given back. Even if goods are disposed of by a legal contract, the trustee may reverse the contract where it is designed to frustrate the bankruptcy. If a car worth £10,000 is sold to the debtor's brother for £1,000 four years before bankruptcy, the trustee will reverse the sale and claim the car back. The brother will rank as an unsecured creditor for his £1,000, which will usually mean that he receives little or none of his money back.

A trustee will not usually seek to reverse gifts or contracts if they appear to be genuine and reasonable transactions. Goods sold to a stranger at a reasonable price will not be reversed. Similarly a £10 Christmas present to a nephew is unlikely to be reclaimed. However, any large gift may be reclaimed. A payment of £10,000 to help a son or daughter buy a house is likely to be reclaimed however innocently that gift was intended and however much of a problem this creates for the son or daughter. The principle is that a bankrupt must be fair to creditors before being generous to his friends.

The restrictions imposed on a bankrupt and the time taken to be discharged can depend on how the bankrupt has behaved. Any blatant attempt to frustrate bankruptcy by disposing of property is seen as bad behaviour and will prolong the bankruptcy. In determining this, the court will look at the facts around the gift or undervalue contract when made. If a parent could reasonably spare £10,000 to help a son or daughter set up home and then was bankrupted by unforeseeable events, there is clearly no frustration, though it is still likely that the son or daughter will be required to hand back the £10,000.

Causes of bankruptcy require disclosure of when the person first became unable to pay debts. It also asks some specific questions on such matters as to whether the debtor gambled. Great care must be exercised in completing this form, as indications of irresponsible behaviour can lead to a bankruptcy restriction order (see page 240).

Creditors' petition

An alternative to the debtor making himself bankrupt is to let the creditors do it.

Bankruptcy is not a means of enforcing a court judgment. Although this has always been the law, it has now been explicitly confirmed by the Court of Appeal in the case *John Henry Popely v Ronald Albert Popely [2004] EWCA Civ 463*.

Also, bankruptcy must be for the benefit of *all* creditors, not just those creditors who present the petition. It is possible for a creditor to bankrupt a person, pay all the costs, and then find that other creditors receive all the money realized. For this reason, a creditor is only likely to institute bankruptcy proceedings if owed a significant sum and the bankrupt has significant assets.

A creditor starts the process by either serving a statutory demand on the debtor or by unsuccessfully attempting to enforce a court judgment by execution against goods (see page 161).

A **statutory demand** is sent by the creditor directly to the debtor. A statutory demand is not issued by the court, or even seen by the court at this stage. It is a formal notice demanding payment of a sum owed, to be paid either in a single payment or in a form acceptable to the creditor, such as by instalments. Strictly, the creditor does not need to have a court judgment to issue a statutory demand. In practice, a creditor is unwise to issue a statutory demand in the absence of a judgment as the debtor could then challenge the debt in the bankruptcy proceedings.

Despite what the Court of Appeal has said, some businesses issue statutory demands as a means of debt collection. Even if you suspect that this is the case, the statutory demand must not be ignored.

If the debtor has concluded that bankruptcy is the best option (i.e. the least worst option), the procedure is to do nothing but let the bankruptcy proceed. Bearing in mind that the behaviour of the bankrupt is closely monitored, it may be better in such cases to write to the creditor explaining that bankruptcy is accepted by the debtor.

If the debtor wishes to avoid bankruptcy, the choices are:

- to apply for an administration order (see page 221)
- to apply for an IVA (see page 224)
- make a payment which clears the debt or reduces it to less than £750
- offer to make payment in instalments
- offer a voluntary charge over any property; or
- apply to set aside the statutory demand.

An application to set aside a statutory demand must be made to the district judge in the local county court on payment of a fee which is £60 in 2007. A debtor can apply for this fee to be waived in certain cases.

The application to set aside a statutory demand must be on one of these grounds:

- there is a real dispute about the amount owed
- the debtor has a claim against the creditor for the same or greater amount
- the creditor holds security sufficient to cover the debt
- the debt is statute-barred (more than six years old); or
- there is a procedural irregularity, such as not signing the demand.

The first of these cannot be used if the creditor already has a court judgment. If a creditor issues a statutory demand without a court judgment, there must be a **genuine triable issue**. This means a real dispute which needs a court to resolve. A debtor cannot set aside a statutory demand by inventing a dispute.

If a debtor admits owing money to the creditor, but disputes the amount, the debtor is expected to pay the undisputed amount. Unless judgment has been granted, the debtor may apply to set aside a statutory demand for the disputed amount.

A statutory demand cannot be set aside on the basis that a creditor has rejected or even refused to consider a reasonable offer of repayment.

The next step is for the creditor to present a petition to the court. This must be accompanied by fees and an affidavit confirming that the facts stated in the petition are true. The petition must be served personally on the debtor. Even at this stage, bankruptcy can be avoided by making a payment, making an acceptable offer or seeking an IVA.

The next step is the **bankruptcy hearing** before a district judge. The creditor must prove that the petition was personally served on the debtor and must file a certificate stating that the debt is still outstanding. It is at this stage that a court can stay bankruptcy proceedings if the debtor makes what seems a reasonable offer of payment to the creditor.

It is quite common for the debtor and creditor to reach a provisional agreement at this point. In such cases, the court will adjourn the hearing. This temporarily stops the bankruptcy from proceeding while keeping the process alive. The court can order further adjournments, but these should not be agreed if there is no realistic prospect of paying the debt to the reasonable satisfaction of the creditor.

In the absence of any stayed or adjourned proceedings, the judge makes a bankruptcy order. The debtor is now a bankrupt and subject to restrictions.

When a bankruptcy order is made

When a bankruptcy order is made, the court notifies the **Official Receiver**, a government officer.

The Official Receiver contacts the bankrupt promptly, often on the same day. The Official Receiver's duties are to:

- investigate the bankrupt's conduct and financial affairs, and report to the court
- obtain control of the bankrupt's property and gain custody of relevant documents.

The bankrupt will be sent a questionnaire to complete. If the debtor presented his own petition, many of the questions will repeat those already given on the statement of affairs (see page 234). The questionnaire is followed by an interview.

If the bankrupt has recently traded or has been bankrupt before, the Official Receiver will usually want to interview the bankrupt in person at the Official Receiver's offices. Otherwise the interview is usually conducted by telephone. The interview checks the answers given and will sometimes seek additional information.

A bankrupt is expected to co-operate with the Official Receiver. Any non-co-operation will almost certainly delay discharge from bankruptcy and could result in tougher bankruptcy restriction orders. In serious cases, the bankrupt may commit a bankruptcy offence which can lead to a criminal prosecution. If the Official Receiver is not satisfied with the bankrupt's answers, an application may be made for the bankrupt to be questioned in court.

For the bankrupt, these court appearances and interviews may be a terrifying ordeal. To the judge, Official Receiver and insolvency practitioner, it is just another day's work. Provided the bankrupt co-operates, there is no reason for any of these people to be unpleasant.

The Official Receiver will:

- register the bankruptcy at the Land Registry
- usually advertise the bankruptcy in the *London Gazette* and one local newspaper
- freeze all the bankrupt's bank accounts
- report any criminal offences discovered to the appropriate authority
- visit any *business* premises of the bankrupt.

The Official Receiver may:

- visit the home of the bankrupt
- seize any items of value belonging to the bankrupt.

Both of these eventualities are rare in practice.

The Official Receiver usually investigates the causes of the bankruptcy unless he considers this unnecessary, such as when the cause is obvious.

Every creditor is sent a letter by the Official Receiver inviting them to **prove** their claims. The word 'prove' here is used in a legal sense. It simply requires the creditors to submit their claims, not to provide any evidence to support them.

Within 12 weeks of the bankruptcy order, the Official Receiver either appoints a trustee in bankruptcy or acts as such himself. A **trustee in bankruptcy** is an insolvency practitioner, typically a qualified accountant with a licence to practise in insolvency work. The trustee owns the bankrupt's property and must apply it for the benefit of creditors.

Once the trustee is appointed, the bankrupt loses ownership of all his property with a few exceptions. The bankrupt is not allowed to sell any property without the trustee's permission (because all the property now legally belongs to the trustee). If an arrangement to sell was made before the appointment, and the sale is a legitimate one, the trustee will usually agree to it. For example, a trader may continue to trade at least up to the appointment of a trustee. Genuine commercial sales agreed before the appointment will be honoured after the appointment.

A bank will dishonour all cheques issued by the bankrupt before the bankruptcy order but presented afterwards, unless the bank did not have notice of the order when the cheque was honoured or it is not reasonably practical for the bank to recover payment.

Bankruptcy restriction orders

In addition to making a person bankrupt, the court may impose bankruptcy restriction orders (BROs) or accept bankruptcy restriction undertakings (BRUs). The difference is that a BRU is offered by the bankrupt himself. A BRO is involuntary. The consequences of a BRO and BRU are otherwise exactly the same, and all references below to a BRO apply equally to a BRU. This regime of BROs and BRUs was introduced on 1 April 2004 and so may be unfamiliar to those with earlier experience of bankruptcy.

A BRO lasts for between two and 15 years. The court makes a BRO if it believes this to be 'appropriate having regard to the conduct of the bankrupt'.

The following factors make a BRO likely:

- failing to keep proper records, as a consequence of which property was lost in the two years before the bankruptcy
- failing to produce records as demanded by the Official Receiver or trustee in bankruptcy
- making a transaction at undervalue
- making excessive pension contributions
- failing to supply goods or services for which the customer has paid, and for which the customer could therefore claim in the bankruptcy
- trading before bankruptcy when the bankrupt knew, or should have known, that he would be unable to pay his debts
- incurring any debt which the bankrupt had no reasonable expectation of being able to pay
- failing properly to account for any loss or insufficiency of property
- gambling, or indulging in any rash or speculative activity after the presentation of the bankruptcy petition
- any extravagant expenditure after presentation of the bankruptcy petition
- any neglect of business affairs which has contributed to or exacerbated the effects of the bankruptcy
- fraud
- breach of trust
- failing to co-operate with the Official Receiver or trustee in bankruptcy.

Some of these factors have specific time limits set on them. For others, there is no set time limit as such, but the longer ago the factor occurred, the less seriously it is likely to be regarded.

The fact that a person has been bankrupted before does not in itself justify a BRO. However, if a person has been bankrupted in the previous six years, that may be considered in determining how seriously one of the above factors should be regarded.

Someone facing bankruptcy may be tempted to blow money on one final extravagance or to place a bet in one last desperate effort to realize funds. The attitude may be 'I have nothing to lose'. In reality there is much to lose, such as early discharge from bankruptcy and freedom from a BRO.

Another temptation is **squirrelling**. This is simply hiding assets where the Official Receiver or trustee in bankruptcy cannot find them. This can be as crude as burying a box containing bank notes. More commonly, squirrelling involves passing money or an asset to a friend or relation and telling them to say that this belongs to them and not the bankrupt. Doing this is a criminal offence by both the bankrupt and the friend. Sometimes assets are hidden in bank deposit boxes or in facilities offered by storage companies. Trustees in bankruptcy are knowledgeable in such ploys and have means to detect them.

At this stage, the bankrupt can feel totally demoralized and humiliated. This is not the purpose of bankruptcy, but can be its consequence. Depending on the bankrupt's personality, this may manifest itself in 'giving up the ghost' and just not bothering at all. Another possibility is that the bankrupt wishes to assert what little dignity he has left by stubbornness or asserting rights he does not have. Both of these possibilities should be strenuously resisted. Although a bankrupt should be treated with civility and understanding, the process will not be stopped because of the consequences. Bankruptcy is already a concession to the debtor in allowing him to escape paying all his debts. The bankrupt should adopt an attitude of meek compliance in the knowledge that he is still a person with all rights and dignities. Meekness and compliance will reduce the effects of bankruptcy and BRO.

Another consequence of bankruptcy is embarrassment. Some bankrupts have compared it with parading naked in public, as details of the bankrupt's failings are exposed to public view. Yet a bankrupt would probably have no objection to undressing for medical treatment. Similarly, the Official Receiver, the trustee in bankruptcy, the judge and probably even the officials who represent major creditors such as the bank or the tax authority will probably have a similar detached and non-judgmental view of the bankrupt's position. They have seen it all before, and are simply doing their job.

Against this, many bankrupts can find this stage a huge relief. The problems are being solved, no creditors are hassling, the trustee in bankruptcy proves to be a very pleasant and reasonable person, normal daily life continues, the end is in sight, and it is all not as bad as they feared. Encourage such a positive attitude.

A BRO continues some of the restrictions of bankruptcy after a person has been discharged from bankruptcy. Such restrictions commonly restrict acting as a director or obtaining credit. Non-compliance with a BRO is a bankruptcy offence.

The BRO starts from the date of discharge, so if the discharge is suspended, this automatically defers the starting date of the BRO.

There is a procedure for a submission of evidence and hearings to determine the scope of a BRO. The Secretary of State for Trade and Industry (or someone acting on his behalf) must present the evidence to the court. It is necessary to show that the bankrupt engaged in misconduct only on the balance of probabilities. Because of the delay in obtaining a BRO, it is possible for an interim BRO to be issued until the matter is settled.

A bankrupt who accepts misconduct may agree to a BRU which avoids the procedure as there is no need to prove what is admitted. It must be understood that there is no question of plea-bargaining in this. A person cannot admit to a lesser offence to get a shorter BRU to avoid a longer BRO. There may be a slight advantage in that agreeing a BRU demonstrates co-operation, but there must never be any pressure on a bankrupt to admit to misconduct unless he honestly agrees with it.

The length of the order depends on the seriousness of the offence. A less serious offence attracts a BRO of 2 to 5 years, a moderately serious offence from 6 to 10 years, and a very serious offence from 11 to 15 years.

Vesting of goods

When the trustee in bankruptcy is appointed, most of the bankrupt's goods legally belong to the trustee and not to the bankrupt. This transfer of ownership is known as **vesting**.

The two exceptions in law are:

- household goods for basic living
- tools of the trade.

A bankrupt must be allowed to continue living normally and to be able to work. In each case, the excepted goods must be necessary for basic living or the trade. Items which the trustee considers are not necessary pass to the trustee.

Household goods includes bedding, clothes, furniture, crockery and cutlery, fridge and cooker, and most other household items. Household goods must be sufficient for the bankrupt and his household. Exceptions may be made for particularly luxurious items, such as antiques, works of art, expensive watches, fur coats or particularly expensive music systems. To protect heirlooms, see page 234.

Although this provision of bankruptcy law has remained unchanged for over 100 years, the scope of basic living has changed hugely. In the 1950s, a radio was considered a luxury. Today a trustee in bankruptcy is likely to allow the bankrupt to keep a colour television, video recorder, DVD player and cable or satellite TV system. In any event, trustees in bankruptcy usually do not take goods where the realizable value is less than £500. So even goods for which the debtor paid £1,500 can be safe.

Tools of a trade include any vehicle which is necessary for the trade, such as a delivery van. There is no exemption for the stock in any trade which is vested in the trustee and usually sold for whatever can be obtained. Many retail and production businesses shut down when the proprietor becomes bankrupt.

A **car** or other vehicle not used for work will usually be vested in the trustee for realization. If a bankrupt believes that a car is essential for his work, he must argue the case with the trustee. The only argument likely to succeed is that travel is essential for work and that public transport is unreliable. Even if the trustee does agree, he will usually insist on an inexpensive car and require any quality car to be sold. A trustee will otherwise require the sale of a car even if its realizable value is less than £500, as ownership of a car represents a continuing liability (such as insurance and road tax) and the trustee's duties include minimizing liabilities. Bankruptcy does not affect the bankrupt's driving licence, so he may still drive a car belonging to someone else.

The trustee in bankruptcy may disclaim **onerous property**. This is where the realizable value of the property is less than any amount owed on it. Suppose a car was bought for £20,000 of which £18,000 is owing to the hire purchase company when the car has a second-hand value of £10,000. The trustee in bankruptcy simply ends the HP agreement and tells the hire purchase company to take the car back. The hire purchase company has no say in the matter. The car is theirs and they have no further claim for their money.

A bankrupt may still have an income from employment, trading, royalties or other sources. This income legally belongs to the bankrupt, at least initially. A bankrupt must be allowed reasonable income to pay for living expenses of his household. The bankrupt is not restricted to the levels laid down for income support. The calculation allows for such contributions from other members of the household as it is reasonable to expect them to make, regardless of what amounts they actually do pay. Income left over is called **available income**. If the available income is at least £100 a month, the trustee in bankruptcy will seek an agreement with the bankrupt for some of the income to be regularly paid to the trustee. The agreed amount is then set out in an **income payments order.**

If a figure cannot be agreed, the trustee in bankruptcy may apply to the court to determine the amount of the payment. Such a payment cannot be made for more than three years, though a further order may then be sought. An order is usually for between half and two-thirds of available income. An order automatically expires when the bankruptcy is discharged. Either the trustee or bankrupt may apply to the court for the order to be varied at any time.

Income payments orders are made in just 10% of bankruptcies. Almost all of them are for amounts agreed between the bankrupt and trustee.

The position on **pensions** depends on whether the scheme has been approved by HMRC (or Inland Revenue before April 2005). If the scheme has been approved, the pension fund itself is protected and does not vest in the trustee in bankruptcy. This applies to both personal pension plans and occupational pension plans. If the pension scheme has not been approved (which is unlikely in practice), the funds do vest in the trustee in bankruptcy. This is the law as it applies from 29 May 2000.

Where payments from a pension scheme are made, they are usually regarded as earnings and can therefore be subject to an income payments order.

From 6 April 2002, a bankrupt may apply to the court for an **exclusion order** to allow for payments from a pension scheme to be not subject to an income payments order, or for an unapproved scheme not to vest in the trustee in bankruptcy.

Student loans are not regarded as part of a bankrupt's estate and so do not vest in the trustee. The downside is that (from 1 July 2004) they are excluded from bankruptcy completely, so a discharged bankrupt is still liable to repay the full amount of the loan.

Owner-occupied homes are part of the bankrupt's estate, even if the home is co-owned by another person, such as a husband or wife. Whatever interest the bankrupt has in the home is vested in the trustee in bankruptcy, who registers that interest with the Land Registry.

The trustee in bankruptcy must try to realize the value of the home. If it is co-owned, the easiest option is to sell it to the co-owner. Suppose a home is worth £300,000 and owned by a bankrupt man and his solvent wife. The trustee in bankruptcy will invite the wife to buy out the half of the house she does not own, possibly by the wife taking out a new mortgage. The trustee in bankruptcy will often be willing to sell a half interest for a little less than half its full value to reflect the saving of time and expenses in selling the home. If the house has negative equity or very little equity, it may be possible for the co-owner to buy out the interest for a nominal sum like £1.

If it is not possible to sell the home to a co-owner, of if there is no co-owner, the trustee in bankruptcy will put the property on the market. Since 1 April 2004, the trustee has three years from the date of the bankruptcy order to sell a property which is the main home of the bankrupt or the bankrupt's husband or wife, or former husband or wife. The trustee does not have to sell the property before the bankruptcy is discharged. It is possible, and frequently happens, that a bankrupt is discharged and his home is subsequently sold and the money distributed between creditors.

If the property is not sold within three years, the property reverts to the bankrupt unless within that period the trustee

(a) realizes the interest, usually by selling what the bankrupt had owned to a partner or someone else; or
(b) applies for an order for the sale or possession of the property; or
(c) applies for a charging order in respect of the bankrupt's interest; or
(d) comes to another agreement with the bankrupt.

These four options are roughly in the order of popularity of the options. Option (d) is most unlikely as the trustee's job is to realize assets for the creditors.

If the bankrupt's interest in the property is less than £1,000, options (b) and (c) are not available to the trustee.

If the bankrupt's property is the home of a husband, wife or civil partner, that person has a limited right to residence even if the partner is not a co-owner. The trustee in bankruptcy usually seeks a court order to sell a co-owned property. If children also live in the home, such a court order is essential. The law is that the interests of the family must be considered for one year. After this, the interests of the creditors take precedence. In practice, this means that homes where other people live are not sold for one year.

In deciding to sell a home which is lived in by (say) the wife of a bankrupt, the court will consider:

- the creditors' interests
- whether the wife contributed to the bankruptcy
- the needs of the wife and of any children
- other relevant circumstances.

The court will not consider the bankrupt's needs.

Someone other than a partner or child of the bankrupt does not have the same right. However, such a person may have contributed to the purchase of the property. If so, this can create an equitable interest giving them a right to payment from the proceeds even when their name is not on the deeds.

If a property is sold, any co-owner is entitled to their share of the net proceeds. The rest is vested in the trustee in bankruptcy.

It is possible for a home to have **negative equity**, that is, when the value of the property is less than the amount still owed on the mortgage (see page 112). In such a case, the Official Receiver will still take ownership of the house but the debtor should approach the Official Receiver with a view to buying back the house for a nominal sum, typically £1, plus solicitor's fees. Failing this, the Official Receiver will keep the property for up to three years. The debtor will lose any benefit from that property increasing in value during that period. If the Official Receiver does not sell the property within the three years, the property must be returned to the debtor.

Discharge from bankruptcy

Under the law from 2004, discharge from bankruptcy is automatic after 12 months unless the Official Receiver or trustee in bankruptcy satisfies the court that the bankrupt has not complied with his obligations. If the court is so persuaded, the discharge may be suspended for either a set period or until the bankrupt complies with a specific condition.

It is possible for a bankrupt to be discharged in less than 12 months if the bankrupt has co-operated fully with the Official Receiver, trustee and creditors, and the creditors have not raised any matter which requires further investigation.

A bankruptcy order may be **annulled** by the court at any time if either

- the estate is found to have realized enough money to pay all the creditors in full; or
- there were insufficient grounds to have made the bankruptcy order in the first place.

If the order is annulled, the person ceases to be bankrupt and becomes fully liable for all his debts again.

There is a separate procedure whereby the court may **rescind** a bankruptcy order where there has been a change of circumstances and rescission is to the benefit of creditors.

Scotland

Scotland has a different personal insolvency law from England and Wales. The main law is the Bankruptcy (Scotland) Acts 1985 and 1993, and Insolvency (Scotland) Rules 1986.

Scottish insolvency is overseen by the Accountant in Bankruptcy (AIB) based in Kilwinning; the website is www.aib.gov.uk. For companies, the insolvency processes such as receivership and liquidation are the same as for England and Wales.

As with other parts of the UK, a debtor is free to negotiate with creditors directly to see if an informal agreement can be reached to pay debts without involving any insolvency procedures.

Failing any informal procedure, there are three formal insolvency procedures:

- debt arrangement scheme
- trust deed
- sequestration.

Debt recovery in Scotland usually starts with a court issuing a **decree**. This is a formal statement of the court that one person owes money to another. It is the equivalent of a judgment in England and Wales.

Debt arrangement scheme

A **debt arrangement scheme (DAS)** is a procedure to help people with less serious financial problems. DASs were introduced from 30 November 2004 under Debt Arrangement Scheme (Scotland) Regulations 2004.

Strictly, this is not an insolvency procedure at all, as no restrictions are imposed on the debtor and it is intended to pay all debts in full. A DAS imposes some discipline on the debtor, gives some certainty to creditors and avoids the expenses and inconvenience of formal insolvency procedures. If there is no prospect of paying all debts in full, a DAS may not be used, and a trust deed should be considered.

Under a DAS, someone with many debts is introduced to a money adviser, usually based in a Citizens' Advice Bureau or Money Advice Centre. A DAS must be agreed by

- the debtor; and
- a majority of creditors.

A dissenting creditor has a limited right of appeal to the courts. Otherwise an agreed DAS is binding on all creditors.

A DAS must be registered with the AIB. The existence of a DAS protects the debtor from formal insolvency proceedings.

No charges are made at all to the debtor and no expenses of the DAS are deducted from the realization of assets. A charge of up to 5 % may be made to *the creditors*.

In a DAS, the debtor and creditors agree on a repayment plan. The DAS lasts for as long as is necessary to clear the debts. The DAS appoints someone as **payments distributor**, who is often the money adviser. The debtor makes regular payments to the payments distributor who then distributes the payment to the creditors in proportion to their debt.

If the debtor is employed, the payments distributor may serve a notice on the employer requiring the employer to make regular deductions from the debtor's pay and send it directly to the payments distributor. Such a notice lasts for one year at a time, but may be revoked by the debtor or money adviser at any time. A form is provided for this purpose. An employer must comply with such a notice. When a DAS is completed and all debts fully paid, the payments distributor must notify the employer, who must not make any further deductions from pay. If an employer does refuse to co-operate, the employer can be forced to pay the sum demanded himself without being able to reclaim it from the debtor.

If the debtor fails to make payments, the DAS may be revoked. The debts remain, and a more formal procedure must be followed to obtain payment.

Trust deed

A **trust deed** is a halfway house between the informal DAS and very formal sequestration. It is less formal than an IVA. Under a trust deed, the debtor usually does not pay the full amount of the debts.

A trust deed is entirely voluntary on the part of the debtor. If the debtor agrees, his estate including all his property, possessions and money, are transferred to a trustee who realizes them for the benefit of creditors. There is no court procedure involved. A trust deed may be registered as a **protected trust deed**. This then makes the trust deed binding on all creditors. Commonly an interim trustee is appointed to act until a permanent trustee can be appointed. Both types of trustee are appointed by the court.

A trust deed which is not protected is called either an **unprotected trust deed** or simply a trust deed. An unprotected trust deed is rare in practice. An unprotected trust deed does not stop creditors starting sequestration procedures; a protected trust deed does. An unprotected trust deed does not require *all* of the debtor's possessions to vest in the trustee; it may transfer only some of them.

Under a protected trust deed, the possessions of the debtor are vested in a trustee. This is an insolvency practitioner, usually a specially trained accountant. Basic living items and tools of trade are protected, as in a sequestration (see page 242). The expenses of the trustee are paid from realizing the debtor's assets. The AIB provides a draft deed.

A trust deed includes such terms as may be agreed between the debtor and creditors. This includes how much of a person's regular income must be paid to the trustee.

The trust deed is signed by the debtor, usually on the advice of the insolvency practitioner, and sent to creditors. It is also published in the *Edinburgh Gazette*. Any creditors who are owed at least £1,500 have five weeks to object and petition for sequestration. They have a further week to lodge the petition.

A trust deed does not become protected if objections are received from either:

- over half of the creditors by number; or
- over one third of creditors in value.

If sufficient creditors do object, the trust deed is unprotected. This allows creditors or the debtor to petition for sequestration as explained below, if the relevant conditions are met.

Protected trust deeds are registered. The register is open for public inspection. Unprotected trust deeds are not registered.

If a debtor does not comply with the terms of a trust deed, the trustee may petition for sequestration.

The trust deed itself will determine how long it lasts. This is usually three years, but can be four or five. The end of the trust deed period wipes out any unpaid debts (other than those which cannot be wiped out, such as fines and overpayments of social security). There is one very rare exception if a creditor can prove to a court that he would have received more money if the debtor had been put into sequestration.

Signing a trust deed does not in itself prevent a person from being a company director or holding any public office. In practice many company articles and many public bodies' own rules prevent this.

Sequestration

Sequestration is very similar to bankruptcy. A trustee is appointed to collect the assets and realize their value for creditors. A debtor who co-operates with the trustee is automatically discharged after three years. The court can extend this period in certain circumstances, such as when there has not been co-operation. Extensions are usually for two years at a time.

Sequestration, like English bankruptcy, may be started by the debtor himself or by a creditor. A debtor may apply for sequestration if he owes at least £1,500 and is 'apparently insolvent', as explained below, and has not been sequestrated in the previous five years. Proceedings initiated by the debtor are called **self-sequestration**.

The creditor must first have obtained a decree from the court confirming that the debt is owed. Alternatively, sequestration can be initiated by a creditor in a DAS where the debtor has not kept to its terms.

If a debtor is not 'apparently insolvent' (see below), a debtor may still apply for self-sequestration if either:

- he has the agreement of a creditor or creditors to whom he owes at least £1,500; or
- he signed a trust deed but it did not become protected because a majority of creditors objected.

A creditor applies to the court's sheriff officer, who serves a **statutory demand** on the debtor, who has 21 days in which to pay.

The next step is for the debtor to be what is technically called **apparently insolvent**. This applies if:

- a creditor has obtained a decree and a **charge for payment** which gives 14 days for payment, and no payment has been made; or
- a government department or local authority has obtained a warrant against the debtor for non-payment of tax, council tax or similar; or
- a sheriff officer has served a statutory demand which has not been paid.

Sequestration may be started by a **qualified creditor**. This is someone to whom the debtor owes at least £1,500 and who has court decrees confirming these debts. Two or more creditors may jointly apply if their combined debts exceed £1,500. Application is made at either the local Sheriff Court or at the Court of Sessions in Edinburgh.

The court sends out a **warrant to cite** to the debtor. This requires the debtor to attend court in person unless he wishes the sequestration to proceed. A debtor may only stop the process at this stage if he attends court and demonstrates that he has either paid the debt or can guarantee payment. In the absence of that, the sequestration starts from the date of the warrant.

The court appoints an insolvency practitioner as trustee. The court may appoint the Accountant in Bankruptcy as trustee, in which case the work is done by her staff. A debtor or creditor may seek the appointment of an insolvency practitioner in the private sector.

The processes of marshalling and realizing the assets are largely identical to those in an English bankruptcy. There is an equivalent duty to co-operate honestly, and equivalent penalties for failing to do so. There is a similar exemption for basic living items and tools of the trade, except that there is a specific £1,000 value for tools which may be kept.

The restrictions during sequestration are also similar to those during English bankruptcy. A sequestrated debtor may not seek credit of more than £250 without disclosing the sequestration (compared with a £500 limit in England and Wales).

Every sequestration is announced in the *Edinburgh Gazette*, but there is no notice in a local newspaper.

Unpaid debts are written off when the sequestration is discharged. Unlike the English system, this may be years after the sequestration has finished.

A record of the sequestration is kept in a register known as the **sederunt book**. This record is permanent and public, and so may be inspected decades after the sequestration.

There is a separate procedure known as **sequestration for rent** which may be initiated by a landlord to recover rent arrears. This is not sequestration in the form of the bankruptcy procedure explained above.

There is also a **summary warrant** which can be granted to government bodies and local authorities for the recovery of taxes and fines.

Northern Ireland

Insolvency law in Northern Ireland changed on 27 March 2006 under the Insolvency (Northern Ireland) Order 2005. The previous law was the Insolvency (Northern Ireland) Order 2002.

This order basically brings Northern Ireland insolvency law into line with that of England and Wales. For example, the normal bankruptcy period is reduced from three years to one year. There is the same provision for bankruptcy restriction orders for up to 15 years.

There are the same options for administration orders, IVAs and bankruptcy.

13

Scams

Introduction

Con artists and scam merchants have been around from the earliest days. What is depressing is that scams are little changed from the earliest times (though they adapt to new situations), and that people still fall for them.

Anything that looks too good to be true probably is not true. In business, there is an expression 'there is no such thing as a free lunch'. This means that something which appears to be free always has a price somewhere.

Credit cards

One day a banker, a priest and a doctor were rowing a boat through shark-infested waters when they lost an oar. They cast lots to see who would risk swimming out to retrieve it. The banker lost and duly jumped overboard and started swimming. The others watched as a shark swam straight towards the banker, but then circled him before swimming away. The priest said, 'It is a miracle'. The doctor replied, 'No, just professional courtesy'.

The main banks, insurance companies and credit card providers do not tell lies. They do not need to with the ingenious ways they have found for telling the truth. Here are some examples.

No interest for six months

Credit cards often attract new business by offering a period of interest-free or low-interest borrowing, particularly on transferred balances, such as an interest-free period for six months.

The first point to note is that the interest may be free, but the transfer itself often is not. Typically a card company may charge 2% of the balance transferred. If you write a credit card cheque, you could find that you are charged £35 for it.

But perhaps more significantly, what they don't tell you is that any payments made during this period are first offset against the interest-free sum and only then against other borrowings.

Suppose you transfer a balance of £6,000 to a credit card on one of these interest-free loans for six months. You also use the card to buy £1,000 worth of goods each month, and pay £1,000 when you receive the statement. The company charges you (say) 1.5% a month interest on any balance other than the interest-free amount.

You might expect to find that the balance after six months is £6,000, as you have paid in full each month for your other purchases. Wrong! Each payment of £1,000 *reduces the interest-free sum first*. Figure 17 shows what happens to your account:

Month	Starting balance	Interest-free balance	Interest-bearing balance	Interest charge	New balance
	£	£	£	£	£
0	6,000.00	6,000.00	0.00	0.00	6,000.00
1	6,000.00	5,000.00	1,000.00	15.00	6,015.00
2	6,015.00	4,000.00	2,015.00	30.22	6,045.22
3	6,045.22	3,000.00	3,045.22	45.68	6,090.90
4	6,090.90	2,000.00	4,090.90	61.37	6,152.27
5	6,152.27	1,000.00	5,152.27	77.29	6,229.56
6	6,229.56	0.00	6,229.56	93.45	6,323.01

Figure 17: Credit card charges with an interest-free loan.

Your 'interest-free loan' has cost you £323.01 in interest in six months! This is the equivalent of an interest rate of over 11% a year.

The reason is that you have not had a loan of £6,000 for six months. The £1,000 you pay each month for your purchases first reduces the interest-free balance, so the part of the balance on which interest is charged does not reduce at all.

The supposed 'interest-free loan' has made life worse. If it were not there, you would at least be paying off some of your £1,000 worth of purchases each month, but with the 'interest-free loan' means that you are in effect paying off none of your purchases, so the interest keeps piling up.

If the credit card company charged you a 2% transfer fee, the situation would be even worse (Figure 18).

Figure 18: Credit card charges with a 2% transfer fee.

Month	Starting balance	Interest-free balance	Interest-bearing balance	Interest charge	New balance
	£	£	£	£	£
0	6,120.00	6,000.00	120.00	1.80	6,121.80
1	6,121.80	5,000.00	1,121.80	16.83	6,138.63
2	6,138.63	4,000.00	2,138.63	32.08	6,170.71
3	6,170.71	3,000.00	3,170.71	47.56	6,218.27
4	6,218.27	2,000.00	4,218.27	63.27	6,281.54
5	6,281.54	1,000.00	5,281.54	79.22	6,360.76
6	6,360.76	0.00	6,360.76	95.41	6,456.17

Here your 'interest-free borrowing' has you cost you £456.17 in interest over six months. This is the equivalent of an APR interest rate of 15.7%.

The Debt Doctor's Advice

If you do use an interest-free period, *do not use that card for anything else until the end of the period.* Make your purchases in another way, such as another card.

It may seem crazy that credit card companies will not waive interest in a way that should discourage anyone from using the card at all, but that is the exact position. It is because so few people realize this that they can legally charge 11% or more interest on 'interest-free borrowing'.

You need never miss a bargain again

This is only true if you pay the whole balance when your credit card statement arrives.

Imagine you have been admiring a coat in a shop window costing £200 but decide you cannot afford it. Then your dream comes true – it is offered in a sale for £100. You do not have £100 in cash on you, but you have your credit card and so you buy it and feel smug because you have saved yourself £100. But have you? Only if you pay the whole of the card bill when you receive it is the answer yes.

Suppose you just pay off the minimum 2% of the balance each month and are charged interest of 1.5% a month. The £100 for your account only appears on your credit card statement once. Thereafter it is simply lost in the balance brought forward each month. Figure 19 shows what happens to the £100.

Figure 19: Paying the minimum amount.

Month	Start balance	Minimum payment (2%)	Balance less payment	Interest charge (1.5%)	New balance
	£	£	£	£	£
1	100.00	2.00	98.00	1.47	99.47
2	99.47	1.99	97.48	1.46	98.94
3	98.94	1.98	96.96	1.45	98.41
4	98.41	1.96	96.45	1.45	97.90
5	97.90	1.96	95.94	1.44	97.38
6	97.38	1.95	95.43	1.43	96.86
7	96.86	1.94	94.92	1.42	96.34
8	96.34	1.92	94.42	1.42	95.84
9	95.84	1.92	93.92	1.41	95.33
10	95.33	1.91	93.42	1.40	94.82
11	94.82	1.90	92.92	1.40	94.32
12	94.32	1.90	92.42	1.40	93.82

These figures were calculated to five decimal places, so there may be some rounding differences.

After one year, you have paid £23.31 interest, but the debt has only reduced by £5.68 to £94.32. It is easy to see that, with an interest rate of 1.5% but only 2% paid off each month, about three-quarters of all your payments are interest charges and only a quarter of your payments reduce your debt.

If you paid off the balance of £94.32 after one year, you would have paid £117.62 for your £200 coat, which is still a bargain. But suppose you don't. Suppose you continue paying just the minimum amount. Using the same rates, Figure 20 shows what happens to the debt as the years pass by.

Figure 20: Cost of long-term use of a credit card.

Years since you bought coat	Total payments to coat	Amount still owed on coat	Cost of coat so far
	£	£	£
1	23.31	94.32	117.62
2	45.18	88.49	133.67
3	65.71	83.03	148.74
4	84.95	77.90	162.85
5	103.02	73.08	176.10
6	119.97	68.57	188.54
7	135.87	64.33	200.20
8	150.79	60.36	211.15
9	164.79	56.63	221.42
10	177.92	53.13	231.05
20	271.95	28.08	300.03
30	321.65	14.84	336.49
40	347.92	7.84	355.76
50	361.80	4.15	365.95
60	369.13	2.19	371.42
70	373.01	1.16	374.17
80	375.06	0.61	375.67
100	376.72	0.17	376.89

After seven years, you have paid more than the full price for the coat, and that may be the time that you throw the coat away! After ten years, you may not even still have the coat, but you still owe £53.13.

After ten years, you have paid off less than half the price.

Even after 30 years, you still owe one seventh of the price. Suppose you bought this fashionable coat when you were starting work at the age of 21, you will still owe £4.15 when you retire at 71, and are wearing different clothes.

The balance never reduces to zero, but the debt falls below half a penny (which is therefore rounded down to zero) after 150 years, by which time the interest payments will be £377.34. After infinite years, the total interest would be about £378.

However young you are when you spend, if you only make the minimum repayment each month on your credit card, the debt is only finally paid when you die.

Some of this cost is lessened by the impact of inflation over the years, but this is only marginal as most of the heavy charges are in the early years. The simple message is not to use a credit card for a 'bargain' unless you pay off the whole balance when you receive your credit card statement.

If you intend to pay just the minimum balance, multiply the bargain price by 3. Only if it is still a bargain should you buy it. If not, save yourself this long-term debt and look for a cheaper coat.

For just 75p a month per £100, we can insure the balance of your card should you be unable to pay

Payment protection insurance (PPI) for credit card balances is a rip-off. Always. No exceptions.

The sum of 75p a month equals £9 a year. If you have a card for 40 years' working life, you have paid £360 in premiums to insure £100 against something that probably never happened. And that is not a good bargain.

Suppose you did take PPI and something does happen, you lose your job or go into hospital. You will find that this protection plan does not simply wipe off the balance on your card. It:

• is subject to many exclusions
• is time-limited
• only pays off the balance.

Interest continues to be charged.

The protection is supposed to provide protection for loss of employment, but PPI is routinely sold to the unemployed and retired. Companies try to smuggle this in without drawing your attention to it.

As our example, we take one of the better (i.e. least bad) policies.

The policy provides cover for unemployment or disability, except for:

• card-holders over the age of 65
• card-holders who worked for fewer than 16 hours a week
• resignation, retirement, voluntary redundancy, or dismissal for misconduct
• unemployment which arises in the first 90 days of the policy.

A self-employed card-holder must prove an inability to find work, which is almost impossible in practice.

The policy provides cover for sickness and disability, except for:

- card-holders over the age of 65
- normal pregnancy and childbirth
- pre-existing medical conditions.

Cover only starts when the card-holder has registered for jobseeker's allowance. Payments are not made during any period covered by a payment in lieu.

The cover pays off 5% of the balance each month for up to 18 months for unemployment, or 24 months for sickness and injury. After this, you are liable to pay off the balance.

Suppose a 35-year-old card-holder with an average balance of £100 unthinkingly pays his 75p a month for 15 years. So he has paid £135 in premiums.

Then at the age of 50, he is made redundant. He is given a payment in lieu equal to three months' pay. He claims on his protection plan. There is no cover for the first three months because of the payment in lieu. (In practice, the card-holder would make some payments during these three months to avoid a late payment charge, but these are ignored below to illustrate the effect of the insurance policy.)

Assume that interest is calculated at 1.5% a month. Figure 21 shows what happens under the policy.

The cover stops when his 18-month period finishes. He still owes £54.29, which the insurance will not pay. In other words, his insurance has covered less than half the debt! If instead of paying his premiums for 15 years he invested each year's premiums at just 4% interest, he would have saved £187.41 guaranteed. Instead he spent it on insurance cover on which most people never claim, and when he did claim he received the equivalent of £45.71.

If instead of becoming redundant, he became sick or injured, cover would last for 24 months. On the basis above, this would reduce his bill to £45.26, which is still nearly half the sum.

If his claim was not delayed by three months but the insurance payments started immediately, the balance would be £51.93 after 18 months or £41.74 after 24 months.

The Debt Doctor's Advice

Payment protection insurance is always a waste of money.

Figure 21: Payment protection insurance.

Month	Balance	Payment from insurance	Balance after payment	Interest charge	New balance
£	£	£	£	£	£
1	100.00	-	100.00	1.50	101.50
2	101.50	-	101.50	1.52	103.02
3	103.02	-	103.02	1.54	104.56
4	104.56	5.23	99.33	1.49	100.82
5	100.82	5.04	95.78	1.44	97.22
6	97.22	4.86	92.36	1.38	93.74
7	93.74	4.69	89.05	1.34	90.39
8	90.39	4.52	85.87	1.29	87.16
9	87.16	4.36	82.80	1.24	84.04
10	84.04	4.20	79.84	1.20	81.04
11	81.04	4.05	76.99	1.15	78.14
12	78.14	3.91	74.23	1.11	75.34
13	75.34	3.77	71.58	1.07	72.65
14	72.65	3.63	69.02	1.04	70.06
15	70.06	3.50	66.56	0.99	67.55
16	67.55	3.38	64.17	0.97	65.14
17	65.14	3.26	61.88	0.93	62.81
18	62.81	3.14	59.67	0.89	60.56
19	60.56	3.03	57.53	0.86	58.39
20	58.39	2.91	55.48	0.83	56.31
21	56.31	2.82	53.49	0.80	54.29

The credit card companies arrange payment protection insurance through an insurance company. In 2003, it was reported that the premium paid by the credit card company was only one fifth of what they collect. So of every 75p you pay, 15p provides insurance cover and 60p inflates the profits of the credit card company.

If you want insurance against unemployment or disability, you can obtain income protection insurance for probably one fifth of the equivalent premium directly from an insurance company.

Buy now, pay later

These deals are commonly offered by stores and mail order companies. You can buy your furniture or computer and pay nothing for six months or a year.

This is what you are not told:

- The deal is actually a credit sale and so is subject to a credit check. If your credit rating is low, you will be refused. In some cases, there are very high thresholds, so many creditworthy customers may be refused. They are enticed by the 'pay later' offer, and rather than go home without the goods they then pay the purchase price normally. The refused credit is a black mark on the person's credit rating.
- If the payment is not made within the six months or year, interest is charged at a high rate, usually over 25%. Interest is charged for the whole period *including the interest-free period*.
- You are not reminded that the full repayment is due. So if you forget and are just one day late, the whole interest-free period is wiped out. Suppose you bought your furniture in one of these offers for £1,000 and forgot the repayment date a year later. You could be hit by an immediate interest payment of perhaps £259.

You should appreciate that suppliers who may offer excellent products at good prices with good customer service may offer poor quality on financial deals.

For example, Argos provides quality goods at keen prices. Details of its 'pay nothing' scheme are found on page 1721 of its catalogue buried in tiny, almost unreadable white print against a red background at the bottom of the page. It says:

Quote from terms for Argos 'Pay Nothing' scheme

If you pay off any PAY NOTHING plan by the due date, then you won't be charged any interest. If you choose to spread the cost for a longer period, then we will simply add the interest *from the date of purchase* and you then make a minimum payment of 4% of the balance or £2 whichever is greater. Typical APR 25.9% *variable*.

The italics are mine, and highlight the crunch words. The whole of the above text covers an area just one centimetre high across half the page.

Argos is quoting typical consumer terms, and its APR is conspicuously stated elsewhere on the page. However, Argos, like all other retailers offering this service, does not draw your attention to any of the three points mentioned above. And Argos is no worse than dozens of other suppliers.

Fraud

The ability of man to cheat his fellow man seems limitless. Some of the more common examples are listed below.

The **Ponzi fraud**, named after its first user, promises high returns, such as 5% per month. The first investors pay £100 and duly receive £5 after one month. They tell their friends and soon the money rolls in. The first investors continue to receive their £5 a month, which is simply paid from their own money. When enough has been collected, the company disappears.

Pyramid selling is when an agent agrees to sell so many products to so many agents who recruit their agents and so on, each taking a commission on their and their agents, and sub-agents' sales. Either the commissions become tiny or the products become too expensive. Agents find they are contracted to buy products they cannot sell. This is illegal.

Chain letters where you pay £10 to a person at the top of the list of four and then send the letter to four more people, removing the top name, moving others up one and adding their own to the bottom. Each person sends £10 and expects to receive over £2,500 when their name is top of the list. The problem is that by the time it gets to you, the number of people required to make the scheme work could exceed the population. The money never arrives.

Herd instinct

Never assume that something is a good deal because 'everybody is doing it'.

In 1719 shares in the South Sea Company soared from £100 to £1,050 even though the company had done almost nothing for eight years. This is known as a **bubble**. It burst in 1720 when many investors were bankrupted.

In 2000 shares in boo.com valued the company at over £100 million. It was just a website selling sportswear. The bubble burst six months later.

Identity theft

From a few documents, it is possible for a person to 'become' you. They can misappropriate your credit cards and incur expenditure in your name. The Home Office estimates that identity theft costs £1.7 billion a year.

Identity theft does not always mean that all your documents have been copied. Identity theft can involve accessing your mobile phone, your eBay account or ordering goods in your name. Legally you are not responsible unless you colluded in the theft or possibly were careless.

Sometimes identity theft involves mail being stolen. You can write a letter to yourself, with typed white envelope and padded to look as though it contains a credit card, and see if it arrives. If you suspect your mail is being stolen, call Royal Mail on 08457 740 740. This can also identify any mail redirection arranged without your knowledge.

Moving house presents opportunities for identity theft. It is advisable to:

- tell everyone you deal with of your new address
- have your mail redirected to the new address for 12 months
- check your credit record with all three agencies after 3 months.

Avoid carrying too many credit cards. Keep details of the emergency numbers all card companies provide, but not in the same wallet as the cards. If a card is lost or stolen, it must be cancelled immediately. Similarly, lost driving licences and passports must be reported immediately.

Certain documents should not be thrown away whole. These include bank statements, credit card statements, bills, receipts, and suchlike. They should be shredded or burned. Even shredding is not that effective as quarter-inch strips can easily be reconstituted back to documents. It is advisable to include other documents in the shredding and put the contents in different bags.

Check all statements on arrival and query any unexpected item.

Keep passwords safe, and never divulge them. The police and credit card companies never ask for the whole password. If in doubt about whether the person is who he says he is, ask for their name and contact details. Contact the organization on a number the organization has provided, not the number given by the person. That number could be a friend who is part of the scam.

Make sure that no-one can overhear you giving out a credit card number or entering a PIN.

Other advice and help on identity theft is available from a special Home Office website, http://www.identity-theft.org.uk.

'You have won a competition'

And pigs can fly. You may receive a telephone call saying you have won a competition. If the telephone operator is a good actor or actress, they may congratulate you in excited tones. Most such calls are scams. If you have won a genuine prize, it simply arrives or (for huge prizes) a representative calls. You do not have to call a telephone number starting 09 for a large prize, nor write in anywhere.

Here is an example reported by *Which?* magazine. Two million people received a letter from Purple Rock Solutions saying that they had 'definitely been selected' to win a prize from a list which included a BMW car and a flat-screen television. The 137,000 people who called in were on a premium rate line (starting 09) for six minutes at £1.50 a minute. All they received was a voucher for a cheap camera which was 'free' on payment of a handling fee of £14.95. The company was fined £10,000 by Icstis, which regulates premium rate services, having pocketed an estimated £500,000 just from the calls.

Prizes are either worthless items or are vouchers which simply offer discounts. A 'guaranteed prize worth at least £1,000' could be just a 10% discount on a £10,000 holiday where you would never pay the other 90%. Another ploy is 'you could win millions of pounds' where your prize is a £1 national lottery ticket.

However, that is not the end of the story. Once a company has your details, you will be bombarded with more 'winnings' and wonderful offers.

Letters are often sent out saying you have won a lottery, particularly the Spanish lottery. They are bogus, and simply seek to find your bank details.

Trading standards officers received an estimated 600,000 complaints about bogus competitions each year. They estimate that every 'winner' loses an average £53.

Phishing

The growth of the Internet and mobile phones has made impersonation frauds easier.

A common trick is to send an e-mail, supposedly from a bank or a reputable retail website like eBay or Amazon, saying that they need to update your security or have detected irregular activity. The e-mail asks you to enter personal details such as passwords. The e-mail is actually routed to a fraudster who can then use those details to order goods in your name on your account.

You should never respond to an e-mail which asks for such details. If you think such a message may be genuine, close the e-mail and contact the website directly.

Another trick is that a text message is sent to a mobile telephone pretending to be an unnamed contact from someone keen to be reunited with you. The message can cost £1.50 to receive. Once you have accepted the message, you can be bombarded with further messages at £1.50 a time. If you do not know the caller, simply refuse to accept a text message. If they want to make contact with you, they can simply phone you.

The 419 scam

This scam takes its name from the relevant section of the penal code of Nigeria, where the scam originated.

You receive an unsolicited letter or e-mail telling you a fanciful tale about funds locked up in an account which can only be liberated to a UK bank account. The amounts are usually millions of pounds. The letters are typically long with poor spelling and grammar. You are promised a share for liberating funds. Below is a letter received by the author (and probably by a few thousand others).

> I am pleased to get across to you for a very urgent and profitable business proposal, though I don't know you neither have I seen you before but my confidence was reposed on you when the Chief Executive of Lagos State chamber of Commerce and Industry handed me your contact for a confidential business.
>
> I am the manager of United Bank for Africa Plc (UBA), Ilupeju branch, Lagos Nigeria.
>
> The intended business is thus; We had a customer, a Foreigner (a Turkish) resident in Nigeria, he was a Contractor with one of the Government Parastatals.He has in his Account in my branch the sum of US 38.6 Million (Thirty Eight Million, Six Hundred Thousand U.S. Dollars).
>
> Unfortunately, the man died four years ago until today non of his next of kin has come forward to claim the money. Having noticed this, I in collaboration with two other top Officials of the bank have covered up the account all this while. Now we want you (being a foreigner) to be fronted as one of his next of kin and forward your account and other relevant documents to be advised to you by us to attest to the Claim.
>
> We will use our positions to get all internal documentations to back up the claims .The whole procedures will last only five working days to get the fund retrieved successfully without trace even now or in future.

Your response is only what we are waiting for as we have arranged all necessary things. As soon as this message comes to you kindly get back to me indicating your interest, then I will furnish you with the whole procedures to ensure that the deal is successfully concluded.

For your assistance we have agreed to give you twenty five percent (25%) of the Total sum at the end of the transaction while 65% would be for my colleagues and I and the remaining 10% would be for any form of expenses that may be incurred during the course of the transaction which would be given to us when the money is transferred into your account before splitting the balance on the agreed percentage of 65% to 25%.

I await your earliest response.

Thanks,
Yours Sincerely

Mr.Ike Collins

What happens is that the process starts and then hits some 'unforeseen snags' and some funds are needed which you are expected to provide. You never see those funds, or any other funds, ever again. Because your involvement is not legal, you are not tempted to report it to the police.

The Nigeria 419 scam can appear in religious guise, particularly if you are a church minister or otherwise have your address published in a Christian directory.

Such letters are often handwritten. They will, as said, often be long with poor spelling and grammar. Sometimes they give heart-rending accounts of starving children, and regularly invoke the blessings of God. They are still scams. Help for Third World causes should be made through proper charities with relevant experience.

If you really must send funds direct to Africa, you should open a separate bank account for that purpose and pay in the funds to send. Many well-meaning donors have sent cheques only to find that the account number, sorting code and signature are used for forged documents to appropriate funds. Banks have a good record in spotting this, but they cannot expect always to detect forgeries.

14

Staying out of trouble

Cut up your credit cards

Credit cards are one of the biggest sources of personal indebtedness. About 59% of card-holders pay the whole balance when they receive the statement. That is responsible use of a card. The other 41% carry forward balances and use the card more, so that 75% of all credit card statements carry some interest. On average, every UK adult has four credit cards.

About 11% of card-holders make just the minimum payment each month. This rises to 18% for those in the 18–25 age range.

If you do not pay off your whole credit card each month, you should cut up your credit cards. Even if you pay off the whole balance each month, you can still be tricked into massive charges. This can be seen as a modern interpretation of Matthew 18.8: 'If your hand or your foot causes your downfall, cut it off and fling it away; it is better for you to enter into life maimed or lame, than to keep two hands or two feet and be thrown into the eternal fire.'

The easiest way out of credit card debt is to throw the cards away and go back to cash, bank notes and coins. This can be used for **jam jar accounting**, from the practice of putting cash into jam jars allocated for specific purposes, such as food, telephone bill, car maintenance etc.

Psychologically it is often a good idea to have funds in ready cash as it often helps to appreciate funds as 'real money' as opposed to numbers on a statement. There is a small additional risk of losing cash from theft, but this is usually much smaller than losing funds from irresponsible credit card use. It is also possible to have cards stolen.

Here are some of the pitfalls of not using credit cards properly:

Increased spending

On average, a credit card user spends 34% more than someone of similar means who uses cash.

The credit card company may say that having a card means that you don't miss unexpected bargains. Let us see what that means. You have admired a £150 coat in a shop window. It is then offered at a sale price of £100, so you buy it on your Barclaycard. Because you are near the limit, you pay only the minimum 2% each month, and are charged interest at 1.24% on the balance each month (the card's standard rate in June 2005). Because the £100 is 'lost' with all the other balances, you think about it no more and regard the coat as paid for.

On the basis of 2% payment each month and 1.24% interest, after ten years (yes, ten years), you will have paid £155 towards the coat and still owe £40. By the time you have cleared it, you will have paid a total of £254, which can take over 97 years. In other words, a 20-year-old person buying a bargain coat could still be paying for it when they die and long after the coat has been thrown away.

And is impulse buying ever a bargain? Almost by definition, an impulse buy is of something you do not *need*. So not buying the coat will save you £100.

Interest charge

It is reasonable for a card to charge you interest when you borrow money, though you should always know the APR for each card. It will usually be between 18% and 36%. The problem is that the different cards have widely different ways of calculating interest.

The credit card company may tell you that you can enjoy up to 56 days' free credit. If you pay the whole bill when you receive it, you do enjoy a free credit period. What you are not told is that if you do not pay on time, the interest is charged from the date of the transaction, not from the date that payment was due.

If there is an old balance overdue from a previous period, the interest may be added to the items on the current statement even though they are not overdue.

Suppose you have a balance on your card of £100, current spending of £500, and interest at 1.24% a month. You could receive a statement like this:

balance brought forward	100.00
interest at 1.24%	7.44
late payment fee	25.00
this month's spending	500.00
balance	632.44

You are being charged £32.44 on a debt of £100. They may quote you a monthly interest rate of 1.24%, equal to an APR of 15.3%. That month, you have paid 32.44% in interest and charges, equal to an APR of 2812.3%!

Late payment fees

If you miss a payment, the credit card company will charge you between £20 and £30 'late payment fee' on top of the high interest. This is just theft, as you receive nothing in return for this 'fee'. In effect, the company is simply imposing a fine on you because it can get away with it. The author does not understand why these charges remain legal.

One person in four is charged this fee each year. If you think this does not matter, take a £20 note and set fire to it. The author's experience is that if you call the credit card company, press all the buttons on their annoying call-answering machines, sit listening to awful music until put through to Tracey in a remote call centre, and then protest loudly, you can get a late payment fee refunded.

Payment protection insurance

A credit card company may offer you 'protection' whereby you insure the balance on your card for, perhaps, 75p per £100. This is a rip-off on a massive scale, and is never justified. The rate of 75p per month is £9 per year. Over a 40-year spending life it means that you have paid £360 to insure £100 against something that will not happen. Do you know anyone who has ever claimed on such a policy?

Not only is this prohibitively expensive insurance but it does not even provide proper cover. Such policies typically pay off between 3% and 10% of the balance each month. And the interest does not stop. Suppose you owe £100 when you become unemployed for a year. At the end of the year, you will still owe £32.74 and will have paid £8.81 interest. See also page 257.

Join a credit union

A credit union is a means by which credit may be advanced to people who lack the resources to obtain finances from commercial sources, and who may therefore be tempted to use a loan shark.

A credit union is a financial co-operative into which members contribute a regular sum into a collective savings account. The members are usually local and known to each other. The members own the credit union. They are regulated by Credit Unions Act 1979 and (from July 2002) are overseen by the Financial Services Authority.

There were 665 credit unions registered with FSA with 463,187 members on 30 September 2003. There were 444 ABCUL-affiliated credit unions in the UK. Their 365,100 members had saved £293 million and borrowed £240 million. The average balance held by a credit union member was £803 on 30 September 2003. Credit unions use the services of about 10,000 volunteers.

Although they have existed since the nineteenth century, credit unions are not common yet in the UK despite their obvious attraction. In the Irish Republic about half the population belongs to a credit union. In the USA, it is about 25% and in the Caribbean 70%. Credit unions are not just for poor people.

The credit union pays dividends to savers, typically at a rate of about 2% to 3%, though some credit unions pay rates up to 8%. Typically, the members also get life insurance equal to the amount saved at the time of death. This means that the member's balance is doubled and paid to whoever the member nominated. The insurance is provided by CUNA Mutual Group.

After a period, members may withdraw sums from the pot for any purpose. The interest rates are low, and the controls are high. A church or other body is an ideal place to start a credit union. The law restricts the maximum charge to no more than 1% on the balance each month (an APR of 12.68%). If someone borrowed £1,000 for a year and repaid it in equal monthly instalments, they would pay just £67 interest. Unlike banks and many other bodies, there are no other charges or penalties. The life insurance clears any unpaid balance at death.

There are two types of credit unions, known as version 1 and version 2. The maximum period for which each type of credit union may lend is:

	Version 1	Version 2
Unsecured loan	3 years	5 years
Secured loan	7 years	15 year

Loans are flexible in that they may be used for any purpose, can be for any amount, and can be for short periods. An application is usually made by completing a form and attending a loan interview. Credit union loans may be allowed to pay off loans from higher-interest lenders.

In addition to saving, borrowing and life insurance, a credit union has a duty to educate its members in the wise use of money. Some credit unions also offer a bill-paying mechanism, which is useful for people without bank accounts.

Each credit union has a **common bond** which states who may join. This is often limited to a geographical area or a common employer. Membership is usually in the hundreds. Credit unions are closely allied to the Co-operative Movement, and many operate from Co-op stores.

It is now difficult to start a credit union from scratch and can take up to three years, so it is usually worthwhile asking an existing credit union to extend its common bond to you. A list of credit unions can be found on the website www.abcul.coop. A credit union must be audited each year by a registered auditor. It must have insurance against theft and fraud. In addition, credit unions are covered by the Financial Services Compensation Scheme. In the unlikely event that a credit union fails, the Scheme pays 100% of balances up to £2,000 to each member and 90% of the next £30,000.

The Financial Services Authority wants to encourage credit unions as well as regulate them more tightly. This means that credit unions will probably become larger.

If you wish to start a credit union from scratch, the steps are:

- define the common bond
- get together an interested group with the right skills mix
- register with ABCUL (for £35)
- prepare a business plan
- talk to the Financial Services Authority
- obtain funding and sponsorship
- appoint officers
- promote the credit union.

Role of the church

The church often does not have a good track record in dealing with debt problems, or indeed in dealing with many financial matters. There is often a lack of sympathy and almost always a lack of understanding.

Every church should consider these responsibilities with regard to debt:

Include those with financial problems in the prayers

As well as praying for people who are sick, regularly include those with debt problems. Many illnesses have the nature of a short-term nuisance against many debt problems which can seem like an endless misery that eats at a person's soul. Remember that a congregation of 100 people can have 20 people with serious debt problems. Have speakers to talk about the issue.

Allow the occasional sermon to be on the subject of debt. Encourage church organizations to invite speakers to talk about it.

Give the minister a discretionary fund

Every church council or similar body should allow its minister a **discretionary fund** from church funds to meet local need. This need not be a large amount – £500 may be enough. If funds run out, the minister can always ask for me.

The following is a recommended code of conduct for a discretionary fund:

Recommended code of conduct for a church discretionary fund (CDF)

- The CDF should come from church funds but be under the control of the minister. If it is desired to give control to other ministers, a separate discretionary fund should be set up for each minister.

- The CDF should be used to make small payments for individuals whom the minister judges to be in need. The fund is not used to make donations to charities or for other purposes.

- Beneficiaries should not be restricted to members of the church.

- The fund should have its own bank account from which the minister may draw cash.

- Wherever possible, the fund should be used to pay a bill or to acquire goods or services, rather than to give cash direct to the person.

- One other person must know the details of each donation from the fund, knowing the name of the donee, the amount and general reason for the donation. This person must be independent of the minister. An ideal person is the church auditor, though others could fill the role. This person must be able to report directly to the church council or equivalent body. This prevents any suspicion of misuse of funds.

- The minister may not use the fund to make donations for the benefit of himself or his immediate family, or for any other minister in the church.

- Other than as stated above, details of recipients and amounts given should remain confidential.

- The fund should be used for single donations, and not be used for repeated payments to assist a person. If the minister believes that the church should provide continuing support for anyone, that should be referred to the church council or equivalent body.

- If a donation is made because a person has debt problems, that person should be encouraged to seek help from a debt counsellor.

- The church accounts should note how much has been allocated to the fund, how much has been spent, and the name of the auditor or other person who shares the confidential information about donees.

The Parable of the Good Samaritan (Luke 10.29–37) contains one often overlooked detail. The parable makes clear that the victim had been mugged, and therefore was blameless in the matter. Despite that, the Samaritan gave two denarii *to the innkeeper* to look after him, not to the victim, and said he would call in again to see if further payment was needed. (Two denarii is about a day's wages.) This illustrates that help should be given in goods and services rather than in cash.

If confronted in the street by someone asking for money for food, it is good policy not to give money which may be used for any purpose, but to provide food if possible.

Support charities that deal with poverty

Churches usually give money to charities, and have many competing claims for limited resources. Charities that are involved in dealing with poverty should be considered among them. This may include specific debt charities such as Credit Action, or welfare organizations like the Salvation Army and Crisis.

The church may wish to provide help more directly by offering free or subsidized food, or by providing meals itself. To do this, the church must comply with certain health and safety legislation, and will usually need a licence from the local authority.

Many people on low incomes do not benefit from being able to travel to out-of-town superstores or by buying in larger quantities. A church could assist by providing transport or by buying in bulk and splitting for resale. Many local authorities offer subsidized transport for disadvantaged groups which is widely used for shopping.

Consider setting up a credit union

The details are given on page 268. This provides an opportunity for church members to provide mutual support within a fellowship. It also offers scope for members to admit debt problems in congenial surroundings to sympathetic friends.

Have professional help available

Most congregations include some lawyers and accountants, and others who understand debt matters. Although it is unreasonable to expect them to provide unlimited free help to others, most professionals are prepared to provide some help, such as a conversation over a cup of coffee.

The minister should be able to call on expertise in helping people. It is possible to contact local firms of accountants and solicitors to see if they are prepared to provide a limited free consultation service. Many firms are willing to offer half an hour free to people in trouble. Quite apart from the moral reasons for doing so (such as tithing one's time and talents), firms can see how this can enhance their reputation and possibly provide them with remunerative business.

Consider setting up or participating in a help scheme

Many churches set up drop-in centres or similar facilities to help anyone in any kind of need. This commendable activity should include help with debt.

Be careful about re-inventing the wheel by duplicating facilities already provided. This is not an area where churches should compete. Rather such facilities should be provided by local churches working together. There is no reason to exclude members of other religions or secular bodies either. Any help scheme should liaise with the local Citizens Advice Bureau and other local help organizations.

A final word

Jesus came to the world and died an agonizing death because of his love for sinners, that is for all of us. Debt can be a time when a person feels little love and sees little light. Yet every debtor is loved by God. Whatever the state of a person's finances, it cannot put them beyond the love of God.

There is always a way out of debt. It may not be easy, it may have a cost, and it may need someone to help, but there is always a way out. Having someone with you makes that journey easier.

Getting out of debt usually involves both following the proper procedures and seeking God's strength and guidance through prayer. Every debtor and every debt adviser has direct access to the greatest debt doctor of all.

Appendix 1

Glossary

419 scam	Fraud involving persuading a person to recover apparently unclaimed funds from overseas. At some point, the victim is asked to pay a fee which is not seen again.
acceptance	In law, agreement to accept an offer which makes a binding contract.
Accountant in Bankruptcy	Scottish official who oversees bankruptcies.
accounting	Process of recording income and expenditure, and other financial statements.
accounting concept	One of five principles which accountants assume have been followed unless specifically stated otherwise.
accused	Person in court facing a criminal charge.
active listening	Counselling skill of listening constructively to a problem.
actual	Amounts of expenditure incurred, as against the budgeted figure.
ad idem	Of the same mind. Two parties to a contract must be ad idem for the contract to be legally enforceable.
additional pension	One of various forms of government-backed additions to state pension funded by national insurance, namely graduated pension, SERPS and state second pension.
administration	(1) Administering the estate of a person who died without making a will. (2) Arrangement where an insolvent company has its management replaced.

administration order	Court-overseen debt management plan when in-debtedness does not exceed £5,000.
advice	Suggestions given to client as to their best course of action.
affirmative interjection	Comments such as 'yes' and 'I see' which indi-cate that a person is still listening but which do not interrupt.
age discrimination	Discriminating against a person because of their age. Generally unlawful from 1 October 2006.
aggression	Manifestation of anger which avoids dealing with a problem.
AIB	Accountant in Bankruptcy.
angel	In finance, someone who invests in a private business.
annual percentage rate	Common method of calculating interest rates to make them comparable.
annuity rate	Amount of income a pension provider will pay for a fixed amount of capital.
annulment	In marriage, end to a marriage on the basis that there was no proper marriage.
apparently insolvent	In Scotland, legal step in sequestration.
Appeal Commissioners	General or Special Commissioners who hear ap-peals against amounts of tax imposed.
approved debts	Debts which a debt factor is prepared to ac-cept.
APR	Annual percentage rate.
articulateness	Skill of being able to express oneself clearly.
asset value	Amount a person's property is believed to be worth, particularly in bankruptcy.
attachment of earnings	Court order requiring some of a person's pay to be used to pay a debt.
attendance allowance	Social security benefit payable to those who look after people who need help with personal care.
austerity	The situation where acquisition of material goods is difficult.
automatic penalty	Additional sum imposed without consideration of factors, such as being late with a tax return.

available income   (1) Amount of a person's income which may be applied to clearing old debts.
(2) Amount of income a bankrupt can provide for creditors.

average earnings   Figure on which entitlement to SERPS and state second pension are calculated.

b/fwd   Brought forward. Indication in bookkeeping of a sub-total taken from a previous page.

bad buy   Product or service which clearly does not represent value for money.

bailiff   Person who enforces a court order.

balance of probabilities   Basis of proof in civil proceedings – you must prove that your case is more likely to be true than not.

bankruptcy hearing   Formal hearing before a judge to check that the requirements of bankruptcy have been followed.

bankruptcy restriction order   Order imposing further restrictions on a bankrupt, during and after the bankruptcy.

bankruptcy restriction undertaking   Restriction agreed with a bankrupt which lasts during his bankruptcy and afterwards.

bankruptcy   Legal process for an insolvent person. Most of his property is taken to pay creditors.

barter   A trade when two people each provide the other with goods or services rather than paying cash.

bereavement allowance   Social security benefit paid for 52 weeks to a young widow or widower.

bereavement payment   Lump-sum **social** security payment paid to widow or widower below retirement age.

beyond reasonable doubt   Basis of proof in criminal proceedings.

bigamy   Having two wives.

binding precedent   Decision of the court which must be followed in a later case if the facts are the same.

body language	Range of mannerisms and physical expressions which indicate what a person is really thinking.
bookkeeping	Keeping financial records.
BRO	Bankruptcy Restriction Order.
BRU	Bankruptcy Restriction Undertaking.
bubble	Company with size but no substance. It keeps growing till it bursts.
budget	Plan for future income and expenditure.
budgeting loan	Interest-free loan from the Social Fund to assist a person on means-tested benefits meet a specific expense.
budget-limited	When financial provision is limited by resources rather than need, particularly discretionary payments from the Social Fund.
business plan	Written strategy for running a business. Often used to secure funding.
buyback store	Another name for retail credit.
c/fwd	Carried forward. Indication in bookkeeping of a sub-total taken to a later page.
capacity to contract	A person or body who is legally able to make a contract.
capsule wardrobe	Economical selection of clothes and accessories designed to blend together in many combinations.
carer's allowance	Social security benefit payable to someone who spends 35 hours or more a week caring for someone.
cash analysis	Exercise book ruled with columns for recording amounts as a means of analysing income and expenditure into categories.
catalogue club	Arrangement whereby goods may be bought from a catalogue and paid by regular instalments.
category A pension	Commonest form of state retirement pension payable from the age of 65.

category B pension State retirement pension payable to a widow or widower who does not qualify for a category A pension.

category D pension Non-contributory state pension payable to people from the age of 80.

caveat emptor The legal principle that a buyer is responsible for choosing what he purchases.

certificated bailiff Person who collects debts for bodies other than the court, such as for a local authority or tax body.

cesser on redemption Legal term for when a mortgage must be repaid.

chain letter Fraud which involves paying money to someone at the top of a short list, and then sending it on to more people, adding your name to the bottom of the list and awaiting a huge sum when your name eventually tops the list.

chaotic lifestyle Category of poor credit risk who can usually only borrow from loan sharks.

charge for payment In Scotland, formal notice of unpaid debt which allows a sequestration to proceed.

charging order Court order which requires some of the proceeds of sale of property to be paid to someone.

charitable giving Donations to charities for worthwhile causes.

cheque shop Retail outlet which allows people to borrow against their own postdated cheques.

child benefit Social security benefit payable to most mothers for their children.

child tax credit Social security benefit for families on medium or low incomes to help pay for children.

civil investigation of fraud Scheme used by tax authorities allowing a person one final opportunity to confess tax irregularities before criminal proceedings are started.

civil law Law relating to disputes between people, unlike criminal law.

civil partnership Arrangement similar to marriage but between two adults of the same sex.

claimant	(1) Person who brings civil proceedings. (2) Someone who makes a claim, such as on an insurance policy or for social security.
class 1 national insurance	National insurance paid by employees and their employers from salaries and wages.
class 2 national insurance	National insurance paid by the self-employed, who also pay class 4.
class 3 national insurance	Voluntary payments of national insurance to allow a person to maintain a complete national insurance record.
class 4 national insurance	National insurance payable by the self-employed (as well as class 2), but which does not count as a contribution.
client-centred	Counselling ethic which ensures that help stays focused on the client.
cold turkey	Therapy of forcing a person to achieve an objective, such as living on a fixed allowance.
cold weather payment	Social Fund payment to certain categories of people when the weather is expected to be below oC for seven consecutive days.
collectable	Item sold for its value to future collectors. Such items are rarely worth the price charged.
columnar system	Basic form of cash analysis which uses columns of figures to help analyse income and spending to produce category totals.
commercial borrowing	Borrowing funds on terms offered by a commercial lender.
commercial debt	Debt which arises in the course of business.
committal warrant	Court order committing someone to prison.
committed money	Money which is allocated for particular spending.
common bond	Statement on who may join a credit union.
Common Financial Statement	Standard form of debt statement agreed by banks and other bodies. Its use can speed up and simplify debt recovery.
common law	Body of decisions which make up most of the law other than Acts of Parliament.

common law wife	Real wife where the marriage cannot be proved.
commonhold	Leasehold where the leaseholders collectively own the common parts.
community care grant	Lump-sum **discretionary** payment from the Social Fund.
company voluntary arrangement	Arrangement whereby a company is protected from debts while a scheme is worked out with creditors.
composition order	Alternative to a final order when a debtor cannot clear his debts within three years.
compound interest	Where interest is charged on the principal and on interest already applied.
compounding	Arrangement between a debtor and creditors for settling debts other than by full payment when due.
concertina order	Sequence of orders obtained together in an IVA.
confidentiality	An agreement between two parties that information is provided subject to restrictions imposed by the provider.
consolidation loan	Loan made to pay off other loans.
Construction Industry Scheme	System of collecting provisional amounts of income tax from self-employed subcontractors in the building trade.
constructive notice	When someone is made aware of a matter which legally requires them to investigate.
contingency	Sum reserved in a budget to meet unexpected expenses.
continuing commitments	Regular outgoings by someone claiming a budgeting loan from the Social Fund.
contract	Legally enforceable agreement between two or more people.
contractual pay	Pay and benefits a person is entitled to receive from their employer.
contributory benefit	Social security benefit where entitlement depends on having paid sufficient national insurance.

cooling off period   Time in which a customer is allowed to cancel an agreement, such as for consumer credit, doorstep sales or timeshares.

cost of sales   Direct cost of providing goods or services which are sold by a business.

council tax   Tax imposed by a local authority on its residents.

council tax benefit   Social security benefit to help pay council tax.

counselling   Process by which one person discusses an issue with another with a view to finding a solution.

counterclaim   When someone is sued on a summons they issued.

county court   Court which hears most civil disputes, such as unpaid bills.

county court bailiff   Person responsible for enforcing orders from the county court.

county court judgment   Legal recognition that a person owes a debt.

Court of Protection   Court where issues are decided relating to people who have a mental incapacity.

credit   Bookkeeping entry which indicates that an asset has decreased, such as when money is taken out of an account.

credit excluded   People who cannot borrow money through the normal channels.

credit ladder   Informal description of ranks of credit facilities with main financial institutions at the top and loan sharks at the bottom. Typically a borrower climbs down the ladder as the interest rates get higher.

credit reference   Record of a person's credit record, noting loans and cards used.

credit repair   Improving a person's credit record.

credit scoring   Reducing a person's credit record to a number (usually out of 1000) from which a lender decides whether to lend and at what rate.

credit union   Club in which people lend and borrow money.

creditor sheet	Another name for a debt statement.
creditors' meeting	When creditors meet to decide whether to agree to the terms of an IVA or bankruptcy.
creditors' petition	Request by creditors that a person be made bankrupt.
criminal law	Law relating to public offences rather than between people.
crisis loan	Immediate interest-free loan from the Social Fund to meet a pressing short-term need.
CVA	Company Voluntary Arrangement.
DAS	Debt Arrangement Scheme.
dating agency	In finance, a body which matches entrepreneurs to investors.
debit	Bookkeeping entry which indicates that an asset has increased, such as when money is added to an account.
debt	Amount of money owed to someone else.
debt arrangement scheme	Scheme used in Scotland to allow debtors to pay their creditors.
debt consolidation	Turning many debts into one debt.
debt counsellor	Someone who helps a debtor solve his problems.
debt factoring	Commercial arrangement whereby a bank or finance company will advance money against a business's invoicing.
debt management plan	Informal agreement between a debtor and creditors.
debt minimization	Processes to reduce the amount of debts, such as by challenging invoices or offering to return goods.
debt negotiation	Discussion with a creditor, usually restricted to the amount repayable and when it will be repaid.
debt problem	When debt is not easily repayable.
debt recovery	Formal process of recovering from debt.

debt statement	List of debts owed. One of the two financial statements prepared in debt recovery.
debt strategy	Policy for determining how debts should be repaid, such as determining the amounts and order.
debt vulture	Person who preys on people in debt with a view to cheating them out of their little remaining money.
decision-making	Mental process of reaching a conclusion. It is akin to putting weights on to a balance.
decree	Another name for a summary warrant issued in Scotland.
deduction rate	Amount of a person's pay taken to pay a debt when an attachment of earnings order has been imposed.
defendant	Person who is sued in civil proceedings.
deferred debt	Debt which ranks after all other debts.
deferred pension	An entitlement from a previous employer which grows until being claimed in retirement.
deficit	Excess of expenditure over income.
deficit budget	Budget which plans to spend more than is earned.
defined benefit	A pension scheme where the amount received in retirement is fixed.
defined contribution	A pension scheme where the amount of contribution is fixed but the amount of pension ultimately payable is not yet known.
denial	State in which a person refuses to acknowledge a problem.
diagnosis	Identification of problem, the stage between recognition and prognosis.
direct taxes	Taxes on income, such as income tax, national insurance and capital gains tax.
directions	In law, instructions from a judge on how a case should proceed.

disability living allowance	Social security benefit payable to anyone under 65 who needs help with mobility or personal care.
discharged bankrupt	Person whose bankruptcy is over. He may still be subject to certain restriction orders and have difficulty borrowing money.
discretionary payments	Payments made at the discretion of the fund holder, particularly social security benefits from the Social Fund.
disputed debt	Sum owed where there is a genuine disagreement over the amount owed, or if anything is owed.
distress	In law, the process of seizing goods to raise funds to pay a debt.
distress finance	Funding for a business in trouble, usually at a very high rate.
distress sale	Sale designed to generate a quick income, usually because the person is desperate.
distress warrant	Order by a court authorizing bailiffs to seize goods for non-payment of a debt.
distributing	In insolvency, sharing proceeds among creditors.
dole	Colloquial name for jobseeker's allowance.
domicile	The one country a person regards as his natural home.
dominant person	Person who has the more responsible role in a fiduciary relationship.
doorstep lending	Another name for a home credit company.
downsizing	Moving from a larger home to a smaller one to raise funds.
dramatic gesture	Any action in response to a situation which aims to draw attention to a person but is usually counter-productive.
dread illness insurance	Insurance policy against contracting certain illnesses.
duress	Forcing someone to make a contract. Such a contract is invalid.

early retirement	Retirement before normal age; usually a way of making older employees redundant.
earnings-replacement	Social security benefit which is designed to replace income, such as jobseeker's allowance and statutory maternity pay.
earn-out	Financial arrangement allowing a business founder to use the business's profits to buy out an outside investor.
economizing	Reducing expenditure without compromising lifestyle.
enabling act	Act of Parliament which allows laws to be made by someone else, usually a government minister.
enduring power of attorney	Power of attorney which can continue after a person has lost the mental capacity to act for himself.
enforcement	Proceedings to make a person comply with a court judgment.
enforcement officer	Another term for a bailiff.
EPA	Enduring power of attorney.
equity finance	Funding for a business by selling a share of it.
equity release	One of several types of scheme designed to produce money from the value of a person's home.
equity release mortgage	Equity release scheme in the form of a loan.
equity release reversion	Equity release scheme which involves selling an interest in the person's home.
estate	Everything a person owns, particularly on death.
esteem	The second highest level of Maslow's hierarchy when a person feels self-confidence and self-respect.
executor	Person who administers the estate of someone who died and left a will.
expenditure	All spending.
explanation	Counselling skill of being able to communicate information so that it is understandable.

extended warranty	Insurance policy sold with goods to extend the guarantee.
extortionate credit	Consumer agreement at such a high rate of interest that it can be set aside.
facility	Limit on how much may be borrowed, such as on a credit card or overdraft.
family borrowing	Borrowing from a relative or friend on non-commercial terms.
fantasy	Indulging one's imagination in inner game theory.
fiduciary relationship	Relationship based on trust, such as accountant and client. There are special rules regarding contracts.
final charging order	Charging order which is no longer interim.
final notice	Last notice sent to a debtor before the creditor starts legal action to recover a sum due.
final order	In insolvency, a court order allowing an administration order to be made.
final salary scheme	Another name for a defined benefit scheme.
financial product	Insurance, banking, pensions and similar financial services viewed in the same way as consumer goods.
first purchaser	Someone who buys something where someone else has guaranteed payment.
fixation	Irrational behaviour which obstructs finding a solution.
fixed budget	Budget where amounts of income and expenditure are stated in advance and are not intended to be affected by circumstances.
fixture	Something attached to land or a building which cannot be removed without damage.
flexible budget	Budget where some amounts of expenditure are determined by amounts of income.
floodgates	Standard argument used by a creditor to reject an offer of repayment. It is easily countered.
forecast	Estimate of future income and expenditure.

fraudulent trading	Criminal offence when a business is set up for fraud.
free money	Money which is not budgeted for spending.
freehold	Owning land and buildings.
freezing an account	Court order preventing a person drawing money from a bank account or similar.
full-service factoring	Debt factoring where the factor takes over the whole administration of the sales ledger.
funeral expenses grant	Social Fund payment to a person on means-tested benefits who becomes responsible for arranging a funeral.
further business	Debt negotiation strategy that can occasionally work for trade debts.
gambling	Staking a sum of money on an uncertain outcome on the basis that a larger sum may be won or the stake is lost.
garnishee	Old name for a third party debt order.
genuine triable issue	Real dispute which must be resolved before a bankruptcy may proceed.
get-rich-quick scheme	Scheme which promises a large return very quickly. Such schemes are almost always scams.
graduated pension	Small additions to the state retirement pension gained by acquiring units for employment between 1961 and 1975.
gross profit	Profit before overheads are deducted.
guarantee	(1) Period during which faulty goods may be returned. (2) Legal undertaking to pay someone else's debt if they fail to pay it.
guarantee credit	Part of the pension credit related to income.
guarantor	Someone who undertakes to pay someone else's debt if they fail to pay it.
guardian's allowance	Addition to child benefit when the child is an orphan.
haggling	Negotiation restricted to an amount.

hardship payment order	Court order allowing a payment from a frozen account.
heirloom	Asset which is regarded as belonging to succeeding generations of a family rather than to its current owner. A family must make provisions to secure heirlooms in an insolvency.
herd instinct	Simply doing what everyone else does.
High Court	Court which hears serious claims.
hire purchase	Legal arrangement whereby goods are hired while instalments are paid towards the purchase price.
holy poverty	When a person deliberately denies themselves material possessions in the hope of achieving spiritual growth.
home credit company	Company which lends money to people and collects it weekly from their home.
home income plan	An equity release mortgage where the sum is used to buy an annuity.
horse-trading	Another name for haggling.
household debt	Money owed by a household.
household goods	Essentials to everyday living which cannot be seized from a bankrupt.
housing benefit	Means-tested social security benefit to help pay rent for people on low incomes.
hypothecation	Process whereby income is dedicated to a particular expenditure.
identity theft	Fraud where a person assumes the identity of someone else.
imposed penalty	Penalty which is imposed after consideration of the circumstances, unlike an automatic penalty.
incapacity benefit	Means-tested social security benefit payable to people unable to work because of illness or injury.
income	Money a person receives from all sources.

income maximization	Any proposal designed to increase a person's income. This is not usually a significant factor in debt recovery.
income payments order	Order requiring a bankrupt to give up income to pay his creditors.
income support	Social security benefit payable to people with a low income.
income threshold figure	Figure of income set each year, below which a household may claim a tax credit.
indebtedness	State of owing money to others.
independent decisions	The aim of therapeutic counselling, rather than giving advice.
indirect taxes	Taxes on spending, such as value added tax, excise duty and road tax.
individual voluntary agreement	Legal arrangement between a debtor and creditors for paying at least 25% of the debts.
indulgence	Any expenditure intended to give pleasure rather than to meet a need.
influence	Persuading someone to make a contract. Within limits, this does not make the contract invalid.
information	Factual statements provided by counsellor which provide more guidance than therapeutic counselling but just stops short of giving advice.
information order	Court order requiring a debtor to attend court to explain why a debt has not been paid.
initial criteria	The two factors considered by social security officers in deciding whether someone is eligible for a budgeting loan from the Social Fund.
inner game theory	Disciplines of reprogramming the subconscious to help achieve a goal.
insolvency	Owing more than you own.
insolvency practitioner	Accountant who specializes in insolvency work.
Insolvency Service	Agency of the Department of Trade and Industry which oversees insolvencies.
interest	Charge for borrowing money.

interest on late payment	A statutory right for late payment of an invoice properly issued in the course of business.
interest on tax	Additional charge automatically imposed if tax is paid late.
interest-only mortgage	Mortgage where regular payments are only made of interest leaving the whole principal to be repaid at the end.
interest rate	A percentage which determines how much interest is charged on a loan or earned on an investment.
interim charging order	Court order which prevents property being sold which may be subject to a charging order.
interim order	In an IVA, temporary protection from creditors while a formal IVA is being prepared.
invoice discounting	Form of secured lending against a business's debts.
IVA	Individual Voluntary Agreement.
IVA equity release	When a person subject to an IVA raises funds by selling property before the IVA ends.
IVA proposal	Document submitted to the court to obtain an IVA.
jobseeker's allowance	Social security payment to someone looking for work.
judgment	Decision of court, usually requiring a person to make a payment.
junk mail	Stuff that comes in the post which you have not asked for.
Kennedy strategy	Negotiation technique which finds a way out for the other person as well as yourself.
kerb appeal	Making a house for sale look attractive from the street to increase its sale price.
land law	Provisions, some ancient, governing legal rights about land.

late payment fee	Charge made by a credit card company for being late with a repayment.
lease	Legal arrangement whereby someone pays for the use of goods without actually owning them.
leasehold	Having a legal right to occupy land and buildings.
legal date of redemption	Date by which a mortgage must be repaid.
legal relations	An intention to create legal relations is a requirement of a contract.
legal tender	Bank notes and coins which legally constitute money.
letters of administration	Legal appointment of an administrator for someone who dies without leaving a will.
levying distress	The process of a bailiff seizing goods to sell.
liability order	Order from a magistrates' court confirming that unpaid rent is owed and allowing the landlord to continue proceedings.
limitation	In law, a period in which an action must be brought.
linked transaction	When one transaction is made on the back of another, such as an extended warranty on the sale of goods.
liquidation	Process of killing off an insolvent company.
little company argument	Standard argument used by a creditor to reject an offer of debt repayment. It can be countered.
living together	Co-habiting. This can affect certain social security payments.
loan shark	Someone who lends money at high rates and uses unlawful means to enforce repayment.
lodger	Person who lives in your home for payment.
LTAHAW	Living Together as Husband and Wife.
McKenzie friend	Someone who is not legally trained but whom the court is prepared to allow to sit and help a party in a case.

market housing	Accommodation acquired at normal market rates, as opposed to social housing.
marshalling	Finding, identifying and valuing property, particularly in insolvency.
Maslow's hierarchy	Model which identifies the different psychological needs of people.
maternity allowance	Social security benefit which may be paid to women who are not eligible for statutory maternity pay.
means-testing	When provision of any facility depends on the claimant proving that their income is sufficiently low.
mental incapacity	Inability of a person to manage their own affairs because of some mental illness or injury or similar.
microgeneration	Facilities for a home to produce electricity.
mindset budgeting	Budget which is influenced by moral judgments as well as financial considerations.
minimum guarantee	The lowest amount of total income received by a person receiving a tax credit.
minor	Person under 18. They have limited ability to make a contract.
misrepresentation	Representing something falsely. It can void a contract or give rise to a claim for damages.
mitigation	When a charge is reduced, such as a tax penalty where the taxpayer has been co-operative.
modesty	In debt recovery, the requirement that personal expenditure is not extravagant.
money purchase	Another name for a defined contribution pension scheme.
monopsony	Being dependent on one customer.
mortgage	Secured loan, usually on a person's home.
mortgage rescue	Scheme which allows a mortgagor to sell all or some of his interest in the home and continue living there as a tenant.
mortgagee	Person to whom a property is mortgaged, such as a bank or building society.

mortgagor	Person who mortgages a property, the owner or occupier.
national insurance	Tax on income to fund social security benefits.
necessary	In law, goods for which a minor may make a contract.
negative equity	When the amount owed in a mortgage or other secured loan is less than the value of the secured asset.
negotiation	Formal process of resolving a dispute between two parties by discussion when both parties want the dispute resolved.
net profit	Gross profit less overheads.
nominee	Name given to insolvency practitioner at the start of the IVA process.
non-certificated bailiff	Person who can collect money but whose powers to seize goods are limited.
non-contributory benefit	Social security benefit where entitlement does not depend on how much national insurance has been paid.
non-judgmental	Counselling attitude which avoids any suggestions of right or wrong to allow the problem to be addressed.
non-priority debt	Debt whose non-payment does not have immediate serious consequences for the debtor.
objectivity	Sufficient detachment between a counsellor and client to allow each not to be unduly influenced by the other.
offer	An invitation to make a contract.
Official Receiver	Government officer who deals with a person who has just become bankrupt.
one-off expenses	Unique expenses. These are usually budgeted for by a contingency.
onerous property	Property of an insolvent person subject to such restrictions that the trustee in insolvency may disclaim them rather than realize them.

order for sale	Court order requiring property to be sold to pay a debt.
organic growth	When a business grows from re-investing its profits rather than by acquiring other businesses.
over-dependence	Risk that a business is too dependent on one customer or supplier.
overheads	Expenses which relate to being in business rather than to the trade of the business.
pari passu	Latin for 'with equal step'. Applies to the principle that creditors in the same rank are paid at the same rate from distributions in an insolvency.
participation quiz	Another name for a television quiz.
particulars of claim	Details which support a legal action.
pawnbroker	Someone who lends money against goods. If not redeemed, the pawnbroker may sell the goods.
Pay As You Earn	System of collecting income tax from employees, administered by the employer.
payment in kind	Settling a debt by providing goods or services rather than cash.
payments distributor	Person who makes payments to creditors in a DAS.
pension credit	Means-tested social security benefit for pensioners on low income.
Pension Tracing Service	Government scheme to help people find details of old pension schemes.
personal accounting	Recording the income and expenditure of a person.
personal capacity	Legal ability which it is assumed all adults have to manage their affairs until the contrary is demonstrated.
personal debt	Debt owed by individuals rather than businesses.
personal discipline	Procedures a person imposes on himself to achieve an objective.
personal loan	Money lent to an individual.

persuasive precedent   Decision of a court which influences future decisions of courts where the facts are similar.

phishing   Internet fraud of pretending to be an authoritative body to get a person to reveal codes and passwords.

physiological need   Basic needs of a person, such as food and warmth. If these needs are not met, no higher need can be addressed.

pledge   In money lending, another word for 'pawn'.

polyandry   Having more than one husband.

polygamy   Having more than one wife.

Ponzi fraud   Investment fraud where supposedly high returns are simply paying early 'investors' from money from later investors.

power of attorney   Legal arrangement allowing someone to administer another person's affairs.

PPI   Payment protection insurance.

preference   In debt recovery, favouring one creditor over another. This is unlawful once insolvency proceedings have started.

preferential debt   Expense which ranks before all other debts except the fees and expenses of the insolvency practitioner.

premium rate number   Telephone number which starts 09 which is very expensive to dial.

prenuptial agreement   Agreement made between two people before they marry on what happens if they separate.

pre-preferential debt   Expenses and fees of the insolvency practitioner, which are paid before all other debts.

pretend money   Forms of money which a person does not recognize as such, and therefore spends more freely than 'real money'.

pre-trial review   Private hearing with the judge before a court case.

primary lease period   First period of a lease in which the payments are related to the value of goods being leased.

principal	Sum of money from which other payments are calculated. The principal in a loan is the sum borrowed from which interest is calculated.
priority debt	Debt whose non-payment has serious consequences for debtor. These are given priority in any debt management.
privacy	Human right of individuals not to have certain personal details made generally known.
private bailiff	Bailiff who works for the court but is not employed by it.
probate	Legal recognition of a will.
problem-focused	Ethic to ensure that counselling sticks to the problem.
prognosis	Proposed solution which follows a diagnosis.
property disposed of	In insolvency, any sale or gift in the previous five years which appears unreasonable or may have been intended to frustrate the insolvency. Such sale or gift may be reversed.
prosecute	Bring proceedings in criminal law.
prosperity gospel	Questionable teaching that generous donations to Christian causes will lead to riches for the donor.
protected trust deed	In Scotland, a trust deed which is registered and therefore binding on all creditors.
payment protection insurance	Insurance sold to pay off the balance owed on a credit card. A rip-off.
prove	In bankruptcy, state the amount owed.
prudence	Accounting concept which requires the preparer of a financial statement to err on the side of caution.
Public Guardianship Office	Government body which oversees arrangements for looking after the affairs of the mentally handicapped.
pyramid selling	Selling to agents who are required to recruit their own agents, and so on. These schemes are illegal.

qualified creditor	In Scotland, someone who is owed at least £1,500 and may start sequestration proceedings.
quantifying	Process of attributing values to known items, such as establishing how much is owed on each debt.
rank	In insolvency, a class of debt determining the order in which it is paid.
real money	Forms of money which are perceived to be real, as opposed to pretend money.
real terms	Amount expressed in terms which allow for inflation.
realizing	In finance, turning assets into cash.
realism	In debt recovery, the requirement that a repayment offer is likely to be met.
receiver	Person who deals with the affairs of another who is either insolvent or suffering from mental incapacity.
receivership	When an insolvent company is taken over by an insolvency practitioner who may run parts of it or sell it as will generate most return.
recognition	First stage in counselling, which recognizes that there is a problem.
reconciliation	Process of agreeing bank statements and similar reports to your own records.
recourse factoring	Commonest form of debt factoring.
re-expression	Counselling skill of articulating a client's problem.
reflection	First counselling skill used in prognosis, allowing a client to identify where a problem lies.
Registry Trust	Where insolvencies are recorded.
regression	Childish behaviour, such as sulking, which avoids dealing with a problem.
regulated agreement	Consumer agreement with the scope of Consumer Credit Acts.

regulated payment	Payment from the Social Fund to meet one of four specific categories of need.
reminder	Notice drawing a person's attention to an unpaid amount due. This is a requirement in many legal procedures to recover a debt.
rent arrears	Amount of rent which should have been paid but has not been.
repayment mortgage	Mortgage where each payment includes some repayment of capital as well as interest.
repayment schedule	Offer made by a debtor to a creditor saying how he intends to clear the debt.
repossession	When a landlord, lender or mortgagee takes back property for unpaid amounts due.
reservation of title	Clause in a contract which says that ownership of supplied goods only passes when they have been paid for.
resignation	Self-pity and similar behaviour which avoids dealing with a problem.
respect	Attitude of mutual acceptance which is essential in a counselling relationship.
restriction	In law, a notice to the Land Registry that a charging order has been made on a property.
retail credit	Arrangement to buy goods and pay by instalments. The goods are taken back if payment is not made.
retention of title	Another name for reservation of title.
return	Total amount received from an investment from all sources.
risk	Chance that something adverse will happen. Risk can rarely be avoided but can usually be mitigated.
Romalpa clause	Reservation of title clause in a contract for sale of goods.
running costs	Cost of using an asset (particularly a car) as opposed to the costs of owning it.

safety need	Second level under Maslow's hierarchy. The security a person needs to feel to be able to address social needs.
savings credit	Part of the pension credit designed to reward those who saved for their retirement.
savings plans	Package of financial products, which typically have high charges and a poor return.
second purchaser	A guarantor in a sale.
secondary lease period	Period of a lease when only nominal payments are paid for the use of goods.
secrecy	Withholding information for its own sake, which is neither privacy nor confidentiality.
secured debt	Debt, non-payment of which allows the creditor to take property.
secured loan	Loan made on the basis that certain goods may be seized by the lender if not paid. A mortgage is a secured loan on a home.
sederunt book	In Scotland, register of sequestrations.
self-actualization	Highest level of Maslow's hierarchy, when a person is sufficiently motivated to achieve their goals.
self-sequestration	In Scotland, sequestration proceedings started by the debtor.
sentimental value	When the value to a person exceeds its cash value. In insolvency, a family or friend should bid for such items.
sequestration	In Scotland, procedure similar to bankruptcy.
sequestration for rent	In Scotland, insolvency procedure started by a landlord.
serious debt	Debt which is causing serious problems to a person's everyday life.
SERPS	Government pension scheme for employees from 1978 to 2002 which can provide significant addition to state retirement pension.
SHIP code of practice	Code for businesses which offer various equity release schemes.

short order	Court order giving a person limited powers to deal with the affairs of a person who lacks mental incapacity.
simple interest	Where interest is charged on the principal but not on any interest already applied.
soap opera	The mentality of picking needless quarrels and resisting all efforts to resolve them.
Social Fund	Social security provision designed to meet needs not otherwise covered.
social housing	Accommodation offered on terms to make it affordable to those who cannot afford market terms.
social need	Third level under Maslow's hierarchy. It includes love and friendship. This level must be met before a person can feel esteem.
split the difference	The usual end to haggling where the parties take an average of their last offers.
squirrelling	Hiding away assets, particularly in insolvency.
stamp duty land tax	Tax paid on buying land and buildings.
standard debt	Debt which causes concern but is not too serious.
standing charges	Cost of owning an asset (particularly a car) as opposed to the costs of running it.
state retirement pension	Social security benefit payable to most people on retirement.
state second pension	The scheme which replaced SERPS in 2002, when the scheme was recast to favour lower-paid workers and to include carers.
statement of affairs	Formal statement provided to court to support an IVA proposal.
statute	Act of Parliament, primary source of law.
statutory adoption pay	Social security benefit paid to a man or woman who adopts a child.
statutory demand	Formal notice sent by creditors before starting bankruptcy proceedings.
Statutory Instrument	Rules made under an Act of Parliament.

statutory maternity pay	Amount an employee may receive from the state during absence for childbirth.
statutory paternity pay	Social security benefit for two weeks payable for absence by the father of a natural child or adopted child, or by a woman whose partner has adopted a child.
statutory payment	General term for statutory sick pay, statutory maternity pay, statutory paternity pay and statutory adoption pay.
statutory sick pay	Social security benefit paid to an employee from a fourth day of sickness.
stay	When a court temporarily suspends a legal action or process.
stop order	Order preventing sale of shares or payment of dividend if a charging order has been made.
subconscious	Mental processes of which a person is unaware.
subject to contract	Negotiation or agreement towards a contract but which does not yet make a contract.
sub-prime lending	Lending to people who cannot use the normal facilities for borrowing.
substantially unfurnished	Premises which contains insufficient furnishing to allow someone to live there. Such a premises may qualify for a lower rate of council tax for six months.
sue	Issue proceedings in civil law.
summarizing	Counselling skill of identifying main elements in a problem.
summary warrant	In Scotland, order granted to a government body or local authority to recover a debt.
summons	Legal notice from a court served on a person who must respond.
sundry	Category of expenditure for items which do not have their own category.
supervisor	In an IVA, insolvency practitioner appointed to oversee the IVA.
Sure Start maternity grant	Social Fund payment to a woman on means-tested benefits who gives birth.

surplus	Excess of income over expenditure.
suspended order	Order committing a debtor to prison for non-attendance at court, but which will not be enforced if debtor attends on a second request.
SWOT analysis	Consideration of strengths, weaknesses, opportunities and threats.
tax	Priority debt of amount owed by a person to the state.
tax appeal	Formal process for contesting a tax demand.
tax code	Used by an employer to calculate how much income tax must be deducted from wages under the PAYE scheme.
tax credit	Means-tested social security benefits. (They have nothing to do with tax, and are not credits.)
tax penalty	Additional sum imposed for non-compliance with tax law.
tea and sympathy	Colloquial term for most elementary form of counselling.
television quiz	Quiz show on television which promises prizes to people who phone in on a premium rate number, most of whom incur a bill and can't get through.
therapeutic counselling	Counselling which does not include giving advice.
third party debt order	Court order requiring a third party, such as a bank, to pay money to discharge a debt.
Time to Pay	Scheme offered by the tax authorities to help a person pay arrears of tax.
tithing	Practice of donating 10% of one's income to charity.
tools of trade	Essentials to a person's work which cannot be seized from a bankrupt.
trigger figure	Amount of household expenditure. If a Common Financial Statement includes a figure above this amount, an explanation must be provided.

trust deed	In Scotland, a voluntary arrangement for payment of creditors by an insolvent person.
trustee in bankruptcy	Insolvency practitioner who deals with the property of a bankrupt.
turnover	Annual income from a business.
undischarged bankrupt	Person who is bankrupt, from which state he has not yet been discharged. He is under severe restrictions.
undue influence	Persuading someone to make a contract in a manner which goes beyond what is lawful.
unemployment benefit	Old social security benefit, now replaced by jobseeker's allowance.
unfair relationship	New Consumer Credit Act test from 6 April 2007, whose non-compliance can make an agreement unenforceable.
unjust steward	Parable from Luke 16.1–8 which provides a Christian insight into debt recovery.
unpressured	Ethic of allowing counselling to proceed at its own natural pace.
unprotected trust deed	In Scotland, a trust deed which is not registered and therefore does not stop a creditor starting sequestration proceedings.
unsecured debt	Debt which is not pre-preferential, preferential or secured. Most debt comes into this category.
unsecured loan	Loan which is not secured on any asset. If the loan is not paid, the lender cannot seize any of the debtor's property.
upping the ante	Practice of deliberately making a problem worse to force someone to take it seriously.
utilities	Basic services provided to a household, such as gas, electricity, water and telephone.
variance	Difference between actual income or expenditure and the budgeted figure.
vesting	Legal process by which ownership is transferred, such as in bankruptcy.

void	Of no legal effect.
walking possession	When a bailiff 'seizes' goods but allows a person to retain use of them until the debt is paid.
war pension	State pension paid to the dependants of someone killed or injured on military service.
warrant to cite	In Scotland, an order for a debtor to attend court in sequestration proceedings.
we are not a charity	Common argument used by a creditor when rejecting an offer to repay a debt. It is irrelevant and easily countered.
week's pay	Figure set by the government from 1 February each year used to calculate redundancy pay and which is also used to determine how much of a person's wages rank as a preferential debt.
weighting	When a figure is multiplied by a factor to reflect its importance. Social Fund budgeting loans use weighting.
widowed parent's allowance	Social security benefit paid to a widow or widower with children.
windfall clause	Term common in an IVA which provides that any windfall, such as inheritance or win, must be given to creditors.
winter fuel payment	Lump-sum **payment** from Social Fund to people over 60 regardless of their income or wealth.
without prejudice	Comment on a letter which stops it being shown to a judge. It is used to conduct separate negotiations while a court case is proceeding.
won't pay, can't pay	Argument sometimes used by a creditor when rejecting an offer to repay a debt. It is irrelevant to the process.
working tax credit	Means-tested social security benefit payable to someone in work on a low income.
write off	Process for removing a balance from the accounts, such as when a business accepts that a bad debt will not be paid.
wrongful trading	Offence of allowing a business to continue when it is obvious that it cannot meet its liabilities.

zero-based budget Budget where all expenditure starts at zero and must justify itself afresh each year, rather than just uplifting last year's figure.

Appendix 2

Useful addresses

The author

Robert Leach, 19 Chestnut Avenue, Ewell, Epsom, KT19 0SY
020 8224 5695. E-mail: robert.leach1@btinternet.com
*The author is happy to explain anything in this book, to talk to groups,
or to assist any debt professional.*

Free debt counselling services

Consumer Credit Counselling Services
0800 138 1111
www.cccs.co.uk

National Debtline
0808 808 4000
www.nationaldebtline.co.uk

Citizens Advice Bureau
See your local phone book
www.adviceguide.org.uk

Christian money education charity

Credit Action, Howard House, The Point,
Weaver Road, Lincoln, LN6 3QN
E-mail: office@creditaction.org.uk
www.creditaction.org.uk

Credit reference agencies

Experian Ltd, Consumer Help Service,
PO Box 8000, Nottingham, NG80 7WF
0870 241 6212
www.experian.co.uk
You can order your credit file on the Internet or by telephone.

Equifax plc, Credit File Advice Centre,
PO Box 1140, Bradford, BD1 5US
0870 010 0583
www.equifax.co.uk
You can order your credit file on the Internet.

Callcredit plc, Consumer Services Team,
PO Box 491, Leeds LS1 5XX
0870 060 1414
www.callcredit.plc.uk
You can order your credit file on the Internet.

Social security help

Freephone 0800 882200

Help for students

Student Support Line (part of DfES)
0800 731 9133
www.dfes.gov.uk/studentsupport

Educational Grants Advisory Service,
501–505 Kingsland Road, Dalston, London, E8 4AU
020 7249 6636
www.egas-online.org.uk

National Union of Students,
461 Holloway Road, London, N7 6LZ
020 7272 8900

Other bodies

Association of Business Recovery Professionals (R3),
8th Floor, 120 Aldersgate Street, London, EC1A 4JQ
020 7566 4200
www.r3.org.uk

Care for the Family,
Garth House, Leon Avenue, Cardiff, CF4 7RG
029 2081 1733

Child Poverty Action Group,
94 White Lion Street, London, N1 9PE
020 7837 7979, Helpline 020 7833 4627

Financial Services Authority,
25 The North Colonnade, Canary Wharf, London, E14 5HS
0845 606 1234

GamCare,
www.gamcare.org.uk
0845 6000 133

Law Centres Federation,
18–19 Warren Street, London, W1P 5DA
020 7387 8570
www.lawcentres.org.uk

Lone Parents Helpline
0800 018 5026

National Consumer Council,
20 Grosvenor Gardens, London, SW1W 0DH
020 7730 3469
www.ncc.org.uk

National Federation of Housing Associations,
175 Grays Inn Road, London, WC1X 8UX
020 7278 6571

Office of Fair Trading
08457 224499
www.oft.gov.uk

Public Guardianship Office,
Archway Tower, 2 Junction Road, London, N19 5SZ
DX 141150 Archway 2
0845 330 9200. Fax: 0870 739 5780. Textphone: 020 7664 7755
E-mail: custserv@guardianship.gsi.gov.uk
www.guardianship.gov.uk

Relate (marriage guidance),
Herbert Grey College, Little Church Street, Rugby, CV21 3AP
01788 573241
www.relate.org.uk

Seniorline
0808 800 6565

Shelter,
88 Old Street, London, EC1V 9HU
0808 800 444
www.shelter.org.uk

Appendix 3

Counselling

Introduction

Counselling is the process of assisting others to deal with problems. It is a specialist subject, with a considerable volume of research material. There are different schools of counselling theory, and different counselling methods.

All of us probably receive and give counselling in its simplest forms, simply by our everyday conversations. The simplest form of counselling is **tea and sympathy,** or where any person talks about a problem with another. However, counselling usually refers to a more formal relationship where one person (the client) seeks the help of another (the counsellor).

In 2005, the British Association for Counselling and Psychotherapy defined counselling in these terms

> Counselling takes place when a counsellor sees a client in a private and confidential setting to explore a difficulty the client is having, distress they may be experiencing or perhaps their dissatisfaction with life, or loss of a sense of direction or purpose. It is always at the request of the client as no one can be properly 'sent' to counselling.

This definition identifies four types of need which may be addressed by counselling:

- difficulty – a problem or problems
- distress – emotional response to problems
- dissatisfaction with life – unrelated to specific problems
- loss of direction or purpose.

Debt counselling is primarily concerned with the first of these, though the counsellor should realize that the other three types may also be present.

The main aspects of counselling are:

- relationship – between two people
- communication – understanding each other
- listening – particularly by the counsellor
- help – from counsellor to client
- confidentiality – counsellor does not improperly disclose relationship
- empowerment – of the client
- clarification – identifying the problems
- use of training – to help, counsellor is trained to identify problems
- recognition – that every client is unique.

It should be appreciated that some of the population, estimated at around 30%, never needs counselling. Whatever happens, they are resilient and self-sufficient enough to deal with problems. This does not make such people superior, nor are they callous or inhuman, they simply have a different mental constitution.

Never assume that someone must need counselling just because of the problems they face. Sometimes a person simply wants advice. It is counter-productive to attempt counselling if someone just needs an accountancy service.

Problem dealing

The three steps in addressing any type of problem are:

- recognition
- diagnosis
- prognosis.

Recognition simply means acknowledging that there is a problem. No progress can be made in dealing with any problem until it is recognized. This can be more of an issue for those close to the client than for the client himself. It is very difficult for someone close to a problem debtor who refuses to acknowledge the problem.

If someone does not admit to having a debt problem, no progress can be made in resolving the problem.

Diagnosis means identifying the real cause of the debt problem. Failure to do this means that debt counselling is treating the symptoms and not curing the disease. Sometimes what appears to be a cause may itself be a symptom. For example, the commonest cause of debt is overspending. But that may itself be a symptom of an inferiority complex or emotional hurt. Until the real issue is identified, the real illness is still there. The real problem remains unresolved and will probably return.

Prognosis is how to address the real issue once identified. A counsellor must be careful not to get out of his depth, nor to attempt to address problems for which he is not qualified.

Counselling skills are most commonly used in diagnosis. Most of this book deals with prognosis.

Negative reactions

There are basically four negative reactions to problems. Negative reactions are always wrong.

The negative reactions are:

- aggression
- regression
- resignation
- fixation.

Aggression is any manifestation of anger, such as shouting or slamming doors. A person may justify this as 'letting off steam', but that is more effectively done in less dramatic ways such as lying down or going for a walk. Aggression is very upsetting for those around and so can create new problems at the time when they are least wanted.

Regression is any form of childish behaviour, such as sulking. It may appear to be escapism but is actually an obstacle to debt recovery. It is more productive to spend three hours on the debt recovery plan and then 'escape' by rewarding your efforts by watching a good film.

Resignation includes self-pity, giving up and believing that the entire universe meets in secret conclave every day to conspire against you. This may appear to be the inevitable consequences of a problem, but it is not. Resignation is a personal choice which sets the person on the wrong direction. If a person has a debt problem, it is *their* problem and they must solve it, albeit with your help.

Fixation is any irrational behaviour. This includes shouting abuse at creditors, threatening legal action on no grounds, lecturing people on the evils of society and suchlike. It is the expenditure of energy which should be directed to solving the problem.

The elimination (or at least significant reduction) of these negative reactions is an essential part in solving any underlying problem.

Counselling skills

The skills of therapeutic counselling involve:

(a) listening
(b) re-expression

(c) summarizing
(d) questioning
(e) clarifying answers
(f) reflection
(g) clarifying thoughts
(h) encouraging focus
(i) challenging the client.

Of these, (a) lies at the heart of all therapeutic counselling. Skills (b) to (e) help establish the factual basis for diagnosis. Skills (f) to (i) start to move to prognosis.

The listening skill is often called **active listening**. The counsellor stays silent for most of the time, but indicates that he is interested in what is being said. This is done by body language (e.g. looking at the person) and by **affirmative interjections** such as 'Yes', 'I see' and 'Quite'.

The skill of **re-expression** is most appropriate when a client is not particularly articulate or where the client is ambiguous. The counsellor could say 'And was this before you lost your job?' Such a question is also an affirmative interjection.

Summarizing should not be routine as it is tedious for a client to have his concerns parroted back. Any summary should be confined to those areas which seem to lie at the heart of the problem. The counsellor may say, 'It seems that you felt very little love in your childhood'. Questioning and asking a client to clarify answers are simply an extension of this skill. Clarifying answers includes getting the client to reflect on what appears to be the real issue.

Reflection is the first step in prognosis. A client may not have realized that his problems arose from emotional issues in childhood. A client will usually need time to reflect on what has been newly realized. Many experiences may need to be reconsidered – 'so that's why she did that', for example. This process should not be rushed. The more the client can reflect on the real problems, the greater will be the determination to address them. The counsellor can find that he or she is back to active listening.

Clarifying thoughts is an extension of reflection. It simply helps a person come to terms with matters during reflection. This leads to encouraging the client to focus on those areas which are important. The last step of challenging a client is to get them to see any issues they are overlooking or playing down too much.

From all this, it can be seen that therapeutic counselling is not a passive discipline. From the beginning of the process, the counsellor is making analysis, sifting evidence, checking this evidence for credibility, looking for more evidence, and so on.

Counselling ethics

All counselling creates a degree of vulnerability for the client. Counselling starts with a client admitting to a problem which cannot be solved on his own. While this is no different from asking an accountant to help with a tax return (which is similar to debt counselling), the client is unlikely to see it that way.

The reality is that asking a counsellor for help with a personal problem indicates no failure any more than asking a garage to repair your car. In modern society, we each develop skills for our personal use but can never develop all the skills needed. If we tried to provide all our food and everything else without any help from anyone else, we would quickly revert to a Stone Age existence. Instead, we develop particular skills of use to others. These skills are then 'traded' so we help each other, either in a formal commercial arrangement or in a less formal domestic arrangement. There is nothing improper in this; it is the basis of civilization.

There are certain ethical considerations which apply in all counselling. In particular, the counselling must be:

- non-judgmental
- respectful
- objective
- confidential
- client-centred
- unpressured
- problem-focused.

A counsellor must not be judgmental. This means that a counsellor must not say or in any way convey any view that a client has done anything wrong. This client *may* have done things wrong. The non-judgmental approach is needed because resolving problems rarely requires blame to be apportioned.

The counsellor ignores issues of right and wrong because they are irrelevant to counselling. This does not condone any wrongdoing, it simply acknowledges that this is not relevant to the matter in hand. If there is wrongdoing, such as criminal acts or mistreatment of individuals, these may need addressing, but that is outside the counselling process and is usually not the responsibility of the counsellor.

A counsellor must equally be careful not to condone the client's behaviour. Saying that a client has done nothing wrong is just as judgmental as saying that the client has. It may also be untrue.

The concept of **respect** is about the attitude to the client, not the counsellor's opinion of him. The starting point for counselling, or indeed any relationship, is mutual acceptance. However stupid and odious a person may be, everyone is a child of God entitled to personal dignity and human rights. Many deep personal problems arise because people simply do not feel accepted in their peer group.

Accepting a person does not mean that you agree with their views, condone their behaviour or approve of their conduct. Friendship and brotherly love depends simply on valuing the human life form. In the passage traditionally included as John 7.53—8.11, Jesus is presented with an adulterous woman. He shows her great love while not denying the need for justice. He ends by saying 'do not sin again', acknowledging that she *had* sinned. St Augustine put it simply: love the sinner, hate the sin.

Non-judgmentalism and respect are such basic ethics of counselling that there is no point in attempting any counselling if they are absent. If you really cannot avoid feeling judgmental or disrespectful about a client, arrange for another counsellor to take over. Some counsellors may have such a repugnance about a client guilty of child abuse or who holds racist views (to mention just two) that they cannot counsel such a client. They should not attempt to do so.

Many people become counsellors because of problems they have overcome in their own life. (You should not counsel if there are problems which you have not overcome.) Despite having overcome the problems and despite any training, it is still possible that a similar experience shared by a client could trigger a negative reaction in the counsellor. If so, the counsellor should seriously consider whether to continue.

The remaining ethics make counselling effective and legal.

A counsellor must be **objective**. This is unlikely to be possible if the counsellor is related to the client or is a close friend, or if the counsellor has been involved in the incidents prompting the counselling.

Counsellors are human and do have their own experiences and emotions. These should not be banished but should be controlled. Very occasionally it may be helpful for a counsellor to share an experience, such as to reassure a client that the counsellor does understand the client's position. But if a client says, 'You don't understand', the better response is usually to say 'Please help me understand'.

The counselling should be **confidential**. A client will not share sensitive information with a counsellor if the client believes that this will be made known to other people.

It is important to understand that confidentiality is different from privacy and secrecy. **Privacy** is simply the human right of individuals not to have certain personal details generally known. The right to privacy is mainly derived from Article 8 of the European Convention for the Protection of Human Rights and Fundamental Freedoms 1950, which is given legal effect in Britain under Human Rights Act 1998.

Secrecy is when one person simply withholds information from others. Apart from official secrets, there is no legal concept of secrecy, and no penalty for publishing secret information.

Confidentiality is not a personal right, but something which must be agreed by the parties to a relationship such as a contract. If you hire a hall there may be conditions that you do not play loud music, sweep the floor and leave by 11 p.m. You only become bound to follow those conditions as a consequence of hiring the hall. Similarly a person may give you information on condition that you do not disclose it. This creates the duty of confidentiality. It is simply what the parties have agreed between them.

Confidentiality does not mean that information may never be disclosed. There is a measure of legal protection for information shared with a lawyer, and for information shared with a priest in confession.

A counsellor should not tell a client that information shared in counselling is absolutely confidential and will never be revealed to any third party. There are some circumstances when a counsellor *must* disclose confidential information, and other circumstances where a counsellor *may* do so.

The following is based on English law and the practice followed by qualified accountants.

A person *must* disclose confidential information:

- if he believes the client has committed treason or terrorism
- if he suspects the client is involved in drug trafficking or money laundering (a person commits a criminal offence under Criminal Justice Act 1993 if he fails to report a reasonable suspicion)
- if so required by a court order (the client will have had the opportunity to challenge such an order in court)
- to a liquidator or trustee in bankruptcy under various provisions of the Insolvency Act 1986.

A person *may* disclose confidential information:

- if it discloses a serious crime (other than those listed above), such as murder or child abuse, and it is in the public interest that this be disclosed
- to defend himself against charges brought by a client
- where permitted by a specific Act of Parliament, provided the disclosure is fully within the scope of the Act
- where required by a statutory body under its legal powers.

If information is sought from the police, tax authorities, regulatory body or similar authority, the counsellor should check that the requester has the legal authority to demand the information and otherwise refuse. A counsellor required to appear as a witness in court action against a client should refuse until a subpoena or summons is served on the counsellor requiring attendance.

Counselling should be **client-centred**. It has been known for a session to comprise the counsellor talking about his problems to the client instead of listening. It is easy for a counselling session to depart from the client's issues to the counsellor's or to a chat about the world in general. Although an occasional comment on these lines may help to introduce an element of perspective to the conversation, this should be brief and quickly return to the client's problems. There is no need to discuss the weather or football at length to establish a relationship with a client. A far better relationship is established by discussing the client's problems.

A counselling session must be **unpressured**. This means that it must proceed at its own natural pace, and not be rushed nor unreasonably slowed down. The session should start on time, and every effort must be made not to cancel a session once booked. Lateness and cancellations convey the impression to the client that you are not taking their concerns seriously. A common recommendation is that counselling sessions should last for 50 minutes with a ten-minute break between sessions.

A counsellor must know the difference between a pause and a silence. Generally the former becomes the latter after four seconds. If there has been silence for four seconds or more, the counsellor must decide whether the client needs time for silent reflection, failing which the counselling should be moved along.

The counsellor must convey that he or she is actively listening to the client. Some much-quoted research says that people communicate:

- 8% by what is said
- 37% by how it is said
- 55% by body language.

Body language is the range of mannerisms and physical expressions which convey what a person is really thinking. Smiling when you meet someone conveys friendship and trust. Looking at the client, and not looking out of the window, at papers or (worst) at the clock all convey loss of interest. If you really need to keep an eye on the time, put a clock in the same line of sight as the client.

To keep a counselling session unpressured, it should be arranged where you are unlikely to be interrupted by other people or by telephone calls.

Counselling sessions must be **problem-focused**. This means that the conversation must be confined to the matters in hand. Apart from some opening courtesies, you are simply wasting time by talking about the weather, sport, holidays and television (unless, exceptionally, these are part of the problem). A client who is embarrassed about his problem may prefer the soft option of talking about something else. The more time wasted on such soft options, the harder it becomes to deal with the real issues.

Counselling problems

Debt problems do not readily fit into the usual role of counselling because the client may have expected purely financial and legal advice and not even be aware that there are deeper problems which must be addressed for a full resolution of the debt problem.

Conversely a client may have sought counselling for a non-financial reason, such as to cope with stress, and the counsellor may determine that debt is the problem.

Problems can easily become entwined. Sometimes two or more problems may be separate symptoms of one underlying problem. For this reason a counsellor should be reluctant to try to narrow the scope of counselling to specific problems.

The issues for which people most commonly seek counselling are:

- destructive relationships
- crisis situations
- bereavement
- unresolved issues from the past
- addictions and compulsions
- obsessions and phobias
- depression and anxiety
- work or career-based problems
- personal growth
- social problems
- coping with illness or disability
- loss of work
- sexual identity
- bullying and harassment.

This list is not exhaustive.

A counsellor should not be surprised if other problems arise in the course of debt counselling. A debt counsellor should always be careful not to go out of his depth. A debt counsellor trained in the accounting and legal knowledge of debt may not be the best person to deal with unresolved issues of child abuse or a violent husband. In such a case, the debt counsellor should refer the person to another counsellor to deal with such issues while continuing to deal with debt. Ideally, the client should authorize the two counsellors to share confidential information.

It should first be understood that if a person says he has a problem, then he *does* have a problem. The problem may not be what the person says. Indeed the problem may be that the person fails to see that there is no real problem at all!

Second, all problems are subjective. What is a crisis to one person is simply routine business to someone else. The subjectivity is generally irrelevant for counselling, though it may help when moving to advice and information.

Advice

The main authority for therapeutic counselling is Sigmund Freud (1856–1939), widely seen as the father of psychoanalysis. Although alternative theories have subsequently been advanced by such people as Adler and Jung, Freud's theories and practices still underpin much of modern counselling.

In 1920, Freud cautioned against counsellors ever giving advice. His view was that clients should be helped to make **independent decisions**. In other words, clients should solve their own problems, albeit with guidance and support from the counsellor. The wisdom of this observation is borne out by subsequent educational research which shows that people remember 20% of what they are told but 70% of what they work out themselves.

It is also true that advice can be counter-productive as it can build up resentment, however well-intentioned the advice may be. The other extreme is the person who uncritically follows all advice, which can be equally counter-productive.

Debt counselling is more than pure therapeutic counselling. It must involve the giving of advice to have any value at all. However, even in debt counselling, it is usually necessary to make a clear distinction between the counselling side – helping a person come to terms with the problem – and the practical advice of getting out of debt.

Information is a halfway house which should be the first option for a debt counsellor. Before looking at a person's finances and coming up with an instant solution, the debt counsellor should consider providing relevant factual information and letting the client work out the solution. Advice is simply the application of relevant information to a particular situation.

While giving advice may be considered bad practice in pure therapeutic counselling, it should be remembered that this is a small element in debt counselling. In some cases, the 'debt doctor' may not be involved in therapeutic counselling at all. Here are two examples of the importance of information in debt counselling from the author's personal experience.

Example: The inheritance

A woman contacted an accountant in a state of extreme panic, because she had spent an inheritance of about £80,000 on her house and had made no provision to pay income tax on the money, which she could not now find without selling the house. The accountant explained that income tax is not payable on inheritances, and the sum was below the threshold for inheritance tax.

Example: The tax bill

A retired businessman was suffering severe anxiety because the Inland Revenue (now HMRC) was chasing him for an old tax bill for £17,000 which he could not pay. He did not even know what the bill was for. The accountant identified the nature of the tax bill and saw a ground for appeal. A single letter was sent to the tax inspector which led to the assessment being vacated (cancelled).

In each case, the problem was simply solved by provision of information or advice without any need for counselling. This can be the case in debt counselling. Most of this book provides that information.

Sometimes the information may come at a later stage when sorting through the debts. Here is another example from the author's experience:

Example: The advertisement

A man ran a small business which failed with large debts. One of the debts was for a series of advertisements which the man particularly resented paying for as they had generated no business at all. The magazine publisher was threatening legal action. The debt counsellor saw that the advertisement had mistyped the business's telephone number. It took just one phone call to have all the invoices cancelled.

Maslow's hierarchy

It is useful for a counsellor to understand Maslow's hierarchy of needs, named after Abraham Maslow (1908–1970) who developed this model in the 1940s. It is still widely used for such purposes as workforce motivation, training and personal development.

The principle of Maslow is that a person has five levels of needs which can only be satisfied from the bottom up.

These are:

- self-actualization
- esteem
- social needs
- safety
- physiological needs.

Physiological needs include food and warmth. If these are lacking, no higher level of motivation is possible. A debtor should not attempt to starve or freeze to save money.

Safety needs are the security that physiological needs will continue to be met. Any creditor who threatens a debtor's needs must be dealt with as a priority.

Social needs include love and friendship. A person who lacks physiological or safety needs will find it difficult to deal with social needs.

Esteem includes self-confidence and self-respect. This is when a person gains quality of life.

Self-actualization is the highest level. It is the stage when a person has the motivation to improve. It is possible for a person to reach this level despite having serious debt.

Personal disciplines

The task of a debt counsellor is not limited to therapeutic counselling and financial advice. In many cases, devising a solution can be straight-forward; the problem can be in exercising the personal disciplines to maintain that solution.

The best way to resist temptation is not to rely on willpower but to remove the temptation in the first place. Someone who overspends on credit cards may be well advised to cut up the cards to make overspending on them impossible.

Research has shown that many of the impulses for irresponsible spending and other negative conduct derives from the **subconscious**. This term describes the mental processes of which a person is not aware. In psychoanalysis, the term describes the part of the mind which includes memories, motives and intentions. Although a person is not consciously aware of them, they can be recalled to awareness in the conscious mind.

The subconscious mind can be reprogrammed. Such techniques are now commercially available. Musicians and other performers may use the techniques outlined in *The Inner Game of Music* (Barry Green, Doubleday, 1986). There are similar books for tennis, golf and other sports. The principle here is that:

performance = potential – distraction.

So performance can be enhanced by removing distraction as well as by enhancing potential. The method involves **fantasy**. The person imagines that the performance or game has gone as well as possible and that they have become a huge success. The subconscious cannot distinguish between fantasy and reality, and this removes the nerves or other distraction.

The same idea lies behind Paul McKenna's methods in *I Can Make You Thin*. In this he addresses the problems of cravings and similar temptations by repeatedly telling the subconscious what is required, enforcing this with simple disciplines and getting the person to imagine themselves as being thinner. McKenna uses similar methods to help people overcome phobias.

When debt is the cause of uncontrolled spending, some tough disciplines can be needed. The BBC 3 television programme *Spenda-holics* provides excellent examples. Every compulsive spender has a psychological report to determine the underlying issues. This deals with the underlying causes while the financial experts deal with the symptoms.

Credit cards are banned. (One suggested method is to tape it to the inside of the freezer which has to be defrosted to retrieve it.) The person must then have at least one week of **cold turkey** when they are given a small amount of cash for their spending. Many manage to survive on sums far less than they thought possible.

Attitude of a debt counsellor

A debt counsellor must have the right attitude and the right skills.

The attitude has at least these five elements:

- non-judgmentalism
- patience
- worldly wisdom
- commitment to the debtor
- a questioning mind.

A **non-judgmental** attitude does not mean that you pretend there is no right or wrong. It just means that you recognize that apportioning blame is not the first priority in remedying the position. It is probably not second, third, fifth or twentieth priority either.

There should be no comments on the lines of 'Well, it's your stupid fault you got into this mess' or 'You've only got yourself to blame' or 'How could you be so daft?' Such comments may be true, but expressing them is unlikely to help the debtor.

Patience is needed in identifying debts, income and expenditure. It is quite common to believe you have identified all debts only for the debtor to say 'Of course, there is also money I owe to my family members'. Be prepared to revisit the same financial statements several times. Records may be chaotic and explanations long and rambling.

Worldly wisdom is common sense with worldly knowledge. A debtor will frequently understate his debts or mis-state his income or expenditure. A certain scepticism is appropriate to ensure that all debts have been identified for their full value. Budgets need careful scrutiny to ensure that the income is not over-optimistic and that no items of expenditure have been omitted.

There must be **commitment to the debtor**. An adviser can only work for one party (with a possible exception for mediation). The debtor must know that everything you do is to help him. It may seem immoral that you only represent one side of the argument, but that is your function. Creditors have their own advisers.

A **questioning mind** is needed to resolve such issues as the underlying cause of the debt problem and whether the debtor has made a full disclosure.

Specific skills of a debt counsellor

Having the right attitude does not make someone a good debt counsellor. The debt counsellor must have the necessary skills.

These may be summarized as:

- explanation
- articulation
- negotiation.

Explanation means that you must understand the legal and financial implications of your work with the debtor. Many individuals have significant misunderstandings about the nature of financial issues. This can range from believing that the debtor could be sent to prison or have all his property seized for being late with a bill, through to the opposite extreme of believing that debt does not matter.

The debt counsellor must understand the nature of all documents received and their financial and legal consequences.

Articulation is the skill needed to put ideas into words. This is particularly important when drafting letters to creditors.

Negotiation is the ability to 'trade' with someone to achieve your desired goal.

Practical skills of debt counsellor

The practical skills of a debt counsellor include:

- a professional attitude – commitment to the principles given above
- knowledge of relevant law and financial matters
- a systematic approach
- ability to elicit facts and truth
- tidy and logical systems of record-keeping
- ability to write letters and negotiate.

Before any meeting with a client, the counsellor should review the file to be familiar with the current issues. Notes should be added to any file while the matter is still fresh in the memory.

Index of Subjects

Index of Bible Quotations, Law Quotations and Court Cases

Bible Quotations

Law Quotations

Court Cases